THE INTERNET IS NOT THE ANSWER

Andrew Keen is one of the wor
commentators on the digital re
books: *Cult of the Amateur*, *Dig*
The Answer. He is executive dir
tion salon FutureCast, the host
"Keen On", a Senior Fellow a
CNN and a much-acclaimed public speaker around the world. In 2015, he was named by *GQ* magazine in their list of the "100 Most Connected Men".

"A devastating new book."

—*Daily Mail*

"A punchy manifesto on the Internet age ... [Keen] guides us through the history and excess of the Net, from its arrival in 1991, through the birth of Instagram in 2010 and onwards, to the specter of privacy concerns and 'big data' that loom over us today ... The book is dazzling in scope ... A must-read for anyone remotely concerned about their lives on the Net."

—*Independent*

"Should be applauded for rowing against the tide of veneration for technological innovation."

—*Daily Telegraph*

"[Keen] can be a telling polemicist and has a sharp eye when it comes to skewering the pretensions and self-delusions of the new digital establishment ... Keen has a sharp ear for the sanctimonious strand of tech happy talk."

—*Financial Times*

"Keen goes among the Silicon Valley hipsters—those who truly believe they are on the verge of joining the one percent who own half the winner-takes-all economy—and he is not impressed."

—*New Scientist*

"Andrew Keen is the Christopher Hitchens of the Internet. Neglect this book with peril. In an industry and world full of prosaic pabulum about the supposedly digitally divine, Keen's work is an important and sharp razor."

—Michael Fertik, CEO, Reputation.com

"This is the best and most readable critique of Silicon Valley yet. Keen is no technophobe nor a stranger to The Valley and this is what makes his book especially devastating. On the other hand it allows him to carve out a small space for optimism."

—David Lowery, founder of Camper Van Beethoven and cofounder of Cracker

"Andrew Keen's pleasingly incisive study argues that, far from being a democratizing force in society, the Internet has only amplified global inequities . . . [Keen] wants to persuade us to transcend our childlike fascination with the baubles of cyberspace so that we can take a long hard look at the weird, dysfunctional, inegalitarian, comprehensively surveilled world that we have been building with digital tools . . . Keen challenges the dominant narrative about the Internet—that it's a technology that liberates, informs and empowers people."

—*Observer*

"*The Internet Is Not the Answer* claims that the only real best friend today's tech titans have is money, and until policymakers intervene, or until the 'digital elite' adopt a more altruistic posture, the Internet will remain a winner-take-all marketplace that's widening a yawning gulf between society's haves and have-nots . . . *The Internet Is Not the Answer* supports its convincing narrative with startling numbers and research cataloged over roughly forty pages worth of endnotes."

—*San Francisco Chronicle*

"[A] brilliant, packed history . . . An outstanding polemic, not only for Internet skeptics (below as well as above the age of sixty) but also for its credulous users."

—*Sydney Morning Herald*

"Keen's larger point stands: The tech world, like industrial capitalism before it, will not become sufficiently equitable unless we legislate it to be that way . . . So instead of waiting for technology to sort us out, Keen argues that it's time to intervene—to manage digital developments in ways that increase rather than undermine human welfare."

—*Globe and Mail*

"[Keen is] the most famous British tech voice in the US."

—*GQ*

"Andrew Keen has again shown himself one of the sharpest critics of Silicon Valley hype, greed, egotism, and inequity. His tales are revealing, his analyses biting. Beneath the criticism is a moral commitment, too, a defense of humane society—the right to be left alone, a fair shot at success, access to the doings of the powerful, and other democratic ideals threatened by the Internet and its moguls."

—Mark Bauerlein, author of *The Dumbest Generation*

"Keen provokes us in every sense of the word—at times maddening, more often thought-provoking, he lets just enough out of the Silicon Valley hot air balloon to start a real conversation about the full impact of digital technology. But will anyone accept the invitation? And, if they do, will anyone thank Andrew Keen for bursting our bubble? If so, maybe there's hope for the digital generation after all."

—Larry Downes, coauthor of *Unleashing the Killer App*

"A provocative title and an even more provocative book. Andrew Keen rightly challenges us to think about how the Internet will shape society. I remain more optimistic, but hope I'm right to be so."

—Mark Read, CEO, WPP Digital

"Andrew Keen has done it again. With great authority he places modern Silicon Valley into a historical context, comparing its structure to the feudal system, which produced a wealthy elite from the efforts of myriad serfs. If you have read *The Circle*, this is your next read. Like me, you may find much to disagree with. But you won't be able to put it down. This is a book that demands a reaction. The Valley will never be the same."

—Keith Teare, cofounder of TechCrunch, Easynet, and RealNames

"Keen makes a deeply important argument and offers a constructive caution that there is no Moore's Law for human progress, that technological determinism is not a good in itself, and that until we fuse technology with humanity the real power in the technology that connects will in many ways be to disconnect us from what matters."

—Dov Seidman, CEO of LRN and author of *How*

"For the past two decades, as we listened to a chorus of pundits tell us the Internet would generate more democracy and opportunity, the real world seems to grow more oppressive and unequal by the day. Drawing on his formidable knowledge of this New Economy, Andrew Keen explains why Uber could make billions destroying taxi unions, to cite just one example—and why some people still see this as progress. If you've ever wondered why the New Economy looks suspiciously like the Old Economy—only with even more for the winners and less for everyone else—put down your shiny new phablet and read this book."

—Robert Levine, author of *Free Ride*

"Keen, himself a veteran of the tech industry, reveals the behind-the-scenes workings of the Internet . . . His best message, however, is that with consideration and the application of care we can still shape a future society that utilizes the strengths of the Internet while not allowing it to overwhelm us and turn us into robotic servants of the very technology that was designed to help us gain freedom and growth as human beings."

—The Daily News Online

"If you're stuck like a fly in the World Wide Web and your life is largely lived online, then *The Internet Is Not the Answer* is a book you won't be able to put down."

—*Journal Record*

"Keen warns of [the] Internet's disastrous impact . . . [he] argues that the digital revolution has been—his words—'an epic fail.' . . . A harsh critique of the digital world."

—Voice of America

"Keen wants you to know that the Internet has not lived up to its early promise. Rather than fostering an environment of intellectual and social democracy, it has spawned a rule-by-mob culture, promoted narcissism and voyeurism, encouraged intolerance and exclusivity, created global monopolies, increased unemployment, and decimated whole industries."

—*Booklist*

"A damning indictment of the Internet and digital technology . . . A well-written, convincing critique of Silicon Valley, and a worthy read for anyone with an email account."

—*Publishers Weekly*

"It is with an acerbic wit, perspective and profound dismay that Keen dismisses the Internet as the revolutionary vehicle for progressing human civilization that it started out to be."

—*Prague Post*

The Internet Is Not the Answer

ALSO BY ANDREW KEEN

The Cult of the Amateur: How Today's Internet Is Killing Our Culture

Digital Vertigo: How Today's Online Social Revolution Is Dividing, Diminishing, and Disorienting Us

In Memory of V Falber & Sons

CONTENTS

Preface: The Question xiii

Introduction: The Building Is the Message 1

1 The Network 11

2 The Money 34

3 The Broken Center 75

4 The Personal Revolution 100

5 The Catastrophe of Abundance 120

6 The One Percent Economy 139

7 Crystal Man 162

8 Epic Fail 184

Conclusion: The Answer 209

Afterword 229

Acknowledgments 235

Notes 237

Index 281

Preface

The Question

The Internet, we've been promised by its many evangelists, is the answer. It democratizes the good and disrupts the bad, they say, thereby creating a more open and egalitarian world. The more people who join the Internet, or so these evangelists, including Silicon Valley billionaires, social media marketers, and network idealists, tell us, the more value it brings to both society and its users. They thus present the Internet as a magically virtuous circle, an infinitely positive loop, an economic and cultural win-win for its billions of users.

But today, as the Internet expands to connect almost everyone and everything on the planet, it's becoming self-evident that this is a false promise. The evangelists are presenting us with what in Silicon Valley is called a "reality distortion field"—a vision that is anything but truthful. Instead of a win-win, the Internet is, in fact, more akin to a negative feedback loop in which we network users are its victims rather than beneficiaries. Rather than the answer, the Internet is actually the central question about our connected twenty-first-century world.

The more we use the contemporary digital network, the less economic value it is bringing to us. Rather than promoting economic fairness, it is a central reason for the growing gulf between rich and poor and the hollowing out of the middle class. Rather than making us wealthier, the distributed capitalism of the new networked economy is making most of us poorer. Rather than generating more jobs, this digital disruption is a principal cause of our structural unemployment crisis. Rather than creating more competition, it has created immensely powerful new monopolists like Google and Amazon.

Its cultural ramifications are equally chilling. Rather than creating transparency and openness, the Internet is creating a panopticon of information-gathering and surveillance services in which we, the users of big data networks like Facebook, have been packaged as their all-too-transparent product. Rather than creating more democracy, it is empowering the rule of the mob. Rather than encouraging tolerance, it has unleashed such a distasteful war on women that many no longer feel welcome on the network. Rather than fostering a renaissance, it has created a selfie-centered culture of voyeurism and narcissism. Rather than establishing more diversity, it is massively enriching a tiny group of young white men in black limousines. Rather than making us happy, it's compounding our rage.

No, the Internet is *not* the answer. Not yet, anyway. This book, which synthesizes the research of many experts and builds upon the material from my two previous books about the Internet,[1] explains why.

The Internet Is Not the Answer

INTRODUCTION

THE BUILDING IS THE MESSAGE

The writing is on the San Francisco wall. The words WE SHAPE OUR BUILDINGS; THEREAFTER THEY SHAPE US have been engraved onto a black slab of marble beside the front door of a social club called the Battery in downtown San Francisco. These words read like an epigram to the club. They are a reminder, perhaps even a warning to visitors that they will be shaped by the memorable building that they are about to enter.

Lauded by the *San Francisco Chronicle* as the city's "newest and biggest social experiment,"[1] the Battery certainly is an ambitious project. Formerly the site of an industrial manufacturer of marble-cutting tools called the Musto Steam Marble Mill, the building has been reinvented by its new owners, two successful Internet entrepreneurs named Michael and Xochi Birch. Having sold the popular social media network Bebo to AOL for $850 million in 2008, the Birches acquired the Musto building on Battery Street for $13.5 million a year later and invested "tens of millions of dollars"[2] to transform it into a social club. Their goal is to create a people's club—a twenty-first-century House of Commons that, they promise, "eschews status,"[3] allowing its members to wear jeans and hoodies and discouraging membership from stuffy old elites who "wear a business suit to work."[4] It's an inclusive social experiment that the Birches, borrowing from Silicon Valley's lexicon of disruption, call an "unclub"—an open and egalitarian place that supposedly breaks all the traditional rules and treats everyone the same, irrespective of their social status or wealth.

"We are fans of the village pub where everyone knows everyone," bubbled Michael Birch. His friends liken his irrepressible optimism to that of Walt Disney or Willy Wonka. "A private club can be the city's replacement for the village pub, where you do, over time, get to know everyone and have a sense of emotional belonging."[5]

The club "offers privacy" but it isn't about "the haves and the have-nots," Xochi Birch added, echoing her husband's egalitarianism. "We want diversity in every sense. I view it as us trying to curate a community."[6]

The Battery is thus imagined by the Birches to be anything but a traditional "gentlemen's club," the kind of exclusive establishment to which a twentieth-century aristocrat—a Winston Churchill, for example—might belong. And yet it was Churchill who, to inaugurate the reconstructed British House of Commons after it had been, as he put it, "blown to smithereens" in May 1941 by bombs dropped from German aircraft, originally said in October 1944 that "we shape our buildings; thereafter they shape us." And so the words of the Right Honorable Sir Winston Leonard Spencer Churchill, the son of the Viscount of Ireland and the grandson of the seventh Duke of Marlborough, had become the epigram for this twenty-first-century San Francisco unclub that claims to eschew status and embrace diversity.

Had the Birches been more prescient, they would have engraved a different Winston Churchill quote outside their club. "A lie gets halfway around the world before the truth has a chance to get its pants on," Churchill's remix of a Mark Twain witticism,[7] perhaps. But that's the problem. In spite of being toolmakers of our digital future, Michael and Xochi Birch aren't *prescient*. And the *truth* about the Battery—whether or not it has had a chance to get its jeans on—is that the well-meaning but deluded Birches have unintentionally created one of the least diverse and most exclusive places on earth.

The twentieth-century media guru Marshall McLuhan, who, in contrast with the Birches, was distinguished by his prescience, famously said that the "medium is the message." But on Battery Street in downtown San Francisco, it's the building that is the message. Rather than an unclub, the Battery is an untruth. It offers a deeply troubling message about the gaping inequalities and injustices of our new networked society.

In spite of its relaxed dress code and self-proclaimed commitment to cultural diversity, the Battery is as opulent as the most marble-encrusted homes of San Francisco's nineteenth-century gilded elite. All that is left of the old Musto building is the immaculately restored exposed brickwork displayed inside the building and the slab of black marble at the club's entrance. The 58,000-square-foot, five-story club now boasts a 200-person domestic staff, a 23,000-pound floating steel staircase, a glass elevator, an eight-foot-tall crystal chandelier, restaurants serving dishes like *wagyu* beef with smoked tofu and *hon shimeji* mushrooms, a state-of-the-art twenty-person Jacuzzi, a secret poker room hidden behind a bookcase, a 3,000-bottle wine cellar boasting a ceiling constructed from old bottles, a menagerie of taxidermied beasts, and a fourteen-room luxury hotel crowned by a glass-pavilioned penthouse suite with panoramic views of San Francisco Bay.

For the vast majority of San Franciscans who will never have the good fortune of setting foot in the Battery, this social experiment certainly isn't very social. Instead of a public House of Commons, the Birches are building a privatized House of Lords, a walled pleasure palace for the digital aristocracy, the privileged one percent of our two-tiered networked age. Rather than a village pub, it's a nonfictional version of the nostalgic British television series *Downton Abbey*—a place of feudal excess and privilege.

Had Churchill joined the Birches' social experiment, he certainly would have found himself among some of the world's richest and best-connected people. The club opened in October 2013 with an exclusive list of founding members that reads like a who's who of what *Vanity Fair* calls the "New Establishment," including the CEO of Instagram, Kevin Systrom; former Facebook president Sean Parker; and the serial Internet entrepreneur Trevor Traina, the owner of the most expensive house in San Francisco, a $35 million mansion on "Billionaire's Row."[8]

It's all too easy, of course, to ridicule the Birches' unclub and their failed social experiment in downtown San Francisco. But unfortunately, it isn't all that funny. "The bigger issue at hand," as the *New Yorker*'s Anisse Gross reminds us about the Battery, is that "San Francisco itself is turning into a private, exclusive club"[9] for wealthy entrepreneurs and venture capitalists. Like its secret poker room, the Battery is a private, exclusive club within a private, exclusive club. It encapsulates what the *New York Times*' Timothy Egan describes as the "dystopia by the Bay"—a San Francisco that is "a one-dimensional town for the 1 percent" and "an allegory of how the rich have changed America for the worse."[10]

The Birches' one-dimensional club is a 58,000-square-foot allegory for the increasingly sharp economic inequities in San Francisco. But there's an even *bigger issue* at stake here than the invisible wall in San Francisco separating the few "haves" from the many "have-nots," including the city's more than five thousand homeless people. The Battery may be San Francisco's biggest experiment, but there's a much bolder social and economic experiment going on in the world outside the club's tinted windows.

This experiment is the creation of a networked society. "The most significant revolution of the 21st century so far is not political. It is the information technology revolution," explains the Cambridge University political scientist David Runciman.[11] We are the brink of a foreign land—a data-saturated place that the British writer John Lanchester calls a "new kind of human society."[12] "The single most important trend in the world today is the fact that globalization and the information technology revolution have gone to a whole new level," adds the *New York Times* columnist Thomas Friedman. Thanks to cloud computing, robotics, Facebook, Google, LinkedIn, Twitter, the iPad, and cheap Internet-enabled smartphones, Friedman says, "the world has gone from connected to hyper-connected."[13]

Runciman, Lanchester, and Friedman are all describing the same great economic, cultural, and, above all, intellectual transformation. "The Internet," Joi Ito, the director of the MIT Media Lab, notes, "is not a technology; it's a belief system."[14] Everything and everyone are being connected in a network revolution that is radically disrupting every aspect of today's world. Education, transportation, health care, finance, retail, and manufacturing are now being reinvented by Internet-based products such as self-driving cars, wearable computing devices, 3-D printers, personal health monitors, massive open online courses (MOOCs), peer-to-peer services like Airbnb and Uber, and currencies like Bitcoin. Revolutionary entrepreneurs like Sean Parker and Kevin Systrom are building this networked society on our behalf. They haven't asked our permission, of course. But then the idea of consent is foreign, even immoral, to many of these architects of what the Columbia University historian Mark Lilla calls our "libertarian age."

"The libertarian dogma of our time," Lilla says, "is turning our polities, economies and cultures upside down."[15] Yes. But the real dogma of our libertarian age lies in glamorizing the turning of things *upside down*, in rejecting the very idea of "permission," in establishing a cult of disruption. Alexis Ohanian, the founder of Reddit, the self-described "front page of the Internet," which, in 2013, amassed 56 billion page views from the 40 million pages of unedited content created by 3 million users,[16] even wrote a manifesto against permission. In *Without Their Permission*,[17] Ohanian boasts that the twenty-first century will be "made," not "managed" by entrepreneurs like himself who use the disruptive qualities of the Internet for the benefit of the public good. But like so much of Internet's mob-produced, user-generated content, Reddit's value to this public good is debatable. The site's most popular series of posts in 2013, for example, concerned its unauthorized misidentification of the Boston Marathon bomber, a public disservice that the *Atlantic* termed a "misinformation disaster."[18]

Like Michael and Xochi Birch's San Francisco unclub, the Internet is presented to us by naïve entrepreneurs as a diverse, transparent, and egalitarian place—a place that eschews tradition and democratizes social and economic opportunity. This view of the Internet encapsulates what Mark Lilla calls the "new kind of hubris" of our libertarian age, with its trinitarian faith in democracy, the free market, and individualism.[19]

Such a distorted view of the Internet is common in Silicon Valley, where doing good and becoming rich are seen as indistinguishable and where disruptive companies like Google, Facebook, and Uber are celebrated for their supposedly public-spirited destruction of archaic rules and institutions. Google, for example, still prides itself as being an "uncompany," a corporation without the traditional structures of power—even though the $400 billion leviathan is, as of June 2014, the world's second most valuable corporation. It's active and in some cases brutally powerful in industries as varied as online search, advertising, publishing, artificial intelligence, news, mobile operating systems, wearable computing, Internet browsers, video, and even—with its fledgling self-driving cars—the automobile industry.

In the digital world, everyone wants to be an unbusiness. Amazon, the largest online store in the world and a notorious bully of small publishing companies, still thinks of itself as the scrappy "unstore." Internet companies like the Amazon-owned shoe store Zappos, and Medium, an online magazine founded by billionaire Twitter founder Ev Williams, are run on so-called holacratic principles—a Silicon Valley version of communism where there are no hierarchies, except, of course, when it comes to wages and stock ownership. Then there are the so-called unconferences of Web publishing magnate Tim O'Reilly—exclusive retreats called the Friends of O'Reilly (FOO) Camp—where nobody is formally in charge and the agenda is set by its carefully curated group of wealthy, young, white, and male technologists. But, like the Birches' club with its 3,000-bottle wine cellar boasting a ceiling constructed from old bottles, massively powerful and wealthy multinationals like Google and Amazon, and exclusively "open" events for the new elite like FOO Camp, aren't quite as revolutionary as they'd have us believe. The new wine in Silicon Valley may be digital, but—when it comes to power and wealth—we've tasted this kind of blatant hypocrisy many times before in history.

"The future is already here—it's just not very evenly distributed," the science fiction writer William Gibson once said. That unevenly distributed future is networked society. In today's digital experiment, the world is being transformed into a winner-take-all, upstairs-downstairs kind of society. This networked future is characterized by an astonishingly unequal distribution of economic value and power in almost every industry that the Internet is disrupting. According to the sociologist Zeynep Tufekci, this inequality is "one of the biggest shifts in power between people and big institutions, perhaps the biggest one yet of the twenty-first century.[20] Like the Battery, it is marketed in the Birches' feel-good language of inclusion, transparency, and openness; but, like the five-storied pleasure palace, this new world is actually exclusive, opaque, and inegalitarian. Rather than a "public service," Silicon Valley's architects of the future are building a privatized networked economy, a society that is a disservice to almost everyone except its powerful, wealthy owners. Like the Battery, the Internet, with its empty promise of making the world a fairer place with more opportunity for more people, has had the unintended consequence of actually making the world less equal and reducing rather than increasing employment and general economic well-being.

Of course, the Internet is not all bad. It has done a tremendous amount of good for society and for individuals, particularly in terms of connecting families, friends, and work colleagues around the world. As a 2014 Pew Report showed, 90% of Americans think that the Web has been good for them personally—with 76% believing it has been good for society.[21] It is true that most of the personal lives of the estimated 3 billion Internet users (more than 40% of the world's population) have been radically transformed by the incredible convenience of email, social media, e-commerce, and mobile apps. Yes, we all rely on and even love our ever-shrinking and increasingly powerful mobile communications devices. It is true that the Internet has played an important and generally positive role in popular political movements around the world—such as the Occupy movement in the United States, or the network-driven reform movements in Russia, Turkey, Egypt, and Brazil. Yes, the Internet—from Wikipedia to Twitter to Google to the excellent websites of professionally curated newspapers like the *New York Times* and the *Guardian*—can, if used critically, be a source of great enlightenment. And I certainly couldn't have written this book without the miracles of email and the Web. And yes, the mobile Web has enormous potential to radically transform the lives of the two and a half billion new Internet users who, according to the Swedish mobile operator Ericsson, will be on the network by 2018. Indeed, the app economy is already beginning to generate innovative solutions to some of the most pervasive problems on the planet—such as mapping clean water stations in Kenya and providing access to credit for entrepreneurs in India.[22]

But, as this book will show, the hidden negatives outweigh the self-evident positives and those 76% of Americans who believe that the Internet has been good for society may not be seeing the bigger picture. Take, for example, the issue of network privacy, the most persistently corrosive aspect of the "big data" world that the Internet is inventing. If San Francisco is "dystopia by the Bay," then the Internet is rapidly becoming dystopia on the network.

"We are fans of the village pub where everyone knows everyone," Michael Birch says. But our networked society—envisioned by Marshall McLuhan as a "global village" in which we return to the oral tradition of the preliterate age—has already become that claustrophobic village pub, a frighteningly transparent community where there are no longer either secrets or anonymity. Everyone, from the National Security Agency to Silicon Valley data companies, does indeed seem to *know* everything about us already. Internet companies like Google and Facebook know us particularly well—even more intimately, so they boast, than we know ourselves.

No wonder Xochi Birch offers her privileged, wealthy members "privacy" from the data-infested world outside the Battery. In an "Internet of Everything" shadowed by the constant surveillance of an increasingly intelligent network—in a future of smart cars, smart clothing, smart cities, and smart intelligence networks—I'm afraid that the Battery members may be the only people who will be able to afford to escape living in a brightly lit village where nothing is ever hidden or forgotten and where, as data expert Julia Angwin argues, online privacy is already becoming a "luxury good."[23]

Winston Churchill was right. We do indeed shape our buildings and thereafter they have the power to shape us. Marshall McLuhan put it slightly differently, but with even more relevance to our networked age. Riffing off Churchill's 1944 speech, the Canadian media visionary said that "we shape our tools and thereafter our tools shape us."[24] McLuhan died in 1980, nine years before a young English physicist named Tim Berners-Lee invented the World Wide Web. But McLuhan correctly predicted that electronic communication tools would change things as profoundly as Johannes Gutenberg's printing press revolutionized the fifteenth-century world. These electronic tools, McLuhan predicted, will replace the top-down, linear technology of industrial society with a distributed electronic network shaped by continuous feedback loops of information. "We become what we behold,"[25] he predicted. And these networked tools, McLuhan warned, will rewire us so completely that we might be in danger of becoming their unwitting slave rather than their master.

Today, as the Internet reinvents society, the writing is on the wall for us all. Those words on that black marble slab outside the Battery are a chilling preface to the biggest social and economic experiment of our age. None of us—from university professors, photographers, corporate lawyers, and factory laborers to taxi drivers, fashion designers, hoteliers, musicians, and retailers—is immune to the havoc wreaked by this network upheaval. It changes everything.

The pace of this change in our libertarian age is bewilderingly fast—so fast, indeed, that most of us, while enjoying the Internet's convenience, remain nervous about this "belief system's" violent impact on society. "Without their permission," entrepreneurs like Alexis Ohanian crow about a disruptive economy in which a couple of smart kids in a dorm room can wreck an entire industry employing hundreds of thousands of people. With *our* permission, I say. As we all step into this brave new digital world, our challenge is to shape our networking tools before they shape us.

CHAPTER ONE

THE NETWORK

Networked Society

The wall was dotted with a constellation of flashing lights linked together by a looping maze of blue, pink, and purple lines. The picture could have been a snapshot of the universe with its kaleidoscope of shining stars joined into a swirl of interlinking galaxies. It was, indeed, a kind of universe. But rather than the celestial firmament, it was a graphical image of our twenty-first-century networked world.

I was in Stockholm, at the global headquarters of Ericsson, the world's largest provider of mobile networks to Internet service providers (ISPs) and telecoms like AT&T, Deutsche Telekom, and Telefonica. Founded in 1876 when a Swedish engineer named Lars Magnus Ericsson opened a telegraph repair workshop in Stockholm, Ericsson had grown by the end of 2013 to employ 114,340 people, with global revenue of over $35 billion from 180 countries. I'd come to meet with Patrik Cerwall, an Ericsson executive in charge of a research group within the company that analyzes trends of what it calls "networked society." A team of his researchers had just authored the company's annual Mobility Report, their overview of the state of the global mobile industry.

But as I waited in the lobby of the Ericsson office to talk with Cerwall, it was the chaos of connected nodes on the company's wall that caught my eye.

The map, created by the Swedish graphic artist Jonas Lindvist, showed Ericsson's local networks and offices around the world. Lindvist had designed the swirling lines connecting cities to represent what he called a feeling of perpetual movement. "Communication is not linear," he said in explaining his work to me; "it is coincidental and chaotic." Every place, it seemed, no matter how remote or distant, was connected. With the exception of a symbolic spot for Stockholm in its center, the map was all edge. It had no heart, no organizing principle, no hierarchy. Towns in countries as geographically disconnected as Panama, Guinea Bissau, Peru, Serbia, Zambia, Estonia, Colombia, Costa Rica, Bahrain, Bulgaria, and Ghana were linked on a map that recognized neither time nor space. Every place, it seemed, was connected to everywhere else. The world had been redrawn as a distributed network.

My meeting with Patrik Cerwall confirmed the astonishing ubiquity of today's mobile Internet. Each year, his Ericsson team publishes a comprehensive report on the state of mobile networks. In 2013, Cerwall told me, there were 1.7 billion mobile broadband subscriptions sold, with 50% of mobile phones acquired that year being smartphones offering Internet access. By 2018, the Ericsson Mobility Report forecasted, mobile broadband subscriptions are expected to increase to 4.5 billion, with the majority of the two and a half billion new subscribers being from the Middle East, Asia, and Africa.[1] Over 60% of the world's more than 7 billion people will, therefore, be online by 2018. And given the dramatic drop in the cost of smartphones, with prices expected to fall to under fifty dollars for high-quality connected devices,[2] and the astonishing statistic from a United Nations report that more people had cell phones (6 billion) than had access to a flushing toilet (4.5 billion),[3] it's not unreasonable to assume that, by the mid-2020s, the vast majority of adults on the planet will have their own powerful pocket computer with access to the network.

And not just everyone, but everything. An Ericsson white paper predicts that, by 2020, there will be 50 billion intelligent devices on the network.[4] Homes, cars, roads, offices, consumer products, clothing, health-care devices, electric grids, even those industrial cutting tools once manufactured in the Musto Steam Marble Mill company, will all be connected on what now is being called the Internet of Things. The number of active cellular machine-to-machine devices will grow 3 to 4 times between 2014 and 2019. "The physical world," a McKinsey report confirms, "is becoming a type of information system."[5]

The economics of this networked society are already staggering. Another McKinsey report studying thirteen of the most advanced industrial economies found that $8 trillion is already being spent through e-commerce. If the Internet were an economic sector, this 2011 report notes, it would have contributed to an average of 3.4% of the world's gross domestic product in 2009, higher than education (3%), agriculture (2.2%), or utilities (2.1%). And in Jonas Lindvist's Sweden, that number is almost double, with the Internet making up 6.3% of the country's 2009 GDP.[6]

If Lindvist's graphical map had been a truly literal representation of our networked society, it might have resembled a pointillist painting. The image would have been made up of so many billions of dots that, to the naked eye, they would have merged into a single collective whole. Everything that can be connected is being connected and the amount of data being produced online is mind-boggling. Every minute of every day in 2014, for example, the 3 billion Internet users in the world sent 204 million emails, uploaded 72 hours of new YouTube videos, made over 4 million Google searches, shared 2,460,000 pieces of Facebook content, downloaded 48,000 Apple apps, spent $83,000 on Amazon, tweeted 277,000 messages, and posted 216,000 new Instagram photos.[7] We used to talk about a "New York minute," but today's "Internet minute" in Marshall McLuhan's global village makes New York City seem like a sleepy village in which barely anything ever happens.

It may be hard to imagine, especially for those so-called digital natives who have grown up taking the Internet's networking tools for granted, but the world hasn't always been a data-rich information system. Indeed, three-quarters of a century ago, back in May 1941, when those German bombers blew the British House of Commons to smithereens, nobody and nothing was connected on the network. There weren't any digital devices able to communicate with one another at all, let alone real-time Twitter or Instagram feeds keeping us in the electronic information loop.

So how did we get from zero to those billions and billions of connected people and things? Where do the origins of the Internet lie?

Forebears

They lie with those Luftwaffe bombers flying at up to 250 miles an hour and at altitudes of over 30,000 feet above London at the beginning of World War II. In 1940, an eccentric Massachusetts Institute of Technology (MIT) professor of mathematics named Norbert Wiener, "the original computer geek," according to the *New York Times*,[8] began working on a system to track the German aircraft that controlled the skies above London. The son of a Jewish immigrant from Białystok in Poland, Wiener had become so obsessed with lending his scientific knowledge to the war against Germany that he'd been forced to seek psychoanalytical help to control his anti-Nazi fixation.[9] Technology could do good, he was convinced. It might even help defeat Hitler.

A math prodigy who graduated from Tufts University at the age of fourteen, received a Harvard doctorate at seventeen, and later studied with Bertrand Russell in Cambridge, Wiener was part of a pioneering group of technologists at MIT that included the electrical engineer and science mandarin Vannevar Bush and the psychologist J. C. R. Licklider. Without quite knowing what they were doing, these men invented many of the key principles of our networked society. What distinguished them, particularly Wiener, was a daring intellectual eclecticism. By defiantly crossing traditional academic disciplines, they were able to imagine and, in some ways, create our connected future.

"From the 1920's onwards, MIT increasingly attracted the brightest and best of America's scientists and engineers. In the middle decades of this century, the Institute became a seething cauldron of ideas about information, computing, communications and control," explains the Internet historian John Naughton. "And when we dip into it seeking the origins of the Net, three names always come up. They are Vannevar Bush, Norbert Wiener and J. C. R. Licklider."[10]

In the 1930s, Wiener had been part of the team that worked on Vannevar Bush's "differential analyser," a 100-ton electromagnetic analog computer cobbled together out of pulleys, shafts, wheels, and gears and which was designed to solve differential equations. And in 1941 Wiener had even pitched a prototype of a digital computer to Bush, more than five years before the world's first working digital device, the 1,800-square-foot, $500,000 Electronic Numerical Integrator and Computer (ENIAC), funded by the US Army and described by the press as a "giant brain," was unveiled in 1946.

But it was the issue of German bombers that obsessed Wiener after the German air force's massive bombing of London in the fall of 1940. He wasn't alone in his preoccupation with German aircraft. The US president, Franklin Delano Roosevelt, believed that it had been the overwhelming threat of German airpower that had led to the British appeasement of Hitler at Munich in 1938. So not only did Roosevelt commit the US military to producing ten thousand aircraft per year, but he also set up the National Defense Research Committee (NDRC), directed by Vannevar Bush, who by then had become the president's chief scientific advisor, to invest in more cooperation between the US government and six thousand of the country's leading research scientists.

While dean of the School of Engineering at MIT, Bush had set up the Radiation Lab, a group dedicated to figuring out how to enable antiaircraft guns to track and destroy those German bombers in the London sky. Recognizing that computers were potentially more than simply calculating machines, Wiener saw it as an information system challenge and invented a flight path predictor device that relied on a continuous stream of information that flowed back and forth between the gun and its operator. The polymath, with his interest in biology, philosophy, and mathematics, had serendipitously stumbled onto a new science of connectivity. In his eponymous bestselling 1948 book, Wiener called it "Cybernetics,"[11] and this new communications theory had a profound influence on everything from Marshall McLuhan's idea of information loops and J. C. R. Licklider's work on the symbiosis between man and computer to the mechanics of the Google search engine and the development of artificial intelligence. There may not have been an electronic communications network yet, but the idea of a self-correcting information system between man and machine, "a thing of almost natural beauty that constantly righted its errors through feedback from its environment," in the words of the technology writer James Harkin,[12] was born with Wiener's revolutionary flight path predictor machine.

While Norbert Wiener's technical challenge was making sense of scarce information, Vannevar Bush was worried about its overabundance. In September 1945, Bush published an article titled "As We May Think," in the *Atlantic Monthly* magazine. The purpose of the essay was to answer the question "What are scientists to do next?" in the postwar age. Rather than making "strange destructive gadgets," Bush called on American scientists to build thinking machines that would enrich human knowledge.

A seminal essay that was covered as a major news story by both *Time* and *Life* magazines on its release and was compared by the *Atlantic Monthly* editor to Emerson's iconic 1837 "The American Scholar" address in its historical significance, "As We May Think" offers an introduction to an information network uncannily reminiscent of the World Wide Web. Bush argued that the greatest challenge for his country's scientists in 1945 was to build tools for the new information age. Modern media products like radio, books, newspapers, and cameras were creating a massively indigestible overload of content. There was too much data and not enough time, he believed, highlighting a problem associated with what contemporary Internet scholars like Michael Goldhaber now call the "attention economy."

"The summation of human experience is being expanded at a prodigious rate," Bush explained, "and the means we use for threading through the consequent maze to the momentarily important item is the same as was used in the days of square-rigged ships."[13]

At the heart of Bush's vision was a network of intelligent links. "The process of tying two items together is the important thing," he said in explaining his idea of organizing content together into what he called "trails," which, he stressed, would never "fade." Using new technologies like microphotography and cathode ray tubes, Bush believed that scientists could compress the entire *Encyclopaedia Britannica* to "the volume of a matchbox" or condense a million-book library into "one end of a desk." Imagining a machine "which types when talked to" and that acts as a "mechanized private file and library," Bush called his mechanized information storage device a "Memex." Describing it as "an enlarged intimate supplement to his memory" that would mimic the "intricate web of trails carried by the cells of the brain," Bush imagined it as a physical desktop product not unlike a personal computer, and which would have a keyboard, levers, a series of buttons, and a translucent screen.

Along with its remarkable prescience, what is so striking about "As We May Think" is its unadulterated technological optimism. In contrast with Norbert Wiener, who later became an outspoken critic of government investment in scientific and particularly military research and who worried about the impact of digital computers upon jobs,[14] Vannevar Bush believed that government investment in science represented an unambiguously progressive force. In July 1945, Bush also wrote an influential paper for President Roosevelt entitled "Science, The Endless Frontier,"[15] in which he argued that what he called "the public welfare," particularly in the context of "full employment" and the role of science in generating jobs, would be improved by government investment in technological research. "One of our hopes is that after the war there will be full employment," Bush wrote to the president. "To reach that goal, the full creative and productive energies of the American people must be released."

"As We May Think" reflects this same rather naïve optimism about the economics of the information society. Vannevar Bush insists that everyone—particularly trained professionals like physicians, lawyers, historians, chemists, and a new blogger-style profession he dubbed "trail blazers"—would benefit from the Memex's automated organization of content. The particularly paradoxical thing about his essay is that while Bush prophesied a radically new technological future, he didn't imagine that the economics of this information society would be much different from his own. Yes, he acknowledged, compression would reduce the cost of the microfilm version of the *Encyclopaedia Britannica* to a nickel. But people would still pay for content, he assumed, and this would be beneficial to *Britannica*'s publishers and writers.

The third member of the MIT trinity of Net forebears was J. C. R. Licklider. A generation younger than Bush and Wiener, Licklider came in 1950 to MIT, where he was heavily influenced by Norbert Wiener's work on cybernetics and by Wiener's legendary Tuesday night dinners at a Chinese restaurant in Cambridge, which brought together an eclectic group of scientists and technologists. Licklider fitted comfortably into this unconventional crowd. Trained as a psychologist, mathematician, and physicist, he had earned a doctorate in psychoacoustics and headed up the human engineering group at MIT's Lincoln Laboratory, a facility that specialized in air defense research. He worked closely with the SAGE (Semi-Automatic Ground Environment) computer system, an Air Force–sponsored network of twenty-three control and radar stations designed to track Russian nuclear bombers. Weighing more than 250 tons and featuring 55,000 vacuum tubes, the SAGE system was the culmination of six years of development, 7,000 man-years of computer programming, and $61 billion in funding. It was, quite literally, a network of machines that one walked into.[16]

Licklider had become obsessed with computers after a chance encounter at MIT in the mid-1950s with a young researcher named Wesley Clark, who was working on one of Lincoln Labs's new state-of-the-art TX-2 digital computers. While the TX-2 contained only 64,000 bytes of storage (that's over a million times smaller than my current 64-gigabyte iPhone 5S), it was nonetheless one of the very earliest computers that both featured a video screen and enabled interactive graphics work. Licklider's fascination with the TX-2 led him to an obsession with the potential of computing and, like Marshall McLuhan, the belief that electronic media "would save humanity."[17]

Licklider articulated his vision of the future in his now-classic 1960 paper, "Man-Computer Symbiosis." "The hope is that in not too many years, human brains and computing machines will be coupled . . . tightly," he wrote, "and that the resulting partnership will think as no human brain has ever thought and process data in a way not approached by the information-handling machines we know today."[18]

Just as Norbert Wiener saw computers as more than calculating devices able to solve differential equations and Vannevar Bush believed they could effectively organize information, Licklider recognized that these new thinking machines were, first and foremost, communications devices. A division of labor between men and computers, he argued, could save us time, refine our democracy, and improve our decision making.

In 1958, Licklider left MIT. He first worked at a Cambridge, Massachusetts–based consulting group called Bolt, Beranek and Newman (BBN). Then, in 1962, he moved to Washington, D.C., where he took charge of both the command and control and the behavioral sciences divisions of the Advanced Research Projects Agency (ARPA), a civilian group established by President Dwight Eisenhower in early 1958 to aggregate the best scientific talent for the public good. At ARPA, where he controlled a government budget of $10 million and came to head up the Information Processing Techniques Office, Licklider's goal was the development of new programs that used computers as more than simply calculating machines. He gave ARPA contracts to the most advanced computer centers from universities like MIT, Stanford, Berkeley, and UCLA, and established an inner circle of computer scientists that a colleague dubbed "Lick's Priesthood" and Licklider himself imagined as "The Intergalactic Computer Network."[19]

There was, however, one problem with an intergalactic network. Digital computers—those big brains that Licklider called "information-handling machines"—could only handle their own information. Even the state-of-the-art devices like the

TX-2 had no means of communicating with other computers. In 1962, computers still did not have a common language. Programmers could share individual computers among each other by "time-sharing," which allowed them to work concurrently on a single machine. But every computer spoke in its own disparate language and featured software and protocols unintelligible to other computers.

But J. C. R. Licklider's Intergalactic Computer Network was about to become a reality. The peace that Vannevar Bush welcomed in July 1945 had never really materialized. America had instead quickly become embroiled in a new war—the Cold War. And it was this grand geostrategic conflict with the Soviet Union that created the man-computer symbiosis that gave birth to the Internet.

From Sputnik to the ARPANET

On Friday, October 4, 1957, the Soviet Union launched their Sputnik satellite into earth's orbit. The Sputnik Crisis, as President Eisenhower dubbed this historic Soviet victory in the space race, shook America's self-confidence to the core. American faith in its military, its science, its technology, its political system, even its fundamental values was severely undermined by the crisis. "Never before had so small and so harmless an object created such consternation," observed Daniel Boorstin in *The Americans*, writing about the loss of national self-confidence and self-belief that the crisis triggered.[20]

But along with all the doom and gloom, Sputnik also sparked a renaissance in American science, with the government's research and development budget rising from $5 billion in 1958 to more than $13 billion annually between 1959 and 1964.[21] ARPA, for example, with its initial $520 million investment and $2 billion budget plan, was created by President Eisenhower in the immediate aftermath of the crisis as a way of identifying and investing in scientific innovation.

But rather than innovation, the story of the Internet begins with fear. If the Soviets could launch such an advanced technology as Sputnik into space, then what was to stop them from launching nuclear missiles at the United States? This paranoia of a military apocalypse, "the specter of wholesale destruction," as Eisenhower put it, so brilliantly satirized in Stanley Kubrick's 1964 movie, *Dr. Strangelove*, dominated American public life after the Sputnik launch. "Hysterical prophesies of Soviet domination and the destruction of democracy were common," noted Katie Hafner and Matthew Lyon in *Where Wizards Stay Up Late*, their lucid history of the Internet's origins. "Sputnik was proof of Russia's ability to launch intercontinental ballistic missiles, said the pessimists, and it was just a matter of time before the Soviets would threaten the United States."[22]

The Cold War was at its chilliest in the late fifties and early sixties. In 1960, the Soviets shot down an American U-2 surveillance plane over the Urals. On August 17, 1961, the Berlin Wall, the Cold War's most graphic image of the division between East and West, was constructed overnight by the German Democratic Republic's communist regime. In 1962, the Cuban Missile Crisis sparked a terrifying contest of nuclear brinksmanship between Kennedy and Khrushchev. Nuclear war, once unthinkable, was being reimagined as a logistical challenge by game theorists at military research institutes like the RAND Corporation, the Santa Monica, California–based think tank set up by the US Air Force in 1964 to "provide intellectual muscle"[23] for American nuclear planners.

By the late 1950s, as the United States developed hair-trigger nuclear arsenals that could be launched in a matter of minutes, it was becoming clear that one of the weakest links in the American military system lay with its long-distance communications network. Kubrick's *Dr. Strangelove* had parodied a nuclear-armed America where the telephones didn't work, but the vulnerability of its communications system to military attack wasn't really a laughing matter.

As Paul Baran, a young computer consultant at RAND, recognized, America's analog long-distance telephone and telegraph system would be one of the first targets of a Soviet nuclear attack. It was a contradiction worthy of Joseph Heller's great World War II novel *Catch-22.* In the event of a nuclear attack on America, the key response should come from the president through the country's communications system. Yet such a response would be impossible, Baran realized, because the communications system itself would be one the first casualties of any Soviet attack.

The real issue, for Baran, was making America's long-distance communications network invulnerable against a Soviet nuclear attack. And so he set about building what he called "more survivable networks." It certainly was an audacious challenge. In 1959, the thirty-year-old, Polish-born Baran—who had only just started as a consultant at RAND, having dropped out of UCLA's doctoral program in electric engineering after he couldn't find a parking spot one day on its Los Angeles campus[24]—set out to rebuild the entire long-distance American communications network.

This strange story has an even stranger ending. Not only did Baran succeed in building a brilliantly original blueprint for this survivable network, but he also accidentally, along the way, invented the Internet. "The phrase 'father of the Internet' has become so debased with over-use as to be almost meaningless," notes John Naughton, "but nobody has a stronger claim to it than Paul Baran."[25]

Baran wasn't alone at RAND in recognizing the vulnerability of the nation's long-distance network. The conventional RAND approach to rebuilding this network was to invest in a traditional top-down hardware solution. A 1960 RAND report, for example, suggested that a nuclear-resistant buried cable network would cost $2.4 billion. But Baran was, quite literarily, speaking another language from the other analysts at RAND. "Many of the things I thought possible would tend to sound like utter nonsense, or impractical, depending on the generosity of spirit in those brought up in an earlier world,"[26] he acknowledged. His vision was to use digital computer technology to build a communications network that would be invulnerable to Soviet nuclear attack. "Computers were key," Hafner and Lyon write about Baran's breakthrough. "Independently of Licklider and others in computer's avant-garde, Baran saw well beyond mainstream computing, to the future of digital technologies and the symbiosis between humans and machines."[27]

Digital technologies transform all types of information into a series of ones and zeros, thus enabling computer devices to store and replicate information with perfect accuracy. In the context of communications, digitally encoded information is much less liable to degrade than analog data. Baran's computer-to-computer solution, which he viewed as a "public utility,"[28] was to build a digital network that would radically change the shape and identity of the preexisting analog system. Based on what he called "user-to-user rather than . . . center-to-center operation,"[29] this network would be survivable in a nuclear attack because it wouldn't have a heart. Rather than being built around a central communication switch, it would be what he called a "distributed network" with many nodes, each connected to its neighbor. Baran's grand design, articulated in his 1964 paper "On Distributed Communications," prefigures the chaotic map that Jonas Lindvist would later design for Ericsson's office. It would have no heart, no hierarchy, no central dot.

The second revolutionary aspect of Baran's survivable system was its method for communicating information from computer to computer. Rather than sending a single message, Baran's new system broke up this content into many digital pieces, flooding the network with what he called "message blocks," which would travel arbitrarily across its many nodes and be reassembled by the receiving computer into readable form. Coined as "packet switching" by Donald Davies, a government-funded information scientist at Britain's National Physical Laboratory, who had serendipitously been working on a remarkably similar set of ideas, the technology was driven by a process Baran called "hot potato routing," which rapidly sent packets of information from node to node, guaranteeing the security of the message from spies.

"We shape our tools and thereafter our tools shape us," McLuhan said. And, in a sense, the fate of Baran's grand idea on computer-to-computer communication that he developed in the early 1960s mirrored the technology itself. For a few years, bits and pieces of his ideas pinged around the computer science community. And then, in the midsixties, they were reassembled back at ARPA.

J. C. R. Licklider, who never stayed in a job more than a few years, was long gone, but his idea of "the Intergalactic Computer Network" remained attractive to Bob Taylor, an ex–NASA computer scientist, who now was in charge of ARPA's Information Processing Techniques Office. As more and more scientists around America were relying on computers for their research, Taylor recognized that there was a growing need for these computers to be able to communicate with one another. Taylor's concerns were more prosaic than an imminent Russian nuclear attack. He believed that computer-to-computer communication would cut costs and increase efficiency within the scientific community.

At the time, computers weren't small and they weren't cheap. And so one day in 1966, Taylor pitched the ARPA director, Charles Herzfeld, on the idea of connecting them.

"Why not try tying them all together?" he said.

"Is it going to be hard to do?" Herzfeld asked.

"Oh no. We already know how to do it," Taylor promised.

"Great idea," Herzfeld said. "Get it going. You've got a million dollars more in your budget right now. Go."[30]

And Taylor did indeed *get it going*. He assembled a team of engineers including Paul Baran and Wesley Clark, the programmer who had gotten J. C. R. Licklider hooked on the TX-2 computer back in the fifties. Relying on Baran's distributed packet-switching technology, the team developed a plan to develop a trial network of four sites—UCLA, Stanford Research Institute (SRI), the University of Utah, and the University of California, Santa Barbara. They were linked together by something called an Interface Message Processor (IMP), which today we call routers—those little boxes with blinking lights that connect up the networked devices in our homes. In December 1968, Licklider's old Boston consultancy BBN won the contract to build the network. By October 1969, the network, which became known as ARPANET, and was hosted by refrigerator-sized 900-pound Honeywell computers, was ready to go live.

The first computer-to-computer message was sent from UCLA to SRI on October 1, 1969. While trying to type "login," the SRI computer crashed after the UCLA programmer had managed to type "log." For the first, but certainly not for the last time, an electronic message sent from one computer to another was a miscommunication.

The launch of ARPANET didn't have the same dramatic impact as the Sputnik launch twelve years earlier. By the late sixties, American attention had shifted to transformational issues like the Vietnam War, the sexual revolution, and Black Power. So, in late 1969, nobody—with the exception of a few unfashionable geeks in the military-industrial complex—cared much about two 900-pound computers miscommunicating with each other.

But the achievement of Bob Taylor and his engineering team cannot be underestimated. More than Sputnik and the wasteful space race, the successful building of ARPANET would change the world. It was one of the smartest million dollars ever invested. Had that money come from venture capitalists, it would have returned many billions of dollars to its original investors.

The Internet

In September 1994, Bob Taylor's team reassembled in a Boston hotel to celebrate the twenty-fifth anniversary of ARPANET. By then, those two original nodes at UCLA and SRI had grown to over a million computers hosting Internet content and there was significant media interest in the event. At one point, an Associated Press reporter innocently asked Taylor and Robert Kahn, another of the original ARPANET team members, about the history of the Internet. What was the critical moment in its creation, this reporter wanted to know.

Kahn lectured the reporter on the difference between ARPANET and the Internet and suggested that it was something called "TCP/IP" that represented the "true beginnings of the Internet."

"Not true," Taylor interrupted, insisting that the "Internet's roots" lay with the ARPANET.[31]

Both Taylor and Kahn are, in a sense, correct. The Internet would never have been built without ARPANET. Growing from its four original IMPs in 1969, it reached 29 by 1972, 57 by 1975, and 213 IMPs by 1981 before it was shut down and replaced as the Internet's backbone by the National Science Foundation Network (NSFNET) in 1985. But the problem was that ARPANET's success led to the creation of other packet-switching networks—such as the commercial TELENET, the French CYCLADES, the radio-based PRNET, and the satellite network SATNET—which complicated internetworked communication. So Kahn was right.

ARPANET wasn't the Internet. And he was right, too, about TCP/IP, the two protocols that finally realized Licklider's dream of an intergalactic computer network.

Bob Kahn and Vint Cerf met at UCLA in 1970 while working on the ARPANET project. In 1974 they published "A Protocol for Packet Network Intercommunication," which laid out their vision of two complementary internetworking protocols that they called the Transmission Control Protocol (TCP) and the Internet Protocol (IP)—TCP being the service that guarantees the sending of the stream and IP organizing its delivery.

Just as Paul Baran designed his survivable network to have a distributed structure, so the same was true of Kahn and Cerf's TCP/IP. "We wanted as little as possible at the center," they wrote about the unerringly open architecture of these new universal standards that treated all network traffic equally.[32] The addition of these protocols to the ARPANET in January 1983 was, according to Internet historians Hafner and Lyon, "probably the most important event that would take place in the development of the Internet for years to come."[33] TCP/IP enabled a network of networks that enabled users of every network—from ARPANET, SATNET, and PRNET to TELENET and CYCLADES—to communicate with each other.

Kahn and Cerf's universal rulebook for digital communications fueled the meteoric growth of the Internet. In 1985, there were around 2,000 computers able to access the Internet. By 1987 this had risen to almost 30,000 computers and by October 1989 to 159,000.[34] Many of these computers were attached to local area networks as well as early commercial dial-up services like CompuServe, Prodigy, and America Online. The first so-called killer app, a term popularized by Larry Downes and Chunka Mui in their bestseller about the revolutionary impact of digital technology on traditional business,[35] was electronic mail. A 1982 ARPANET report reviewing the network's first decade noted that email had come to eclipse all other applications in the volume of its traffic and described it as a "smashing success."[36] Thirty years later, email had become, if anything, an even bigger hit. By 2012 there were more than 3 billion email accounts around the world sending 294 billion emails, of which around 78% were spam.[37]

Another popular feature was the Bulletin Board System (BBS), which enabled users with similar interests to connect and collectively share information and opinions. Among the best known of these was the Whole Earth 'Lectronic Link (the WELL), begun in 1985 by the *Whole Earth Catalog* founder Stewart Brand. The WELL captured much of the countercultural utopianism of early online users who believed that the distributed structure of the technology created by Internet architects like Paul Baran, with its absence of a central dot, represented the end of traditional government power and authority. This was most memorably articulated by John Perry Barlow, an early WELL member and lyricist for the Grateful Dead, in his later 1996 libertarian manifesto "Declaration of the Independence of Cyberspace."

"Governments of the Industrial World, you weary giants of flesh and steel, I come from Cyberspace, the new home of mind," Barlow announced from, of all places, Davos, the little town in the Swiss Alps where the wealthiest and most powerful people meet at the World Economic Forum each year. "I ask you of the past to leave us alone. You are not welcome among us. You have no sovereignty where we gather."[38]

The real explanation of the Internet's early popularity was, however, more prosaic. Much of it was both the cause and the effect of a profound revolution in computer hardware. Rather than being dependent on "giant brains" that one "walked into" like the 1,800-square-foot ENIAC, the invention of the transistor by a Bell Labs team in 1947—"the very substructure of the future,"[39] in the words of the technology writer David Kaplan—resulted in computers simultaneously becoming smaller and smaller and more and more powerful. "Few scientific achievements this century were as momentous," Kaplan suggests about this breakthrough. Between 1967 and 1995, the capacity of computer hard drives rose an average of 35% every year, with Intel's annual sales growing from under $3,000 in 1968 to $135 million six years later. Intel's success in developing faster and faster microprocessors confirmed the prescient 1965 statement of its cofounder Gordon Moore, "Moore's law," which predicted that chip speed would double every year or eighteen months. And so, by the early 1980s, hardware manufacturers like IBM and Apple were able to build "personal computers"—relatively affordable desktop devices that, with a modem, allowed anyone access to the Internet.

By the end of the 1980s, the Internet had connected 800 networks, 150,000 registered addresses, and several million computers. But this project to network the world wasn't quite complete. There was one thing still missing—Vannevar Bush's Memex. There were no trails yet on the Internet, no network of intelligent links, no process of tying two items together on the network.

The World Wide Web

In 1960, a "discombobulated genius" named Ted Nelson came up with the idea of "nonsequential writing," which he coined "hypertext."[40] Riffing off Vannevar Bush's notion of "information trails," Nelson replaced Bush's reliance on analog devices like levers and microfilm with his own faith in the power of digital technology to make these nonlinear connections. Like Bush, who believed that the trails on his Memex "do not fade,"[41] the highly eccentric Nelson saw himself as a "rebel against forgetting."[42] His lifelong quest to create hypertext, which he code-named Xanadu, was indeed a kind of rebellion against forgetfulness. In Nelson's Xanadu system, there was no "concept of deletion." Everything would be remembered.

In 1980, twenty years after Nelson's invention of the hypertext idea, a much less eccentric genius, Tim Berners-Lee, arrived as a consultant at the European Particles Physics Laboratory (CERN) in Geneva. Like Nelson, Berners-Lee, who had earned a degree in physics from Oxford University's Queens College in 1976, was concerned with protecting his own personal forgetfulness. The problem, Berners-Lee wrote in his autobiography, *Weaving the Web*, was remembering "the connections among the various people, computers, and projects at the lab."[43] This interest in memory inspired Berners-Lee to build what he called his first website program, Enquire. But it also planted what he called "larger vision" in his "consciousness":

> *Suppose all the information stored on computers everywhere were linked*, I thought. *Suppose I could program my computer to create a space in which anything could be linked to anything.* All the bits of information in every computer at CERN, and on the planet, would be available to me and to anyone else. There would be a single global information space.[44]

In 1984, when Berners-Lee returned to CERN and discovered the Internet, he also returned to his larger vision of a single global information space. By this time, he'd discovered the work of Vannevar Bush and Ted Nelson and become familiar with what he called "the advances" of technology giants like Donald Davies, Paul Baran, Bob Kahn, and Vint Cerf.

"I happened to come along with time, and the right interest and inclination, after hypertext and the Internet had come of age," Berners-Lee modestly acknowledged. "The task left to me was to marry them together."[45]

The fruit of that marriage was the World Wide Web, the information management system so integral to the Internet that many people think that the Web actually *is* the Internet. "If I have seen further it is by standing on the shoulders of giants," Isaac Newton once said. And Berners-Lee not only built upon the achievements of the Internet's founding fathers, but he designed the Web to ride on top of the Internet to create what the Sussex University economist Mariana Mazzucato calls a "foundational technology."[46]

His program leveraged the Internet's preexisting packet-switching technology, its TCP/IP protocols, and, above all, its completely decentralized structure and commitment to treating all data equally. The Web's architecture was made up of three elements: first, a computer language for marking up hypertext files, which he called Hypertext Markup Language (HTML); second, a taxonomy for traveling between these hypertext files, which he called Hypertext Transfer Protocol (HTTP); third, a special address code linked to each hypertext file that would be able to instantly call up any other file on the Web, which he called a Universal Resource Locator (URL).[47] By labeling files and by using hypertext as a link between these files, Berners-Lee radically simplified Internet usage. His great achievement was to begin the process of taking the Internet out of the university and into the world.

Berners-Lee wrote his initial proposal for the Web in March 1989, revising the proposal and building the first Web browser, named WorldWideWeb, in 1990. In January 1991 the Web went public and in November 1991 the first website, an information resource about CERN with the address Info.cern.ch, was launched. Even more than email, the Web has been the Internet's ultimate killer app over the last quarter of a century. With the creation of the Web, concludes John Naughton, the Internet achieved "liftoff."[48] Without Berners-Lee's brilliantly simple innovation there would be no Google, Amazon, Facebook, or the millions of other websites and online businesses that we use on a daily basis. Without the Web, we wouldn't all be living in Ericsson's Networked Society.

Tim Berners-Lee wrote his initial Web proposal in March 1989 at CERN. Six months later, a few hundred miles to the northeast of Geneva, the Berlin Wall fell and the Cold War came to an end. Back then, with the dramatic destruction of the Wall in November, it was thought that 1989 would be remembered as a watershed year that marked the end of the Cold War and the victory of free-market liberalism. The Stanford University political scientist Francis Fukuyama, assuming that the great debate between capitalists and socialists over the best way to organize industrial society had finally been settled, described the moment that the Wall came down as the "End of History."

But the converse is actually true. Nineteen eighty-nine actually represents the birth of a new period of history, the Networked Computer Age. The Internet has created new values, new wealth, new debates, new elites, new scarcities, new markets, and above all, a new kind of economy. Well-intentioned technologists like Vannevar Bush, Norbert Wiener, J. C. R. Licklider, Paul Baran, Robert Kahn, and Tim Berners-Lee had little interest in money, but one of the most significant consequences of their creation has been the radical reshaping of economic life. Yes, the Internet may, as one historian suggests, be the "greatest co-operative enterprise in the history of mankind."[49] But distributed technology doesn't necessarily lead to distributed economics, and the cooperative nature of its technology isn't reflected in its impact on the economy. No, with the creation of the Web came the creation of a new kind of capitalism. And it has been anything but a cooperative venture.

CHAPTER TWO

THE MONEY

The One Percent Economy

San Francisco's venerable Commonwealth Club, standing at the southern end of Battery Street, a few blocks from the Battery social club, rarely sells out of tickets for its speaking events. But in February 2014, the club hosted a controversial eighty-two-year-old multibillionaire speaker who gave a sold-out speech titled "The War on the One Percent," requiring the presence of three police officers to protect him from a bellicose, standing-room-only crowd.[1]

A month earlier, Tom Perkins, the cofounder of the Kleiner Perkins Caufield & Byers (KPCB) venture capital firm and "the man most responsible for creating Silicon Valley," according to his biographer,[2] had written an angry letter of complaint to the *Wall Street Journal* about what he described as San Francisco's "Progressive Kristallnacht." The letter was a defense of Silicon Valley's technological elite—the venture capitalists, entrepreneurs, programmers, and Internet executives of KPCB-backed local Internet companies like Google, Twitter, and Facebook, identified by Perkins as "the successful one percent."[3] It turned out to be the most commented upon letter ever published in the *Journal*, sparking an intense debate about the nature of the new digital economy.

"From the Occupy movement to the demonization of the rich embedded in virtually every word of our local newspaper, the *San Francisco Chronicle*, I perceive a rising tide of hatred of the successful one percent. This is a very dangerous drift in our American thinking. *Kristallnacht* was unthinkable in 1930; is its descendant 'progressive' radicalism unthinkable now?," Perkins wrote about the growing popular resentment in the Bay Area to dominant Internet companies like Google and Facebook.

Tom Perkins's February 2014 speech at the Commonwealth Club also made news around the world. While Perkins apologized for his incendiary Kristallnacht analogy, he nonetheless defended the main premise of his *Journal* letter, telling the audience that "the one percent are not causing inequality—they're the job creators."[4]

Many of those in the audience disagreed, seeing local Internet companies like Google, Facebook, and Twitter as the cause of rather than solution to the exorbitant real estate prices and the high levels of poverty and unemployment in the Bay Area. "We've never seen anything remotely like this before," explained the San Francisco cultural historian Gary Kamiya. "Techies used to seem endearing geeks, who made money and cute little products but couldn't get the girls. Now they're the lord and masters."[5]

Perkins, a former Hewlett-Packard executive who cofounded KPCB in 1972, made the same argument about the value of the one percent in his 2007 autobiography, *Valley Boy*. Describing some of his venture capital firm's greatest triumphs, including the financing of Netscape, Amazon, and Google, he boasted that KPCB investments have created $300 billion in market value, an annual revenue stream of $100 billion, and more than 250,000 jobs.[6] It's a win-win, he wrote in *Valley Boy*, insisting that the new digital economy is a cooperative venture. It's resulting in more jobs, more revenue, more wealth, and more general prosperity.

KPCB's successful bets on Netscape, Amazon, and Google certainly have been a personal win-win for Perkins. These lucrative investments enabled the self-styled "Valley Boy" to build the *Maltese Falcon*, a $130 million yacht as long as a football field, made out of the same militarized carbon-fiber material as a B-1 bomber,[7] and *Dr No*, his current "adventure yacht," which carries his own private submarine to explore the South Pole. They financed the purchase of his Richard Mille watch, which he claims is worth as much as a "6-pack of Rolexes,"[8] his 5,500-square-foot apartment on the sixtieth floor of San Francisco's Millennium Tower with its spectacular views of the Bay, and his multimillion-dollar mansion in exclusive Marin County, just over the Golden Gate Bridge from San Francisco.

But Perkins was wrong about the broader benefits of the network economy that KPCB played such an important role in creating. A quarter century after Tim Berners-Lee's invention of the Web, it's becoming increasingly clear that the Internet economy is anything but a cooperative venture. The structure of this economy is the reverse of the technological open architecture created by the Internet's pioneers. Instead, it's a top-down system that is concentrating wealth instead of spreading it. Unfortunately, the supposed "new rules" for this new economy aren't very new. Rather than producing more jobs or prosperity, the Internet is dominated by winner-take-all companies like Amazon and Google that are now monopolizing vast swaths of our information economy.

But why has this happened? How has a network designed to have neither a heart, a hierarchy, nor a central dot created such a top-down, winner-take-all economy run by a plutocracy of new lords and masters?

Monetization

In *The Everything Store*, his definitive 2013 biography of Amazon founder and CEO Jeff Bezos, Brad Stone recounts a conversation he had with Bezos about the writing of his book. "How do you plan to handle the narrative fallacy?" the Internet entrepreneur asked, leaning forward on his elbows and staring in his bug-eyed way at Stone.[9]

There was a nervous silence as Stone looked at Bezos blankly.

The "narrative fallacy," Bezos explained to Stone, is the tendency, particularly of authors, "to turn complex realities" into "easily understandable narratives." As a fan of Nassim Nicholas Taleb's *The Black Swan*, a book that introduced the concept, Jeff Bezos believes that the world—like that map on the wall of Ericsson's Stockholm office—is so random and chaotic that it can't be easily summarized (except, of course, as being randomly chaotic). The history of Amazon is too complicated and fortuitous to be squeezed into an understandable narrative, Bezos was warning Stone. And he would, no doubt, argue that the history of the Internet, in which he and his Everything Store have played such a central role since Amazon.com went live on July 16, 1995, is equally complex and incomprehensible.

But Bezos, the founder and CEO of the largest bookstore in the world, is wrong to be so skeptical of easily understandable stories. The narrative fallacy is actually a fallacy. Sometimes a story that appears to be complex is, in reality, quite simple. Sometimes it can be summarized in a sentence. Or even a single word.

The history of the Internet, which certainly appears to be as random and chaotic as any story ever told, is actually two simple stories. The first story—from World War II through the end of the Cold War in the early nineties—is a narrative of public-spirited technologists and academics like Vannevar Bush, Paul Baran, and Tim Berners-Lee, and of publicly funded institutions like NDRC, ARPA, and NSFNET. This is primarily a story of how the Internet was invented for national security and civic goals. It's a story of how public money—like the million-dollar ARPA investment in Bob Taylor's project to link computers—paid to build a global electronic network. And it's a story of these well-meaning pioneers' relative indifference and occasional hostility to the lucrative economic opportunities offered by their creation. Berners-Lee, who fought hard to make his World Wide Web technology available to anyone for free, even argued that charging for licensing fees for Web browser technology "was an act of treason in the academic community and the Internet community."[10] Indeed, up until 1991, Internet commerce was an "oxymoron" since the US government maintained legal control of the Internet and required companies that sought access to NSFNET, the Net's backbone, to sign an "Acceptable Use Policy" that limited such use to "research and education."[11]

"There are very few second acts in the world of high technology," argues Jim Clark, one of Silicon Valley's most colorful entrepreneurs and founder of Silicon Graphics, Netscape Communications, and Healtheon. But Clark is wrong. High tech is dominated by successful financial second acts—his own, Steve Jobs's, and, most significantly, that of the Internet itself.

The Internet's second act began in the early nineties when the American government closed NSFNET and handed over the running of the Internet backbone to commercial Internet service providers. John Doerr, a general partner at KPCB who was originally hired by Tom Perkins, summarized this second act in a single sentence: "The largest creation of legal wealth in the history of the planet." In this phrase Doerr captures how an electronic network, thanks to Doerr's investments as a KPCB partner in Internet companies like Netscape, Amazon, Google, Twitter, and Facebook, has made him among the richest people on earth, with a personal fortune of some $3 billion and an annual income of close to $100 million.[12]

This story can even be summarized in a single word: *money*. The Internet, to borrow one of Silicon Valley's most hackneyed vulgarisms, has become "monetized." It's a curious historical coincidence. Just as the end of the Cold War led to the scramble by Russian financial oligarchs to buy up state-owned assets, so the privatization of the Internet at the end of the Cold War triggered the rush by a new class of technological oligarchs in the United States to acquire prime online real estate.

"Silicon Valley in 2014 is like Wall Street in the 80's," observes Kevin Roose, the author of *Young Money*. "It's the obvious destination for the work-hard-play-hard set."[13]

Like an express suddenly roaring past a freight train, the second version of the Internet replaced the first with remarkable speed. What is particularly striking is how few people successfully jumped from one train to the other. But one person who did make the leap was Marc Andreessen. Indeed, more than any other single individual, Andreessen was responsible for transforming the nonprofit Internet into a winner-take-all economy.

Andreessen had become familiar with the World Wide Web in the early nineties as a computer science student at the University of Illinois, where he was also earning $6.85 an hour working as a programmer at the National Center for Supercomputing Applications (NCSA), a National Science Foundation–funded research center attached to the university. The major problem with Berners-Lee's WorldWideWeb browser, he recognized, was that it was forbiddingly hard for anyone without advanced programing skills to use. So, in 1993, Andreessen and a team of young programmers at the NCSA developed a graphics-based Web browser called Mosaic, with an easy-to-use interface that enabled websites to feature color pictures. "It spread," Andreessen said, "like a virus,"[14] generating an estimated 342,000 percent increase of Web traffic in a year. At the beginning of 1993, before Mosaic's release, less than 1 percent of Internet users were on the Web and there were only around 50 websites. A year later, Mosaic's viral success had spawned 10,000 websites, with the Web now being surfed by 25% of Internet users.

But the NCSA refused to give the Mosaic team any credit for their remarkably successful creation and so in early 1994 a disillusioned Andreessen quit and moved out west, to Silicon Valley. A couple of months later, he received an email from a stranger. It was his ticket to ride on the express train.

> Marc:
>
> You may not know me, but I'm the founder and former chairman of Silicon Graphics. As you may have read in the press lately, I'm leaving SGI. I plan to form a new company. I would like to discuss the possibility of you joining me.
>
> Jim Clark

In his autobiography, Clark suggests, with characteristic immodesty, that this email might be comparable in its epochal significance to when Alexander Graham Bell said to his assistant, "Watson, come in here. I need you"—the first words ever uttered over the telephone.[15] It wasn't, of course. But the email did have profound consequences for the future of the Internet economy. Clark, recognizing both Marc Andreessen's precocity and the astonishing growth of the Web, saw an opportunity to finally make a Tom Perkins–sized fortune.

"So the hell with the commune," Clark wrote in his autobiography as he turned his back on the nonprofit World Wide Web created by Tim Berners-Lee. "This was business."[16]

Clark and Andreessen created Netscape Communications, one of the most iconic commercial ventures of the last quarter of the twentieth century. Founding it in April 1994 with $3 million of Clark's own money, they reassembled Andreessen's original NCSA Mosaic team out in Silicon Valley and built a far superior version of the original Web browser from scratch, code-named Mozilla, and later called Navigator. In the fall of 1994, Clark secured a $5 million investment from John Doerr—which was not only KPCB's first investment in an Internet company but also among the first significant ventures of any kind in a Web venture. Released in December 1994, Netscape Navigator 1.0 distributed more than 3 million copies in three months, mostly for free. By May 1995, Netscape had 5 million users and its market share had risen to 60% of the Web browser market. Unlike many of the later dot-com companies, Netscape even had real revenue—some $7 million in its first year, mostly from licensing deals to corporations. As *Time* magazine quipped in the summer of 1995 for the first of its many cover stories about the company, Netscape was "growing faster than O.J. Simpson's legal fees."[17] The eighteen-month-old startup went public in August 1995 because Clark rightly feared that Microsoft, back then the world's most powerful computer software company, nicknamed Godzilla by its competitors because of its fearsome business practices, was about to get into the browser business in order to crush Netscape.

Mozilla did indeed elude Godzilla. The public offering was so spectacularly successful that it is now known as the "Netscape Moment" and holds its own mythological place in both Wall Street and Silicon Valley folklore. The IPO realized a payout of $765 million for Kleiner Perkins, which was more than double the value of the entire fund from which the original investment came.[18] Clark's investment of $3 million came to be worth $633 million—which explains why the incorrigibly self-aggrandizing entrepreneur put the identifying number 633MN on the tail of an executive jet he bought with some of his proceeds from the IPO.[19] And the just turned twenty-four-year-old Marc Andreessen, who two years earlier had been making $6.85 an hour as a NCSA programmer, was suddenly worth $58 million, thus becoming the first in a long line of boy tycoons minted by the Internet.[20]

"What happened to Netscape Communications was without parallel," notes David Kaplan, "and came to define modern Silicon Valley."[21] Netscape's success drove the first great commercial expansion of the Internet. The number of Internet users grew from 16 million in 1995 to 361 million in 2000. This growth confirmed Metcalfe's law—Ethernet inventor Bob Metcalfe's eponymous rule that each new person who joins a network increases the power of that network exponentially. It triggered the dot-com boom, a half decade of irrational exuberance that created Amazon, Yahoo, eBay, and thousands of failed Internet startups, including my own, an online music website backed by Intel and SAP called AudioCafe. And it crowned Marc Andreessen, who was featured sitting shoeless on the cover of *Time* magazine in February 1996, as the young disruptive hero of the Internet revolution.

But the Netscape Moment marked the death of something, too. Discussing Tim Berners-Lee's decision to give away his technology for free, Jim Clark—who disliked venture capitalists, believing them to be vultures that "make hyenas look good"[22]—suggests that "any entrepreneur might wonder about his (Berners-Lee's) sanity while admiring his soul."[23] What the Internet lost in the early nineties, with the passing of its mantle from researchers like Tim Berners-Lee to businessmen like Jim Clark, can be simply summarized. As Wall Street moved west, the Internet lost a sense of common purpose, a general decency, perhaps even its soul. Money replaced all these things. It gushed from the spigots of venture capitalist firms like KPCB, which—with successful Internet companies like Amazon, Facebook, and Google—came to replace the government as the main source for investment in innovation.

Jeff Bezos, if he happened to be reading this, would probably accuse me of inventing a narrative fallacy, of reducing the Internet's complex reality to an easy-to-understand morality tale. But Bezos and his Everything Store are exhibits A and B in my argument. He was a Wall Street analyst who moved out west and amassed a $30 billion personal fortune through his Internet ventures. And his own 1994 startup, Amazon, the winner-take-all store that had revenue of $74.45 billion in 2013—in spite of its convenience, great prices, and reliability—reflects much of what has gone wrong with the Internet in its monetized second act.

The Winner-Take-All Network

After the Netscape Moment, everything, it seemed, was possible. Venture capital investments rose in America from $10 billion in 1995 to $105.8 billion in 2000.[24] Internet companies went public with barely any revenue. Hundreds of millions of dollars were poured into supposedly "innovative" Web businesses trying to sell everything from pet food to toilet paper. One influential futurist, the MIT professor of technology Nicholas Negroponte, even described the digital age in his bestselling 1995 book *Being Digital* as being a "force of nature." "It has four very powerful qualities that will guarantee its ultimate triumph," Negroponte promised about this revolution. It would be "decentralizing, globalizing, harmonizing and empowering."[25]

One of the most frequently quoted books about the Internet economy published in the wake of the August 1995 IPO was Kevin Kelly's *New Rules for the New Economy*.[26] Kelly's economic manifesto, which came out as a series of articles he wrote as the founding executive editor for *Wired* magazine, became an appropriately magical handbook for startup entrepreneurs in the surreal dot-com era. The personally very gracious and well-meaning Kelly, one of the founders of the countercultural WELL BBS and a born-again Christian techno-mystic who would later write a book about how technology has a mind of its own,[27] stoked the already irrational exuberance of the late nineties with a new economy manifesto that today reads like a parody of digital utopianism. Kelly's mistake was to assume that the Internet's open technology would automatically be reflected by what he, borrowing Negroponte's messianic verbiage, called the "decentralized ownership and equity" of a "global economic culture."[28] More digital shaman than economist, Kelly presented the new economy as an uneconomy—one in which the traditional laws of supply and demand and abundance and scarcity no longer applied. With rules like "Embrace the Swarm," "Opportunities Before Efficiencies," and "Plenitude, Not Scarcity," Kelly's book—part McLuhan, part Mao, part plain meshuggah—described the Internet economy as a collectivist cornucopia that would climax in what he called "a thousand points of wealth."

But not everyone embraced the swarm and learned to speak this kind of gobbledygook. In 1995, two American economists published a less hyped but much more prescient book about the depressingly old rules of our new economy. In *The Winner-Take-All Society*,[29] Robert Frank and Philip Cook argue that the defining feature of late-twentieth-century global capitalism was a growing financial chasm between a narrow elite and the rest of society. Rather than Kevin Kelly's "thousand points of wealth," Frank and Cook found that wealth in the winner-take-all society actually had very few points. They agreed with Tom Perkins about the enormous power and influence of this new elite. But in contrast with Perkins, Frank, and Cook—whose observations about this emerging plutocracy are supported by the later research of many distinguished economists, including Paul Krugman, Joseph

Stiglitz, Robert Reich, and Thomas Piketty—didn't celebrate this one percent, trickle-down economy.

Frank and Cook argued that the new information economy was central in the creation of the new inequality. "Perhaps the most profound changes in the underlying forces that give rise to winner-take-all effects have stemmed from technological developments in two areas—telecommunications and electronic computing," they argued.[30] Scale is critical in an instantly global market like the Internet. But the bigger the Internet became, they predicted, the fewer dominant online companies there would be. What Frank and Cook described as our natural "mental shelf-space constraints" means that in an increasingly information-rich economy, "for any given number of sellers trying to get our attention, an increasingly small fraction of each category can hope to succeed."[31]

As *Dot.Con* author John Cassidy notes, this winner-take-all model was already powerful in the pre-Internet tech economy, where "consumers tended to settle on one or two dominant products, such as Microsoft Windows, which generate big profits." After the 1995 Netscape Moment triggered the dot-com mania, venture capitalists bet that this winner-take-all model would enable the dominance of a single company in each online sector. Alongside the general stock market hysteria, this thinking contributed to the massive increase in venture capital commitments in America between 1995 and 2000. The obsession with getting big quick also explains some of the most surreal Internet deals in the bubble, such as AOL's catastrophic $164 billion acquisition of Time Warner in January 2000 and the $1.2 billion invested by venture capitalists in the online grocer Webvan, which the technology site CNET ranks as the "most epic fail in the dotcom bubble fiasco."[32] Founded in 1997 by Louis Borders, a founder of Borders Books, Webvan went public in November 1999, even though in the first six months of 1999, the e-commerce grocer lost $35 million on sales of $395,000. On November 5, 1999, the day of its IPO, Webvan was valued at almost $8 billion.[33] A little over a year and a half later, on July 10, 2001, Webvan filed for bankruptcy protection and shut down.

In spite of the Webvan disaster, the winner-take-all model had a particular resonance in the e-commerce sector, where the so-called Queen of the Net, the influential Morgan Stanley research analyst Mary Meeker (who is now a partner at KPCB), saw first-mover advantage as critical in dominating online marketplaces. And it was this winner-take-all thinking that led Jeff Bezos, in 1996, to accept an $8 million investment from John Doerr in exchange for 13% of Amazon, a deal that valued the year-old e-commerce startup at $60 million.[34]

"The cash from Kleiner Perkins hit the place like a dose of entrepreneurial steroids, making Jeff more determined than ever," noted one early Amazon employee about the impact of the 1996 KPCB investment.[35] "Get Big Fast" immediately became Bezos's mantra. Which is exactly what he did, with Amazon's value growing to over $150 billion by June 2014, making the Everything Store by far the dominant retailer on the Internet, crushing or acquiring its competitors, monopolizing the mental shelf space of online consumers, selling everything from books, baby gear, and beauty products to shoes, software, and sporting goods.

Mary Meeker was right about first-mover advantage on the Internet and its consequence of a winner-take-all economy dominated by a coterie of massively powerful global companies. What Kevin Kelly incorrectly predicted as the Internet's "decentralized ownership and equity" structure has, in fact, turned out to be a rigidly centralized economy controlled by what Fred Wilson, the New York City–based cofounder of Union Square Ventures and one of the smartest early-stage investors in the Internet economy, calls "dominant networks that are emerging all around us," like "Google, Twitter, YouTube, SoundCloud [and] Uber."[36] Wilson explains that "for all of its democratizing power, the Internet, in its current form, has simply replaced the old boss with a new boss and these new bosses have market power that, in time, will be vastly larger than that of the old boss."[37]

The rules of this new economy are thus those of the old industrial economy—on steroids. The bigger Amazon has become, the cheaper its prices and the more reliable its services, the more invulnerable it has become to competition. "Amazon is increasingly looking like a monopoly in publishing," Wilson explains, warning that the Internet has gone "from laughable toys to dominant monopolies in less than a decade."[38]

Scale matters more than ever in the online economy, particularly in e-commerce, where the margins are extremely tight. "Opportunities before efficiencies" was one of Kevin Kelly's new rules for the new economy. But Amazon, while certainly not averse to the strategic opportunities in the digital market, has built its economic power upon the tactical efficiencies of a company that, in 2013, booked $75 billion in sales, but a profit of just $274 million.[39] In 2002, Amazon's growing financial clout enabled it to take on United Parcel Service, wringing significant price concessions from the shipping giant, thereby giving it a major cost advantage over its rivals and, as Brad Stone notes, teaching Amazon "an enduring lesson about the power of scale and the reality of Darwinian survival in the world of big business."[40] Amazon's financial resources allowed the notoriously parsimonious company in 2001 to even build its own, customized back-end fulfillment software, which, Stone notes, allowed it "innumerable advantages," such as being able to promise its customers when their packages will arrive and enabling the introduction of its lucrative subscription-based Amazon Prime two-day delivery service.[41]

The winner-take-all economy is a euphemism for a market that tends toward monopoly—and that's exactly what Amazon, with its tighter and tighter control of online commerce, is becoming. Neoliberals like Tom Perkins would argue that Amazon is creating jobs, enriching our culture, and improving everyone's prosperity. But he'd be wrong. The reverse is actually true. Amazon, in spite of its undoubted convenience, reliability, and great value, is actually having a disturbingly negative impact on the broader economy.

The Amazon narrative is best encapsulated by its impact on the publishing industry over the last twenty years. There's no denying that, in many ways, Amazon has been beneficial for book publishers, especially smaller ones. Bezos created a universal bookstore that offered the most comprehensive selection of books ever available in one place, particularly for readers like myself interested in buying hard-to-find new and secondhand books. Amazon empowered smaller publishers, giving them a relatively level playing field to widely distribute their books. And Amazon's significant investment in its excellent Kindle reader, which it launched in 2007, was key to the book industry's relatively smooth transition to digital. But the problem is that the more successful Amazon has become, the more power it has amassed over book publishers both large and small. Unfortunately, what Fred Wilson calls Amazon's "monopoly in publishing" is ultimately bad news not only for publishers, but also for authors and even readers, who are all now suffering as Bezos takes advantage of his increasingly monopolistic power to squeeze publishers of their profits.

The book industry, which was initially quite enthusiastic about Bezos's venture, has mostly soured on Amazon. "An abusive, alcoholic father; a snake-oil salesman; a predatory lion; Nazi Germany," are, according to *Forbes* staff writer Jeff Bercovici, some of the insults that publishers and retailers are now throwing at Amazon.[42] And it's not hard to see why some literary folks are reverting to these kind of clichés. In the United States, where Amazon now accounts for 65% of all digital purchases in a market that now makes up 30% of all book sales,[43] there were around four thousand bookstores in the mid-1990s, when Bezos launched Amazon.com. But today there are half that number, resulting in thousands of lost retail jobs.[44] In Britain, things are no better, with fewer than 1,000 bookstores surviving in 2014, a third fewer than in 2005.[45] The Everything Store hasn't been any kinder to the publishing industry, where, in 2004, Amazon's books group division unleashed what it dubbed a "Gazelle Project" designed to crush small publishers that wouldn't agree to their stringent demands on pricing and bill payment. This project got its name, Brad Stone explains, because Jeff Bezos instructed one of his staff that "Amazon should approach these small publishers the way a cheetah would pursue a sickly gazelle."[46]

Bezos's brutally efficient business methodology, what Brad Stone politely describes as "eliminating more costs from the supply chain,"[47] is now squeezing jobs in every retail sector—from clothing, electronics, and toys to garden furniture and jewelry. As a 2013 study from the US Institute of Local Self-Reliance (ILSR) reports, while brick-and-mortar retailers employ 47 people for every $10 million in sales, Amazon only employs 14 people to generate the same $10 million sales revenue. Amazon, according to the ILSR report, is a job killer rather than job creator, having destroyed a net 27,000 jobs in the American economy in 2012.[48]

Even more chilling is Amazon's heartless treatment of its nonunionized workforce, particularly its utilization of monitoring technologies to observe the company's warehouse workers' most minute activities. Simon Head, a senior fellow at the Institute for Public Knowledge at New York University, argues that this makes Amazon, with Walmart, the "most egregiously ruthless corporation in America." This shop-floor surveillance, Head says, is an "extreme variant" of nineteenth- and twentieth-century Taylorism—the scientific management system invented by Frederick Winslow Taylor, which Aldous Huxley savagely parodied as "Fordism" in *Brave New World*.[49]

Yet even without these monitoring technologies, work in the Amazon fulfillment centers is notoriously unpleasant. Nonunionized Amazon workers in Pennsylvania, for example, have been subjected to such high warehouse temperatures that the company has ambulances permanently parked outside the facility ready to speed overheated workers to the emergency ward.[50] In its Kentucky delivery center, Amazon's hyperefficient work culture has created what one former manager described as the "huge problems" of permanently injured workers.[51] In Germany, Amazon's second-largest market, 1,300 workers organized a series of strikes in 2013 over pay and working conditions as well as to protest a security firm hired to police the company's distribution centers.[52] In Britain, a 2013 BBC undercover investigation into an Amazon warehouse revealed disturbingly harsh working conditions that one stress expert warned could lead to "mental and physical illness" for workers.[53]

But I don't suppose the libertarian venture capitalists care much about the many casualties of this war of the one percent—such as Pam Wetherington, a middle-aged woman at Amazon's Kentucky operation who suffered stress fractures in both feet through walking for miles on the warehouse's concrete floor, yet received no compensation from Bezos's company when she could no longer work.[54] Or Jennifer Owen, a ten-year veteran employee at the Kentucky warehouse who was summarily fired after returning to work from an Amazon-approved medical leave after a car accident.[55] While Amazon is a nightmare for nonunionized workers like Wetherington and Owen, it has been a financial dream for investors like Tom Perkins's KPCB, whose original $6 million investment would, by 2014, be worth around $20 billion.

Yet, in spite of Amazon's phenomenal success, what isn't available in the Everything Store, at least in June 2014, were most of the books owned by Hachette Book Group, the publisher of Brad Stone's *Everything Store*. That's because Amazon was locked in an ongoing contractual dispute with Hachette over the pricing of electronic books. "What seems clear is that Amazon is using its market power," a June 2014 *New York Times* editorial notes about Amazon's decision to unstock Hachette's books, "to get the best deal for itself while it squeezes publishers, annoys its customers and hurts authors by limiting their sales."[56]

"Amazon's Power Play" is how the *New York Times* summarized this bullying behavior. This is an accurate summary not only of the Internet's winner-take-all economy, but also of Amazon's dominant place in it. So much for those "decentralizing, globalizing, harmonizing and empowering" qualities that Nicholas Negroponte promised would be a "force of nature" of the digital age. Jeff Bezos would, of course, disagree, arguing, no doubt, that such a generalization is a narrative fallacy. But he'd be wrong. The real *force of nature* in the digital age is a winner-take-all economy that is creating increasingly monopolistic companies like Amazon and multibillionaire plutocrats like Bezos himself.

The Code Is Cracked

Despite the metaphysical promises of digital prophets like Nicholas Negroponte and Kevin Kelly, the early generation of Internet businesses in what is now called the "Web 1.0" age, such as Amazon, Netscape, Yahoo, and eBay, weren't very innovative. Nobody has ever used terms like Amazonomics, Netscapenomics, or eBaynomics to compliment their business models; nobody has ever claimed that these companies had cracked the code on Internet profits.

For all its economic and cultural significance, Amazon was and still mostly is a very low-margin business—a digital version of Walmart focused on gaining mental shelf space, building its economies of scale, and underselling its rivals so aggressively that the American blogger Matthew Yglesias has even anointed Jeff

Bezos as "the prophet of no profit" and suggested that Amazon's "pace of growth will almost certainly slow," particularly "if Bezos were to turn his interest to other things."[57] Netscape, in spite of its transformational role in Internet history, pursued the very orthodox business models of either selling software subscriptions or advertising on its Web pages. eBay, which grew from 41,000 users trading $7.2 million worth of goods in 1995 to 22 million users trading $5.4 billion worth of goods in 2000,[58] was essentially an electronic platform bringing together traditional buyers and sellers of goods. Like Amazon and Netscape, eBay—which took a cut of each transaction conducted on its site—didn't represent a fundamental break with the economics of the past.

Many of the most highly trafficked sites in this Web 1.0 period were owned by traditional media companies that saw the Internet as little more than an electronic shop window through which to market and sell their content. Others, like Yahoo, an acronym for "Yet Another Hierarchical Officious Oracle," founded in 1994 by Jerry Yang and David Filo and originally known as "Jerry and David's Guide to the World Wide Web," began—as its odd name suggests—as a curated directory designed to help users find interesting new websites. But even by 1998, when Yahoo was the most highly trafficked site on the Web with close to 100 million page views per day,[59] its business model remained that of a glorified electronic magazine, relying on site-based advertising and the selling of online services like email hosting for its revenue.

All this was to change with Google, the revolutionary Internet search engine that not only successfully cracked the code on Internet profits, but ushered in the word *Googlenomics*,[60] a term describing the reinvention of Internet economics. Created in 1996 as an academic project by Larry Page and Sergey Brin, two unusually gifted Stanford University computer science doctoral students, Google began with the kind of audacious idea that would have challenged the intellects of Internet pioneers like J. C. R. Licklider and Vannevar Bush.

Like Bush, Page and Brin were concerned with the problem of information overload. The digital universe was exploding—the number of computers connected to the Internet increasing from 3.8 million in 1994 to 19.6 million by 1997,[61] and the number of websites growing from 18,957 in 1995 to over 3,350,000 sites producing around 60 million pages of online content by 1998. This prodigious growth of sites, pages, and hyperlinks was central to Page and Brin's project and it's why they named their search engine Google—Sergey Brin's unintentional misspelling of the word *googol*, a mathematical term signifying the number1.0×10^{100}, which has come to mean an unimaginably large number.

What if all the content on the Web, all those 26 million pages with their hundreds of millions of hyperlinks, could be sorted and indexed? Page and Brin wondered. What if Google could organize all the world's digital information?

There already were technologies from well-funded startups like Lycos, AltaVista, Excite, and Yahoo, vying to build a winner-take-all search engine for navigating the Web. But Brin and Page beat them all to it with an astonishingly original method for determining the relevance and reliability of a Web page's content. Just as Vannevar Bush's Memex worked through an intricate system of "trails," Page and Brin saw the logic of the Web in terms of hyperlinks. By crawling the entire Web and indexing all its pages and links, they turned the Web into what Brin, a National Science Foundation fellow at Stanford, identified as "a big equation." The end result of this gigantic math project was an algorithm they called PageRank, which determined the relevance of the Web page based on the number and quality of its incoming links. "The more prominent the status of the page that made the link, the more valuable the link was and the higher it would rise when calculating the ultimate PageRank number of the web page itself," explains Steven Levy in *In the Plex*, his definitive history of Google.[62]

In the spirit of Norbert Wiener's flight path predictor device, which relied on a continuous stream of information that flowed back and forth between the gun and its operator, the logic of the Google algorithm was dependent on a self-regulating system of hyperlinks flowing around the Web. Page and Brin's creation represented the realization of Licklider's man-computer symbiosis. As an information map that mirrored the distributed nature of the electronic network, it was the opposite of a centralized Web portal like Yahoo—anything but *yet another hierarchical officious oracle*.

"The idea behind PageRank was that you can estimate the importance of a web page by the web pages that link to it," Brin explained. "We convert the entire web into a big equation with several hundred million variables, which are the PageRanks of all the web pages, and billions of terms, which are all the links."[63]

"It's all recursive," Brin said, revealing the logic of his search engine, "it's all a big circle."[64] And the real beauty of this virtuous circle is that it became more efficient the more the Web grew and the more Web pages and links there were. It was infinitely scalable. The more links the algorithm had to crunch, the more data it was fed, the more accurately the search engine could identify the relevant pages to a query.

"Google search really did feel like magic," notes Levy about the reaction of the Stanford academic community to the search engine.[65] By 1998, Google was dealing with up to 10,000 daily queries and hogging half of Stanford's Internet capacity. Having begun as a possible doctoral dissertation, the project, like its technology, became a virtuous circle, acquiring its own momentum. *What next?* Brin and Page started to ask themselves in 1997. *Maybe this is real.*[66]

Both Page's and Brin's fathers were university scientists and both had always intended to become academics themselves. They wanted to do "something that mattered," which would change the world. In a different age, they might have had public careers like Vannevar Bush or J. C. R. Licklider, spent inside nonprofit universities and government agencies, working for the public good as the world's librarians by organizing all its information. But this was the Stanford of the 1990s rather than the MIT of the 1940s. And that meant launching Google as a for-profit startup and becoming billionaires rather than electronic librarians.

Having raised a million-dollar seed round from investors that included Jeff Bezos, Page and Brin incorporated Google in September 1998 and began to build a team of engineers to transform their academic project into a viable commercial product. But they quickly needed more capital to invest in both engineers and hardware, which inevitably led them to KPCB's John Doerr.

"How big do you think this could be?" Doerr asked them when they met in 1999.

"Ten billion," Larry Page immediately shot back about a "business" that, at that point, not only didn't have any revenue, but didn't even have a coherent model for making money. "And I don't mean market cap. I mean revenues."

Doerr, Steven Levy noted, "just about fell off his chair" at Page's boldness.[67] But he nonetheless invested in Google, joining Michael Moritz from Sequoia Capital in a joint $25 million Series A round. But two years after the investment, in spite of Google's establishing itself as the Web's dominant search engine with 70 million daily search requests, the company—which by now had appointed the "grown-up" Eric Schmidt as CEO—hadn't figured out a successful business model for monetizing the popularity of its free technology.

As always with Google, the solution was both totally obvious (at least in retrospect) and completely counterintuitive. Both Brin and Page—who took great pride in the fast-loading, minimalist aesthetic of the Google home page—had been hostile to the online advertising model pursued by portals like Yahoo that cluttered up the Web with CPM-priced (cost per thousand impressions) banner and interstitial advertisements. The solution was Google AdWords, a do-it-yourself marketplace for advertisers introduced in 2000 that enabled the placement of keyword-associated ads on the right-hand side of the search result page. Advertising thus became baked into search and Google, for all its technical brilliance, became an electronic advertising sales company.

Doing away with the CPM pricing, Google introduced the auction sales model to AdWords, which some of America's leading academic economists later described as "spectacularly successful" and "the dominant transaction mechanism in a large and rapidly growing industry."[68] Rather than buying online advertising at a set price, advertisers were now able to bid in what Steven Levy calls a real-time "unique auction" that simultaneously made online advertising more effective and profitable.[69]

Alongside AdWords, Google also developed an increasingly successful product called AdSense, which provided the tools to buy and measure advertising on websites not affiliated with the search engine. Google's advertising network was becoming as ubiquitous as Google search. AdWords and AdSense together represented what Levy calls a "cash cow" to fund the next decade's worth of Web projects, which included the acquisition of YouTube and the creation of the Android mobile operating system, Gmail, Google+, Blogger, the Chrome browser, Google self-driving cars, Google Glass, Waze, and its most recent roll-up of artificial intelligence companies including DeepMind, Boston Dynamics, and Nest Labs.[70]

More than just cracking the code on Internet profits, Google had discovered the holy grail of the information economy. In 2001, revenues were just \$86 million. They rose to \$347 million in 2002, then to just under a billion dollars in 2003 and to almost \$2 billion in 2004, when the six-year-old company went public in a $1.67 billion offering that valued it at $23 billion. By 2014, Google had become the world's second most valuable company, after Apple, with a market cap of over $400 billion, and Brin and Page were the two wealthiest young men in the world, with fortunes of around $30 billion apiece. In vivid contrast with Amazon, Google's profits were also astonishing. In 2012, its operational profits were just under $14 billion from revenues of $50 billion. In 2013, Google "demolished" Wall Street expectations and returned operational profits of over $15 billion from revenues of nearly $60 billion.[71] Larry Page's response to John Doerr's question when they first met in 1999 had turned out to be a dramatic underestimation of just "how big" Google could become. And the company is still growing.

By 2014, Google had joined Amazon as a winner-take-all company. It was processing around 40,000 search queries each second, which computes into 3.5 billion daily searches or 1.2 trillion annual searches. The leviathan controls around 65% of search globally, with its dominance of some markets, such as Italy or Spain, being higher than 90%.[72] Google's domination of the Internet reveals the new power laws of this networked economy. Idealists like Kevin Kelly and Nicholas Negroponte believed that the "decentralizing" architecture of the Web would result in a "thousand points of wealth" economy. But the reverse is true. By mimicking the distributed architecture of the Web itself, Google has become a monopolist of information. So when thinkers like Moises Naim describe "the end of power"[73] in our digital age, they are wrong. Power hasn't ended. It's simply changed its form, going from a top-down to a recursive, circular structure.

Google's power is increased every time we use it. As a symbiosis of human and computer intelligence, the Google search engine becomes more knowledgeable and thus more useful the more it is used. So every time we make a Google search we are, in a sense, "working" on improving the product. Even more valuable, from Google's point of view, is what Google learns about us each time we make that search. Like Vannevar Bush's Memex, the Google trails never "fade" and Google, for better or worse, never forgets.

All our digital trails are crunched into statistical products like Google Analytics, which provide both Google and its corporate clients with our so-called data exhaust. As *Big Data* authors Viktor Mayer-Schönberger and Kenneth Cukier note, Google has become the "undisputed leader in the data exhaust business. It applies the principle of recursively 'learning from the data' to many of its services," they explain. "Every action a user performs is considered a signal to be analyzed and fed back into the system."[74]

We shape Google's tools and thereafter those tools shape us.

Data Factories

Google changed everything. Among the earliest people to recognize this was Dale Dougherty, a Web pioneer who had founded the Global Network Navigator (GNN), the world's first commercial website, back in 1993. In a brainstorming session with the media mogul Tim O'Reilly a couple of years after the bursting of the dot-com bubble, Dougherty came up with the term "Web 2.0" to describe the new networked economy that Google was ushering in. The term stuck and has become the standard shorthand for describing the radical rebirth of the Web after the NASDAQ crash in the spring of 2000.

In his seminal article "What is Web 2.0,"[75] Tim O'Reilly describes Google as the "standard bearer for Web 2.0." Using Netscape as the equivalent model of what he calls a Web 1.0 company, O'Reilly argues that Jim Clark's startup saw itself in the "old software paradigm" of leveraging its dominance of the browser economy to "give Netscape the kind of market power enjoyed by Microsoft in the PC market" and then make money through the licensing of its software. Netscape's framing of itself as an aspiring Microsoft, O'Reilly writes, is reminiscent of the way the automobile industry first marketed its products as "horseless carriages" to ensure familiarity for consumers. In contrast, O'Reilly writes, Google, as the paradigmatic Web 2.0 Internet company, presented itself as anything but a reassuringly familiar horseless carriage.

So what exactly is Google? "Much like a phone call, which happens not just on the phones at either end of the call, but on the network in between, Google happens in the space between browser and search engine and destination content server, as an enabler or middleman between the user and his or her online experience," is how O'Reilly describes the virtuous circle powering Google. By being simultaneously invisible and ubiquitous, by being an *enabler* and a *middleman*, he suggests, Google represents a new category. It is the first truly native Internet product because its economic value lies in the network itself.

In the first fifteen years of the twenty-first century, the Internet has been dominated by enabling products and middleman services like Google. In this period, participatory Web 2.0 sites have superseded traditional top-down Web 1.0 publications. Web 1.0–style portals like AOL or Yahoo have been overshadowed by personalized 2.0 social networks such as Facebook, Tumblr, and the Birches' Bebo, a social network founded in 2005 that at its 2007 zenith was the most popular network in the United Kingdom, with more than 10 million members, and by 2.0 self-publishing platforms like Reddit, Twitter, SoundCloud, and YouTube. Professional 1.0 resources such as Kodak's photo processing Ofoto service, *Britannica* online, and Monster.com have been replaced by collaborative 2.0 equivalents like Yelp, Instagram, Wikipedia, and LinkedIn.

Most of these Web 2.0 businesses have pursued a Google-style business strategy of giving away their tools and services for free and relying on advertising sales as their main source of revenue. "The best minds of my generation are thinking about how to make people click ads," one of Facebook's engineers dryly notes.[76] Like Google, networks such as Facebook and YouTube have become big data companies able to target their users' behavior and taste through the collection of their data exhaust.

While none of the other Web 2.0 companies, even Facebook, have had quite the same stratospheric financial success as Google, many have created significant wealth for their founders and investors. Facebook's 2012 $100 billion IPO might have been overvalued both in terms of its economics and hype, but it was, nonetheless, the largest in Internet history. Bebo's $850 million sale to AOL in 2008 enabled Michael and Xochi Birch to finance the Battery. Google bought YouTube for $1.65 billion in 2006, Facebook acquired Instagram for $1 billion in 2012, and Yahoo purchased Tumblr for $1.1 billion in 2013. By the summer of 2014, both the publicly traded LinkedIn and Twitter had market caps of around $20 billion.

Sequoia Capital chairman Michael Moritz, Google's other Series A investor and, along with KPCB's John Doerr, the most successful Silicon Valley venture capitalist, places this new generation of Web companies like Google and Facebook into a broader historical context by comparing them with factories from the industrial age. In the old manufacturing economy, Moritz explains, factories were discrete places in which entrepreneurs invested in machinery and labor for the production of goods that were then sold in the marketplace. At night, the gates of these factories would be locked, its machinery shut down and its laborers sent home.

But in the networked age, Moritz says, the logistics of the industrial economy have been turned inside out. The gates of what

Moritz calls our new "data factories" have been flung open. The factory's tools are now available to everyone. It's what Moritz—a former *Time* magazine technology journalist who made his fortune being right as an early investor in Google, PayPal, Zappos, LinkedIn, and Yahoo—describes as the "Personal Revolution." We can all enjoy the free tools and services with which Google and Facebook equip us to search for information and network with our friends and colleagues. Indeed, the more we use the Google search engine, the more accurate the product becomes. And the more of us who join Facebook, the more Metcalfe's law kicks into place and so the more valuable Facebook becomes to us.

"Right here between San Francisco and San Jose something utterly remarkable has been going on, is going on and will go on. It's something that has only occurred in one or two places in the whole course of human history,"[77] Moritz says in describing this personal revolution engineered by data factories like Google, Facebook, LinkedIn, Instagram, and Yelp.

It seems like a win-win for everyone, of course—one of those supposedly virtuous circles that Sergey Brin and Larry Page built into PageRank. We all get free tools and the Internet entrepreneurs get to become superrich. KPCB cofounder Tom Perkins, whose venture fund has made billions from its investments in Google, Facebook, and Twitter, would no doubt claim that the achievement of what he called Silicon Valley's "successful one percent" is resulting in more jobs and general prosperity.

But as always with something that's too good to be true, there's a catch. The problem, of course, is that we are all working for Facebook and Google for free, manufacturing the very personal data that makes their companies so valuable. So Google, with its mid-2014 market cap of over $400 billion, needs to employ only 46,000 people. An industrial giant like General Motors, on the other hand, with its market cap hovering around $55 billion, employs just over 200,000 people to manufacture cars in its factories. Google is around seven times larger than GM, but employs less than a quarter of the number of workers.

This new data factory economy changes everything—even the monetary supply of our global financial system. In early 2014, the global economy's top five companies' gross cash holdings—those of Apple, Google, Microsoft, as well as the US telecom giant Verizon and the Korean electronics conglomerate Samsung—came to $387 billion, the equivalent of the 2013 GDP of the United Arab Emirates.[78] This capital imbalance puts the fate of the world economy in the hands of the few cash hoarders like Apple and Google, whose profits are mostly kept offshore to avoid paying US tax. "Apple, Google and Facebook are latter-day scrooges," worries the *Financial Times* columnist John Plender about a corporate miserliness that is undermining the growth of the world economy.[79]

"So what does it all mean?" Michael Moritz rhetorically asks about a data factory economy that is immensely profitable for a tiny handful of Silicon Valley companies. What does the personal revolution mean for everyone else, to those who aren't part of what he calls the "extreme minority" inside the Silicon Valley bubble?

"It means that life is very tough for almost everyone in America," the chairman of Sequoia Capital, whom even Tom Perkins couldn't accuse of being a progressive radical, says. "It means life is very tough if you're poor. It means life is very tough if you're middle class. It means you have to have the right education to go and work at Google or Apple."[80]

It means, Michael Moritz might have added, that the Internet is not the answer.

The Cult of the Social

Jeff Bezos isn't entirely wrong about the chaotic nature of history. Determinists like Kevin Kelly argue that network technology has a soul that is transporting us toward a digital promised land. But such narrative fallacies—whether of the left or the right, or of the religious or the secular—are the wishful thinking of eschatologists like the born-again Kelly, whose faith trumps his reason in his reading of history.

The only law of history is that there aren't any laws. Rather than having a mind of its own, history is unknowing, unexpected, and unintentional. In his classic 1904 essay *The Protestant Ethic and the Origins of Capitalism*, the German sociologist Max Weber traces how, unwittingly, ascetic Calvinists laid the groundwork for modern capitalism with their belief that the accumulation of wealth was a sign of redemption. And the history of the Internet is equally arbitrary. Created mostly accidentally by public-minded technologists like Paul Baran, J. C. R. Licklider, and Tim Berners-Lee, who were all indifferent and sometimes even hostile to money, the Internet has triggered one of the greatest accumulations of wealth in human history. The story of the Internet's preeminent company, Google, is also laced with irony. Invented by a couple of idealistic computer science graduate students who so mistrusted online advertisements that they banned them on their home page, Google is now by far the largest and most powerful advertising company in history.

But for the unintentional and the unexpected, nothing beats the history of Facebook, the Internet's dominant social network, which was created by a young man so socially awkward that many consider him autistic. In his aptly named *Accidental Billionaires*, the bestselling story of Facebook's early years on the campus of Harvard University, and on which David Fincher's Academy Award–nominated 2010 movie *The Social Network* movie is based, Ben Mezrich reveals that the twenty-year-old Mark Zuckerberg was seen as a total misfit by Harvard contemporaries. Eduardo Saverin, Zuckerberg's cofounder of "Thefacebook.com," which they launched together in February 2004, thought of his partner as the socially "uncomfortable" and "awkward kid in the class," a "complete mystery" with whom communication "was like talking to a computer," while other Harvard students saw him as a "weird" and "socially autistic" geek with a "dead fish handshake."[81] Even after Zuckerberg dropped out of Harvard later in 2004 and, a decade later, built Facebook into the Internet's dominant social network, he still hadn't shaken off his image as a socially disabled loner suffering from what *Wired* dubs "the Geek Syndrome."[82] Facebook's onetime head of engineering, Yishan Wong, claimed that Zuckerberg has a "touch of Asperger's" and "zero empathy."[83] And other seasoned Zuckerberg watchers, like Nicholas Carlson, the chief business correspondent at *Business Insider*, agree, seeing both his "obvious brilliance" and "his inability to hold conversation" as a "symptom" of his autism.[84]

But, in spite of—or, perhaps, because of—his inability to fashion a conversation, Zuckerberg has created the greatest generator of conversation in history, a social computer network whose 1.3 billion users were, by the summer of 2014, posting 2,460,000 comments to one another every minute of every day. With its mostly advertising revenue of $2.5 billion and record profits of $642 million in the first quarter of 2014,[85] Facebook has become the winner-take-all company in the Internet's social space. By successfully monetizing the data exhaust from our friendships, family relations, and love affairs, Facebook reached a July 2014 market cap of $190 billion, making it more valuable than either Coca-Cola, Disney, or AT&T.

Just as Google wasn't the Internet's first search engine, so Facebook didn't invent the idea of a social network—a place on the Internet where users nurture their social relationships. Reid Hoffman, the cofounder of LinkedIn, created the first online social network in 1997, a dating site called SocialNet. This was followed by Friendster in 2002 and then, in 2003, by the Los Angeles–based MySpace, a social network with a music and Hollywood focus that, at its 2008 peak, when it was acquired by News Corporation for $580 million, had 75.9 million members.[86] But Facebook, which until September 2006 was exclusively made up of high school and university students, offered a less cluttered and more intuitive interface than MySpace. So, having opened its doors to the world outside of schools and universities, the so-called Mark Zuckerberg Production quickly became the Internet's largest social network, amassing 100 million members by August 2008.

And then the network effect, that positive feedback loop that makes the Internet such a classic winner-take-all market, kicked in. By February 2010, the Facebook community had grown to 400 million members, who spent 8 billion minutes each day on a network already operating in 75 different languages.[87] Facebook had become the world's second most popular Internet site after Google, a position that it's maintained ever since. By the summer of 2014 Facebook had grown to rival China's population—hosting more than 1.3 billion members, around 19% of the people in the world, with 50% of them accessing the social network at least six days a week.[88] Like Google, Facebook is becoming ever more powerful. In 2014 it made the successful shift to mobile technology, its app being "far and away the most popular service" on both the iOS and Android platforms, with its users spending an astonishing 17% of all their smartphone time in it. Mark Zuckerberg's ten-year-old Internet company is thus likely to remain, with archrival Google, the Internet's dominant company over the second decade of its remarkable history.

Like Google, Facebook's goal is to establish itself as a platform rather than a single website—a strategy that distinguishes it from failed Web 1.0 "portal"-style networks like MySpace. That's why David Kirkpatrick, the author of the definitive Facebook history, *The Facebook Effect*,[89] argues that the launch of Facebook Connect in 2008 and its Open Stream API in 2009, platforms that enable the creation of websites that resemble Facebook itself, was a "huge transition" and "as radical as any [Facebook] had ever attempted" because it enabled developers to turn the Internet inside out and transform it into an extended version of Facebook. Like Google, Facebook seeks ubiquity. "Facebook everywhere" is how *Fast Company*'s Austin Carr describes its 2014 mobile strategy.[90] It wants to become what Kirkpatrick, echoing Tim O'Reilly's definition of a revolutionary Web 2.0 network, calls "a storehouse of information, like a bank, but also a clearinghouse and transit point, like the post office or the telephone company."[91]

Where Facebook does differ from Google is in its almost religious insistence on the social importance of the network. "Facebook is founded on a radical social premise—that an inevitable enveloping transparency will overtake modern life," explains Kirkpatrick. For Mark Zuckerberg, the network is defined by a collective sharing of our personal data in a brightly lit McLuhanesque village. As Kirkpatrick notes, McLuhan "is a favorite at the company" because "he predicted the development of a universal communications platform that would unite the planet."[92] Zuckerberg shares McLuhan's narrative fallacy, seeing the Internet "as just this massive stream of information. It's almost the stream of all human consciousness and communication, and the products we build are just different views of that."[93] One ominous 2009 Facebook project was thus the Gross Happiness Index, a classically utilitarian attempt to measure the mood of its users by analyzing the words and phrases that they publish on their Facebook page. Another was the even creepier 2012 company study that altered the news feeds of 700,000 Facebook users to experiment with their mood swings.[94]

Sergey Brin's "big circle" of data is, for Mark Zuckerberg, the recursive loop of the social Web. The more people who join Facebook, the more valuable—culturally, economically, and, above all, morally—Zuckerberg believes Facebook will become to us all. He even came up with what has become known as Zuckerberg's law, a social variation of Moore's law, and which suggests that each year our personal data on the network will grow exponentially. In ten years' time, Zuckerberg told Kirkpatrick, "a thousand times more data about Facebook users will flow through the social network. . . . People are going to have to have a device with them at all times that's [automatically] sharing. You can predict that."[95] It's a disturbing prediction that, I'm afraid, is already being realized in Facebook's dominance of the mobile Web and the development of smartphones as "the ultimate surveillance machine," which will know not only exactly where we are but also exactly what we are doing.[96]

The Facebook story is another chapter in the Internet's ironic history. Mark Zuckerberg, the kid who can't communicate, has revolutionized twenty-first-century communication by popularizing a bizarre cult of the social. He has appropriated the ideals of openness and transparency to suit Facebook's commercial interests, thereby making privacy increasingly obsolete. His narrative fallacy is to believe that the network, in the form of Facebook, is uniting us as a human race. We thus almost have a moral obligation to reveal our true selves on the network, to participate in the real-time confessional of our brightly lit global village. That's why the socially autistic Zuckerberg believes that we only have "one identity," telling Kirkpatrick that "having two identities for yourself is an example of a lack of integrity."[97] And it's why Sheryl Sandberg, Facebook's chief operating officer, says that "you can't be on Facebook without being your authentic self."[98]

But this, like so much else that Zuckerberg and Sandberg say, is entirely wrong. Having multiple identities—as a citizen, a friend, a worker, a woman, a parent, an online buddy—is actually an example of somebody with so much integrity that they are unable to compromise their different social roles. And as more and more young people are recognizing, maintaining one's "authenticity" in the digital age may well mean leaving Facebook and finding a less well-lit place to hang out at on the Internet.[99]

Inspired by Max Weber's *Protestant Ethic and the Spirit of Capitalism*, the American sociologist Robert Merton popularized the idea of the "unintended consequences" of purposeful social action. The history of Facebook is an excellent example of Merton's theory. Facebook has been designed to bring us together as a happy global village. But the reverse is true. Rather than uniting us, a 2013 study by the University of Michigan psychologist Ethan Kross shows, Facebook is making us unhappier and more envious of others.[100] Rather than establishing trust, a 2014 Reason-Rupe poll of Americans found, Facebook was trusted with our personal data by only 5% of the respondents, significantly less than either the 35% of people who trusted the Internal Revenue Service or even the 18% who trusted the National Security Agency.[101] Rather than cheering us up, a 2013 study of 600 Facebook users by the Institute of Information Systems at Berlin's Humboldt University found, Facebook made more than 30% of its users feel lonelier, angrier, or more frustrated.[102]

None of this should be surprising. It's what happens when you hand over the conversation to a geek who talks like a computer. It's what happens when you trust somebody with zero empathy.

Distributed Capitalism

To explain the decentralized design of the World Wide Web, Tim Berners-Lee liked to compare it with the capitalist free-market system. "I told people that the Web was like a market economy," he wrote in his autobiography. "In a market economy, anybody can trade with anybody, and they don't have to go to a market square to do it."[103]

But in today's libertarian age, the similarities between the Web and capitalism are more than just architectural. Silicon Valley has become the new Wall Street because Berners-Lee's invention has become the vehicle for a twenty-first-century networked model of capitalism that offers astounding financial rewards to its winner-take-all entrepreneurs. "We live at a time when almost everything can be bought and sold," notes the moral philosopher Michael Sandel about an "era of market triumphalism" that began at the end of the Cold War.[104] And the Internet, John Doerr's "largest legal creation of wealth in the history of the planet," engineered by Cold War scientists and coming of age in the same year that the Berlin Wall fell, has become particularly fertile ground for the triumphalism of free-market ideologues like Tom Perkins. There's much, of course, for Perkins to be triumphant about. Larry Page and Sergey Brin are now worth $30 billion apiece because they successfully cornered the market in the buying and selling of digital advertising. Jeff Bezos has made his $30 billion from an Everything Store that offers better pricing and more choice than its rivals. Facebook founder and CEO Mark Zuckerberg has accumulated his $30 billion by monetizing friendship.

In the quarter century since the invention of the World Wide Web, the Internet has gone full circle from banning all forms of commerce to transforming absolutely everything, especially our privacy, into profitable activity. "Social media businesses represent an aggressive expansion of capitalism into our personal relationships," notes Snapchat CEO Evan Spiegel about this monetization of our inner lives by social networks like Facebook. "We are asked to perform for our friends, to create things they like, to work on a personal brand—and brands teach us that authenticity is the result of consistency. We must honor our true self and represent the same self to all of our friends or risk being discredited."[105]

Berners-Lee's definition of capitalism, however, is too pedestrian. Rather than just a static market economy that enables trading, capitalism is what the Austrian economist Joseph Schumpeter called an "evolutionary" process of economic change that "never can be stationary." In his 1942 magnum opus *Capitalism, Socialism and Democracy*, Schumpeter used the term "Creative Destruction" to describe the constant cycles of disruptive invention and reinvention that drive capitalism. "This process of Creative Destruction is the essential fact about capitalism," Schumpeter insisted. "It is what capitalism consists in and what every capitalist concern has got to live with."[106]

Internet economics, therefore, needs to be understood as a historical narrative rather than as just a static set of market relationships. In both the Web 1.0 and 2.0 periods, the Internet mostly disrupted media, communications, and retail. And so, in the twenty years after Jim Clark and Marc Andreessen founded Netscape in April 1994, Schumpeter's gale of creative destruction mostly swirled around the photography, music, newspaper, telecommunications, movie, publishing, and retail industries.

Over the next twenty-five years, however, that digital gale will grow into a Category 5 hurricane and radically disrupt every industry from education, finance, and transportation to health care, government, and manufacturing. This ongoing storm will be fueled by the relentless improvements in the power of both computing (Moore's law) and the network (Metcalfe's law), the increasing speed of broadband access, and the shift in all computer applications to the cloud. The fall in the price of smartphones and the growth in wireless networks, Patrik Cerwall's research team at Ericsson reminds us, will mean that by 2018 there will be 4.5 billion smartphone subscribers. As computer chips become so small, affordable, and powerful that they can be knitted in our clothing and even ingested, as everything we do on our computing devices will be networked, both the Internet of Everything and an Internet of Everyone will, for better or worse, become inevitable.

Just as the Internet will be everywhere, so will the networked market. This digital marketplace is already beginning to resemble Jonas Lindvist's chaotically decentered graphic image on the wall of Ericsson's Stockholm office. Enablers and middlemen in industries as disparate as finance, transportation, and tourism are now mimicking Google's distributed business model. Distributed capitalism equals ubiquitous capitalism. That's the evolutionary logic of networked economics.

In the financial market, Bitcoin already has its own trading indexes where hundreds of millions of dollars are speculated on the electronically networked currency. Digital money like Bitcoin represent a peer-to-peer alternative to centrally controlled currencies like the US dollar or Swedish krona, an alternative in which middlemen and thus banks and banking fees are eliminated. Writing in the *New York Times* to explain "why Bitcoin matters," Marc Andreessen—who now is the managing partner of Andreessen Horowitz, a $4 billion Silicon Valley venture fund with $50 million invested in Bitcoin-based startups like the virtual wallet Coinbase—argues that this new digital money represents "a classic network effect, a positive feedback loop." As with the Web, Andreessen says, the more people who use the new currency, "the more valuable Bitcoin is for the people who use it."[107]

"A mysterious new technology emerges, seemingly out of nowhere, but actually the result of two decades of intense research and development by nearly anonymous researchers," writes Andreessen, predicting the historical significance of this networked currency. "What technology am I talking about? Personal computers in 1975, the Internet in 1993, and—I believe—Bitcoin in 2014."[108]

What Silicon Valley euphemistically calls the "sharing economy" is a preview of this distributed capitalism system powered by the network effect of positive feedback loops. Investors like Andreessen see the Internet—a supposedly hyperefficient, "frictionless" platform for buyers and sellers—as an upgrade to the structural inefficiencies of the top-down twentieth-century economy. Along with peer-to-peer currencies like Bitcoin, the new distributed model offers crowdfunding networks like the John Doerr investment Indiegogo, which enable anyone to raise money for an idea.

As an enabling platform that sits between the entrepreneur and the market, Indiegogo captures the essence of this new distributed economic system in which anything can not only be bought or sold, but also crowd-financed. Indiegogo offers anyone the opportunity to fund other people's home renovations, sports cars, $10,000 African safari vacations, potato salad (which, in one bizarre July 2014 campaign, raised more than $30,000),[109] even their breast implants.[110] It is the reverse, the exact opposite, of the old top-down system of the post–World War II era in which government-appointed wise men like Vannevar Bush and J. C. R. Licklider funded the invention of major public projects like the Internet rather than potato salad.

Another of Andreessen Horowitz's venture investments is Airbnb, a peer-to-peer marketplace founded in 2007 that allows anyone to rent out a room in their home, transforming it into a hotel. By the end of 2013, Airbnb had topped 10 million guest stays from an active list of 550,000 worldwide properties in 192 countries that included spare rooms in homes, castles, and yurts.[111] And in February 2014, the 700-person startup raised a $475 million round of investment at a valuation of $10 billion,[112] which makes it worth about a half as much as the $22 billion Hilton corporation, a worldwide chain with 3,897 hotels and 152,000 employees. Airbnb cofounder Brian Chesky describes the company as a platform of "trust" in which the reputations of guests and of hosts will be determined by feedback on the network.[113] But Airbnb has been beset by such a scarcity of trust from the authorities that 15,000 New York City hosts were subpoenaed in May 2014 by New York State attorney general Eric Schneiderman because they may not have paid taxes on their rental incomes.

Andreessen Horowitz has also ventured into the car-sharing market, where it is backing a 2012 San Francisco–based middleman called Lyft, a mobile phone app that enables peer-to-peer ride sharing. But the best-known startup in the transportation-sharing sector is Uber, a John Doerr–backed company that also has received a quarter-billion-dollar investment from Google Ventures. Founded in late 2009 by Travis Kalanick, by the summer of 2014 Uber was operating in 130 cities around the world, employing around 1,000 people, and, in a June 2014 investment round of $1.2 billion, was valued at $18.2 billion, a record for a private startup company. It made Kalanick a paper billionaire and gave his four-year-old startup with its 1,000 employees almost the same valuation as that of Avis and Hertz combined,[114] companies which together employ almost 60,000 people.

"Everybody's Private Driver" Uber markets its distributed taxi network, and in July 2013 also introduced "UberCHOPPER," a $3,000 private helicopter service which whirled wealthy New Yorkers over to the exclusive Hamptons.[115] "Blair Waldorf, Don Draper, and Jay Gatsby got nothing on you," Uber boasted in advertising UberCHOPPER. "This is the epitome of luxury, convenience, and style."[116]

"Uber is software [that] eats taxis," an admiring Marc Andreessen stated in describing the San Francisco–based transportation service.[117] Yet that's not all it *eats*. Tom Perkins promised that Silicon Valley's one percent entrepreneurs are "job creators." But tens of thousands of taxi drivers around the world would disagree. Indeed, Uber is so disrupting the livelihoods of these professional taxi drivers that in June 2014 there were strikes and demonstrations in many European cities, including London, Paris, Lyon, Madrid, and Milan, against its introduction.[118]

And yet Uber remains an iconic company in Silicon Valley, where it is "seen as the messiah" and the next $100 billion Internet sensation by San Francisco's tech crowd.[119] Marc Andreessen certainly admires the customer-friendliness of the mobile service. "You watch the car on the map on your phone as it makes its way to you," he said, complimenting the app's real-time user interface. "It's a killer experience."

What's *making its way to us*, however, is more than just an image of an Uber limousine blinking across our mobile screen. It's the creative destruction inflicted by distributed capitalist networks like Uber or Airbnb, in which anyone can become a cabdriver or a hotelier. And Marc Andreessen—whose Mosaic Web browser opened the Internet's moneyed second act—is right. Uber is certainly going to be a "killer experience" for its early investors, who stand to make 2,000 times their initial outlay.[120]

But while a lucky handful of investors turned $20,000 angel investments in Uber into $40 million fortunes, the consequences of this casino-style economy are much more troubling for the rest of us. And the most important Internet story isn't Tom Perkins's "successful one percent." It's the other 99% who haven't invested in Uber, don't own Bitcoins, and aren't renting out spare rooms in their castles on Airbnb.

CHAPTER THREE

THE BROKEN CENTER

The Future

"Everybody's private driver." Thus Uber boasts about its radically disruptive black limousine service. But there were no Uber cars at Greater Rochester International Airport in upstate New York when I arrived hungry and cold one gray afternoon in the winter of 2014 on a drafty United Airlines plane that had rattled all the way from Chicago. Nor were there any UberCHOPPERs available at the airport to twirl me on a three-thousand-dollar helicopter ride to downtown Rochester.

That was fortunate, really, because Rochester's downtown—a landscape of boarded-up stores and homeless people wheeling their earthly possessions in rusty shopping carts along empty streets—resembled a picture from the dystopian future. From *Blade Runner*, perhaps, Ridley Scott's 1982 movie about a twenty-first-century world in which human beings and robots have become indistinguishable. Or from *Neuromancer*, William Gibson's 1984 science fiction novel, the subversive classic about an electronically networked world that not only popularized the word *cyberspace* but also may have foreseen Tim Berners-Lee's invention of the World Wide Web five years later.[1]

"The sky above the port was the color of television, tuned to a dead channel," Gibson—known on Twitter, perhaps not uncoincidentally, as @GreatDismal—began *Neuromancer*. And, like Gibson's dismal image of the future, downtown Rochester was tuned to a dead channel. The heart of this industrial city had been ripped out and not even the most nostalgic of Instagram photographic filters could have brought it back to life. It was a broken place, a town that time had forgotten. Best known for its high unemployment and crime rates—the city's notorious number of robberies being 206% above the US national average and its murder rate almost 350% higher than that of New York City in 2012[2]—the only buzz in the dead sky above downtown Rochester was from police choppers. No wonder the city is now known as "the Murder Capital of New York."

"The future is already here—it's just not very evenly distributed," you'll remember Gibson once said. And there are few places where the future is less *evenly* distributed than in Rochester, a rusting industrial city of some 200,000 souls on the banks of Lake Ontario in upstate New York. No, Rochester's downtown definitely wasn't worth a three-thousand-dollar private helicopter ride—unless perhaps you had, like me, come to the city in search of a quarter century of failure.

One of the most ludicrous Silicon Valley cults—its most "striking mantra," according to the *Guardian*[3]—is its religious veneration of the idea of failure. Peddled by thought leaders like Tim O'Reilly, it's the idea that business failure is a badge of success for entrepreneurs. Idolizing failure is the hottest new meme for the alpha geeks of the Valley. The bigger their success, the more exaggerated their claim to being serial failures. "How I Failed," O'Reilly thus titled a much-hyped 2013 keynote speech at one of his own successful events.[4] But O'Reilly has some stiff competition in this failure Olympiad. Reid Hoffman, the billionaire founder of LinkedIn, advises entrepreneurs to "fail fast."[5] Paul Graham, a multimillionaire angel investor, calls his incubator of startup Internet ventures, which has hatched many successful startups, including Alexis Ohanian's Reddit, "Failure Central,"[6] while Dave McClure, another wealthy angel, not to be outfailed by his successful rival, talks up his equally successful 500 Startups incubator as "Fail Factory."[7] Indeed, the cult of failure has become such a mania in the Valley that there is now even an entire event, a San Francisco conference called FailCon, dedicated to its veneration.

But, of course, winner-take-all entrepreneurs like Reid Hoffman, Tim O'Reilly, and Paul Graham know as much about failure as Michael and Xochi Birch know about running a village pub. And so to find failure, a genuine Failure Central, I'd flown 2,700 miles east, from San Francisco to Rochester. But, on my arrival, the only hint of "failure" in the airport terminal was the glossy cover of a technology business magazine displayed in the window of an airport bookstore.

Silicon Valley had come to Rochester. Or, at least, to this bookstore. The image was of an energetic young entrepreneur with a dark goatee and black-framed glasses dressed in a hoodie, frayed jeans, and old sneakers. The guy, who might have been outfitted to hang out at the Battery, was wielding a sledgehammer with which he was energetically smashing some plastic objects into smithereens.

REALLY CREATIVE DESTRUCTION, the magazine's headline screamed in letters as black as the dude's goatee and glasses.[8]

One doesn't need to be a semiotician to grasp the significance of seeing this picture—with its "move fast and break things" message—in Rochester, of all places.

Much of Rochester's industrial economy had itself been smashed into smithereens over the last twenty-five years by a Schumpeterian hurricane of creative destruction. The significance of that magazine cover was, therefore, hard to miss: the sledgehammer mirrored the destructive might of the digital revolution;

while the plastic objects being destroyed represented the broken city itself.

A picture, they say, is worth a thousand words. And if the people of Rochester knew the value of anything, it was that of a picture. As the global headquarters of the Eastman Kodak Corporation, pictures were to Rochester what cars once were to Detroit or what the Internet is today to Silicon Valley. Known as "the World's Image Center" and "Snapshot City," Rochester had built its prosperity on the many millions of "Kodak moments" captured by all of us over the last 125 years.

"You press the button, we do the rest," Kodak's founder, George Eastman, promised when he introduced his first handheld camera in 1888. And that's exactly what we all did throughout the industrial age—*press the button* on our Kodak cameras and rely on high-quality Kodak film and Kodak imaging and processing services to *do the rest.* We paid for all this, of course—exchanging cash for the developed photographs that then became our property. And so for more than a century, millions of Kodak moments had made Rochester wealthy and famous. But now a darker kind of Kodak moment had transformed Rochester from the World's Image Center into a picture of failure.

Paul Simon sang about Kodak's bringing us lovely "bright colors" in his 1973 hit "Kodachrome." The song was Simon's tribute to what David Wills, the author of *Hollywood in Kodachrome*, described as the "spectacular" Kodak color film first introduced in 1935, a stock, Wills says, "synonymous with sharp detail and brilliant color" that produced "crisp" images and had "minimal grain."[9] For seventy years, Kodachrome accurately captured the world's moments. It was used to take many of the twentieth century's most detailed and memorable pictures—from Neil Armstrong's 1968 snaps of the lunar landscape to the official images of many Hollywood stars.[10] But Simon's lyrics could equally apply to Rochester, where Kodak's control of the global picture business had enriched the city with the brightest colors of all: a thriving local economy and tens of thousands of well-paying jobs.

We haven't stopped taking pictures. The problem is actually the reverse. We took 350 billion snaps in 2011 and an astonishing 1.5 trillion in 2013—more than all the photos ever taken before in all of history. "Pictures are more sexy than words," explains Joshua Chuang, the curator at the University of Arizona's Center for Creative Photography.[11] "I snap therefore I am,"[12] adds the *Wall Street Journal*'s Ellen Gamerman, about a culture in which we are using our camera phones so obsessively that if just the 125 billion photos captured in the United States in 2013 were turned into four-by-six prints, they would extend to the moon and back twenty-five times.

The saddest thing of all about Rochester is that the more photos we take, the fewer jobs there are in Snap City. Don't take my Kodachrome away, pleaded Paul Simon in his song. Since then, however, the digital revolution has taken away not only Kodachrome, but most of Kodak, too. When Simon wrote "Kodachrome," Kodak controlled 90% of the film sales and 85% of the camera sales in the United States.[13] Twenty-five years later, Kodak halted the manufacture of its Kodachrome film, ending a seventy-four-year history of production. And in September 2013, a few months before my arrival in Rochester, an emaciated Kodak emerged from Chapter 11 bankruptcy having sold the vast majority of its assets and laid off most of its employees.

Things look a lot worse in black-and-white, Paul Simon sang. Yes, much, much *worse*. "An entire city," cultural critic Jason Farago writes in an epitaph for Rochester, "has lost its center."[14] The Kodak collapse was "a tragedy of American economic life," mourned the US judge who presided over the company's exit from bankruptcy. The real tragedy, this judge explained, was that up to fifty thousand Kodak retirees, many of whom had worked their entire lives at the company, would either completely lose their pensions or, at best, get a payout of four or five cents on the dollar.[15] To borrow a word from Sequoia Capital chairman Michael Moritz, life has indeed become "tough" for Rochester's old industrial working class.

Another bankruptcy judge, whose grandfather had actually worked for Kodak, put the tragedy in even more somber terms. "The bankruptcy proceeding has been a sorrowful thing," he explained, "like losing a family member."[16]

I had come to Rochester in search of Kodak. I wanted to see for myself this broken place, this epic fail that had torn the heart out of the city. But even with the help of the latest networked mapping software from Google and Apple, failure can sometimes be hard to track down.

Coming to an Office Near You

"In a half a mile, turn left onto Innovation Way," the voice instructed me.

If only finding innovation were that easy. In my search for Kodak, I was navigating a rental car around the "Rochester Technology Park"—a cluster of low-rise office buildings next to a freeway on the outskirts of the city. And my driving directions were being broadcasted from my iPad by an automated female voice.

"In a quarter of a mile, turn right onto Creative Drive," the voice of the Google Maps algorithm continued in her mechanically unflappable way. "Then, in eight hundred yards, turn right onto Initiative Drive."

Rochester Technology Park had been carved up into identical-looking, hopefully named streets like Initiative Drive, Innovation Way, and Creative Drive. But as I drove up and down looking for a Kodak research laboratory that, I'd been told, was located in the complex, I realized that it wasn't just Kodak that was hard to find. Initiative, innovation, and creativity were equally elusive. The sprawling technology park contained a lot of flat office buildings, but it seemed to be missing the most essential ingredient of all: people. In my search for Kodak, I barely saw a living soul. Nobody seemed to be there. It appeared hopeless, in a greatly dismal William Gibson kind of way. As if Silicon Valley had been transported to Rochester but somebody had forgotten to bring the humans. As if human workers had been replaced by robots.

Perhaps they had. "It is an invisible force that goes by many names. Computerization. Automation. Artificial Intelligence. Technology. Innovation. And, everyone's favorite, ROBOTS," wrote the *Atlantic*'s Derek Thompson in 2014 about our increasing concern with the elimination of jobs from the economy.[17] As if to mark (or perhaps mourn) the twenty-fifth anniversary of the Web, it seems as if 2014 is the year that we've finally fully woken up to what the *Wall Street Journal* columnist Daniel Akst dubs "automation anxiety."[18] The cover of the one business magazine that I'd read on the flight from Chicago to Rochester, for example, featured the image of a deadly tornado roaring through a workspace. "Coming to an office near you . . .," it warned about what technology will do to "tomorrow's jobs."[19]

Many others share this automation anxiety. The distinguished *Financial Times* economics columnist Martin Wolf warns that intelligent machines could hollow out middle-class jobs, compound income inequality, make the wealthy "indifferent" to the fate of everyone else, and make a "mockery" of democratic citizenship.[20] "The robots are coming and will terminate your jobs,"[21] worries the generally cheerful economist Tim Harford in response to Google's acquisition in December 2013 of Boston Dynamics, a producer of military robots such as Big Dog, a three-foot-long, 240-pound, four-footed beast that can carry a 340-pound load and climb snowy hiking trails. Harford suspects 2014 might be the year that computers finally become self-aware, a prospect that he understandably finds "sobering" because of its "negative impact of . . . on the job market."[22] He is particularly concerned with how increasingly intelligent technology is hollowing out middle-income jobs such as typists, clerks, travel agents, and bank tellers.

Equally sobering is the involvement of dominant Internet companies like Google and Amazon in a robot-controlled society that the technology writer Nicholas Carr foresees in his 2014 book about "automation and us," *The Glass Cage*. Carr's earlier 2008 work, *The Big Switch*, made the important argument that, with the increasingly ubiquity of cloud computing, the network has indeed become a giant computer, with the World Wide Web thus being "The World Wide Computer."[23] And with automation, Carr warns in *The Glass Cage*, the World Wide Computer is now designing a society that threatens to discard human beings.

"The prevailing methods of computerized communication pretty much ensure that the role of people will go on shrinking," Carr writes in *The Glass Cage*. "Society is reshaping itself to fit the contours of the new computing infrastructure. The infrastructure orchestrates the instantaneous data exchanges that make fleets of self-driving cars and armies of killer robots possible. It provides the raw materials for the predictive algorithms that inform the decisions of individuals and groups. It underpins the automation of classrooms, libraries, hospitals, shops, churches, and homes."[24]

With its massive investment in the development of intelligent labor-saving technologies like self-driving cars and killer robots, Google—which has imported Ray Kurzweil, the controversial evangelist of "singularity," to direct its artificial intelligence engineering strategy[25]—is already invested in the building and management of the glass cage. Not content with the acquisition of Boston Dynamics and seven other robotics companies in the second half of 2013,[26] Google also made two important purchases at the beginning of 2014 to consolidate its lead in this market. It acquired the secretive British company DeepMind, "the last large independent company with a strong focus on artificial intelligence," according to one inside source, for $500 million; and it bought Nest Labs, a leader in smart home devices such as intelligent thermostats, for $3.23 billion. According to the *Wall Street Journal*, Google is even working with Foxconn, the huge Taiwanese contract manufacturer that already makes most of Apple's products, "to carry out the US company's vision for robotics."[27] With all these acquisitions and partnerships, Google clearly is, as the technology journalist Dan Rowinski put it, playing a game of Moneyball[28] in the age of artificial intelligence—setting itself up to be the dominant player in the age of intelligent computing. In the future, then, the origins of that deadly tornado "coming to an office near you" will probably lie in the Googleplex, Google's global headquarters in Mountain View, California, where the automated data feedback loop of Sergey Brin's "big circle" is coming to encircle more and more of society.

And then there's Google's interest in Travis Kalanick's Uber—another play that may turn out to be a massive job killer. In 2013, Google Ventures invested $258 million in Uber, the largest ever outside investment by Google's venture arm. It's not hard to figure out why. As the *Forbes* columnist Chunka Mui suggests: "Google Car + Uber = Killer App."[29] And as T. J. McCue, Mui's colleague at *Forbes*, adds, Google's interest in Uber may lie in Kalanick's transportation network becoming the infrastructure for a revolutionary drone delivery service. Google could, in the not too distant future, take on UPS, FedEx, DHL, and postal services and replace the jobs of hundreds of thousands of delivery drivers and mail carriers around the world with networked drones. Given that UPS and FedEx alone employed almost 700,000 people in 2013,[30] the impact of this drone revolution on middle-class jobs threatens to be particularly corrosive. "FedEx needs Amazon more than Amazon needs FedEx," the *New York Times*' Claire Cain Miller notes about Amazon's ability to negotiate its own special rates with FedEx.[31] And this power asymmetry will become increasingly pronounced as Amazon develops technology and services that directly compete with independent delivery services like FedEx and UPS.

For some, the idea of automatic drones replacing UPS and FedEx drivers is a science fictional fantasy, more suited to 2114 than 2014. But not for Jeff Bezos, another early investor in Uber. In a December 2013 interview with Charlie Rose on the CBS News show *60 Minutes*, Bezos actually floated the idea of deploying drones to deliver packages. Calling this service "Prime Air," Bezos said, "I know this looks like science fiction. It's not."[32] And just as Amazon may one day go robot-to-robot with Google in the delivery drone business, it is also competing with Google in the war of the one percent to eliminate the jobs of everyone else in our economy. In July 2014, Amazon even wrote to the US Federal Aviation Administration asking for permission to test Prime Air. The delivery drones could travel at up to 50 miles an hour and deliver packages of up to 2.3 kilograms.[33]

The Amazon theater of this automation war is as strategically significant as the Google front. Yes, Amazon may be hiring low-income, hourly, nonunionized laborers for its rapidly growing number of warehouses. But, like Google, Amazon is also massively investing in automated labor technology, with Jeff Bezos telling his investors in May 2014 that he expected to be using 10,000 robots in its fulfillment centers by the beginning of 2015.[34] Thus in 2012 Amazon paid $775 million for Kiva Systems, a maker of robots for servicing warehouses. Kiva robots—which, by the way, are already being used by the Amazon-owned online shoe store Zappos (in Zappos's hierarchy-free holacracy, all robots are presumably equal)—can retrieve and pick 200–400 items an hour. As George Packer warns in a 2014 *New Yorker* piece, "Amazon's warehouse jobs are gradually being taken over by robots." The chilling end result, Packer forecasts, is that Amazon will have "eliminated the human factor from shopping, and we will finally be all alone with our purchases."[35] The Everything Store is, in truth, turning out to be the nobody store. It's an automated echo chamber—a store in which we are surrounded by algorithmic mirrors and all we see are our own buying histories. The algorithm knows what we want before we enter the store and then a robot fulfills our order, which, if Jeff Bezos has his way, will be delivered by our own personalized drone.

Like Google and Amazon, Facebook is also aggressively entering the artificial intelligence business. In 2014, Facebook acquired Oculus VR, a virtual reality company, and British-based pilotless drone company Ascenta.[36] Mark Zuckerberg has also co-invested with Tesla Motors's CEO Elon Musk and the Hollywood actor Ashton Kutcher in an artificial intelligence company called Vicarious, which mimics human learning. According to its founder, Scott Phoenix, Vicarious's goal is to replicate the neocortex, thus creating a "computer that thinks like a person . . . except that it doesn't have to sleep."[37] Phoenix told the *Wall Street Journal* that Vicarious will eventually "learn how to cure diseases, create cheap renewable energy, and perform the jobs that employ most human beings."[38] What Phoenix didn't clarify, however, is what exactly human beings will do with themselves all day when every job is performed by Vicarious.

The threat of artificial intelligence to jobs is becoming such a huge problem that even Eric Schmidt, Google's normally glib executive chairman, now acknowledges its seriousness. "The race between computers and people," Schmidt declared at the 2014 World Economic Forum in Davos, will be the "defining one" in the world economy over the next twenty-five years.[39] And "people need to win," he said. But given their massive investment in artificial intelligence, can we really trust Google to be on our side in this race between computers and people over the next quarter century? If we "win" this race, won't that mean Google—having invested in artificial intelligence companies like Boston Dynamics, Nest Labs, and Deep Mind—will have *lost*?

Rather than focusing on "winning," our networked automation anxiety is really all about identifying the losers, the people who will lose their jobs, the failures in our networked economy. Citing a paper by Oxford University's Carl Benedikt Frey and Michael Osborne that predicts that 47% of all American jobs might be lost in the next couple of decades,[40] the *Atlantic*'s Derek Thompson speculates on "which half" of the workforce could be made redundant by robots. Of the ten jobs that have a 99% likelihood of being replaced by networked software and automation over the next quarter century, Thompson includes tax preparers, library technicians, telemarketers, sewers in clothing factories, accounts clerks, and photographic process workers.[41]

While it's all very well to speculate about who will lose their jobs because of automation, Thompson says, "the truth is scarier. We don't have a clue."[42]

But Thompson is wrong. The writing is on the wall about both the winners and the losers in this dehumanizing race between computers and people. We do indeed have more than a clue about its outcome. And that's what really is scary.

The Writing on the Wall

Not everything about our automation anxiety is speculative. Indeed, when it comes to photographic process workers, there's a 100% certainty that they lost the race with computers for jobs. That was why I had come to Snapshot City. Rather than speculating about the destruction of tomorrow's jobs, I'd flown into Rochester to understand how networked technology is killing today's jobs.

I'd begun my search for Kodak's remains earlier that morning at Visit Rochester, a run-down building at ground zero of the city's decimated downtown, on the corner of Main and East Streets, where I did, at least, manage to find a live person.

"Could you tell me where I can find the Kodak offices?" I asked the gray-haired old lady, who was volunteering her labor at the center. Judging by the distraught look on the kindly woman's face, I might have brought up a recent family bereavement. Perhaps I had. Her husband, she told me, had worked at Kodak for more than forty years. "A lifer," she called him, ruefully shaking her head. I wondered if he was one of the fifty thousand retirees who'd lost all his benefits after the bankruptcy.

The woman unfolded a map of Rochester and spread it on the counter between us. But rather than a local geography lesson, she gave me an introduction to her city's troubled history. "Well, there used to be a factory here and labs here and here," she said, not bothering to veil her nostalgia for a city that no longer existed. "And here, and here, too.

"But now," she added, lowering her voice, "now, I'm not so sure."

Twenty-five years ago, of course, it would have been a quite different story. In 1989, when Tim Berners-Lee made his revolutionary breakthrough at CERN, Eastman Kodak employed 145,000 people in research laboratories, offices, and factories all over Rochester. Even in the mid-nineties, the publicly traded company had a market value of more than $31 billion. Since then, however, Kodak's decline has been even more precipitous than that of the global recorded music industry.

The paradox is that Kodak has been a victim of abundance rather than scarcity. The more ubiquitous online photo sharing has become, the easier it's become to take pictures from our smartphones and tablets, the less anyone has needed Kodak. "You press the button, we do the rest," George Eastman famously boasted. But the digital revolution has made photography so easy that there is no longer any *rest* to *do*. And so, between 2003 and 2012—the age of multibillion-dollar Web 2.0 startups like Facebook, Tumblr, and Instagram—Kodak closed thirteen factories and 130 photo labs and cut 47,000 jobs in a failed attempt to turn the company around.[43] And then, having emerged from Chapter 11 bankruptcy in 2013, Kodak committed suicide to avoid being murdered. Trying to reinvent itself as a "commercial imaging company serving business markets like packaging and graphics,"[44] Kodak got out of the consumer picture business entirely. It was as if Kleenex suddenly stopped selling tissues or Coca-Cola withdrew overnight from the fizzy drinks business. Kodak sold its online photo-sharing site and its portfolio of digital imaging patents—what the *New York Times* described as its "crown jewel"[45]—to Silicon Valley vultures like Apple, Facebook, and Google that were eager to pick over the carcass.[46] After all these self-inflicted cuts, there wasn't much left of the company. By October 2013, only 8,500 people worked for Kodak.[47] The game was up. Kodak was dead.

But Kodak—or, at least, its carcass—still existed in Rochester. And after driving around for a while, I did manage to find a company office. The building was at the intersection of State and Factory Streets in the old industrial part of town, a few blocks from the visitors center. KODAK: WORLD HEADQUARTERS, a dull corporate plaque advertised outside a sixteen-story building that, when it was constructed in 1914, had been the tallest place in Rochester. It was constructed from a similar sort of industrial brick that made up the old Musto marble factory in downtown San Francisco. But that's all it had in common with the reinvented 58,000-square-foot Battery club. A desultory American flag flew outside this former skyscraper. On the corner of Factory Street, there was a row of stores that had all been shuttered. SAMBA CAFÉ: IT'S JUST SENSATIONAL, a faded neon sign claimed above a boarded-up Brazilian restaurant. FLOWER CITY, another derelict store advertised over a scratched-out sign that said JEWELERS.

This palimpsest of industrial life was a picture worth at least a thousand words. And so, parking my rental car in the building's empty driveway, I took out my iPhone and began to photograph the desolation. The scene was so real that I didn't even need to switch on the camera's "noir" and "tonal" filters that had been designed to give my amateurish pictures more authenticity. But my shoot didn't last long. After a few minutes, an ancient security guard shuffled out of the old brick building and told me that photography wasn't permitted. I smiled sadly. No snaps allowed in Snap City. It was like outlawing email in Palo Alto or banning driving in Detroit.

I returned to the old woman at the empty visitors center. She brightened up when she saw me. "You'll find people at the Eastman House," she said after I described my people-less drive around Innovation Way and Creative Drive. "That's the only reason anyone comes to Rochester."

It was a good reason—particularly for anyone seeking to make sense of Kodak's fate. Located a couple of miles away from downtown Rochester, the Eastman House was the most meretricious mansion on a wide, leafy street lined with the sprawling trophy homes of Gilded Age industrial magnates. Built by George Eastman between 1902 and 1904, it was declared a National Historic Landmark in 1966. Housing more than 400,000 photographs and 23,000 films as well as a collection of antique Kodak cameras, the Eastman House is now one of the world's leading museums of photography and film.[48]

In "Kodachrome," Paul Simon sang about being able to read what had been written on the wall. And the writing about Kodak's fate was certainly written with a vivid, Kodachrome-like clarity on the Eastman House wall.

On a long white wall at the entrance to the museum was a timeline of the history of photography. Beginning in fifth-century BC China, with the first record of an optical device designed to capture light, the timeline on the wall included the creation of the first image from a camera obscura in 1826, the invention of the modern Zoetrope in 1834, Kodak's introduction of the first mass-market camera for children in 1900, Tim Berners-Lee's formal proposal to develop a protocol of the World Wide Web in 1992, Kodak's decision to stop producing cameras in 2004, and the fact that 380 billion photos, a remarkable 11% of the total photographs ever taken, were snapped in 2011.[49]

The timeline ended in 2012 with four entries that could have been grouped under the headline *REALLY* CREATIVE DESTRUCTION:

— Eastman Kodak company files for bankruptcy under CH 11
— Instagram has over 14 million users and hosts about 1 billion photographs
— There are over 6 billion photographs on Flickr
— There are over 500 billion photographs on Facebook

And that was it. The timeline concluded there. The writing was indeed on the wall for Rochester and Kodak. Silicon Valley sledgehammers like Flickr and Facebook had smashed old Rochester into smithereens. The Kodak economy had been replaced by the Facebook economy with its 500 billion free photographs. No wonder the Eastman House, as a memorial to a now-extinct analog industry, had been transformed into a museum. No wonder the only people who now visit Rochester come to gaze nostalgically at its past rather than imagine its future.

The Broken Center

"So what?" apologists of radical disruption like Tom Perkins will ask about Kodak's usurpation by Internet companies like Instagram, Flickr, and Facebook. Tragedy in Rochester, they will say, equals opportunity for West Coast entrepreneurs. Nostalgia, the determinists will remind us, is a Luddite indulgence. And the writing on the wall, they will remind us, eventually appears for everyone.

In some ways, of course, they are right. For better or worse, technological change—especially in our digital age of creative destruction—is pretty much inevitable. Paul Simon himself once described this to me with a bittersweet regret. "I'm personally against Web 2.0 in the same way as I'm personally against my own death," he said about the damage unleashed by the Internet upon the music industry—a hurricane that has flattened both the traditional labels and the economic value of recorded music.[50] "We're going to 2.0," Simon predicted to me. "Like it or not, that is what is going to happen."[51]

"There will be no more Kodak Moments. After 133 years, the company has run its course," Don Strickland, the Kodak executive who had unsuccessfully encouraged the company to pioneer the digital camera, thus concluded in 2013.[52] "Kodak was caught in a perfect storm of not only technological, but also social and economic change," added Robert Burley, a Canadian photographer whose work memorializes Kodak's decline.[53]

No, nothing lasts forever. And certainly the Kodak tragedy can be seen, at least in part, as a parable of a once-mighty monopolist, a Google of the industrial age, that couldn't adapt to the digital revolution. Yes, Kodak failed to become a leader in digital photography, in spite of the fact that the company actually invented the digital camera, back in 1975.[54] Yes, Kodak is, in part, a victim of what Harvard Business School professor Clayton Christensen calls, in his influential 2011 book about why businesses fail, *The Innovator's Dilemma*,[55] the challenge of a once-dominant incumbent having to disrupt its own business model. Yes, a string of myopic executives failed to reinvent Kodak, with the result that a great company that up until the 1990s was often listed among the world's top five most valuable brands[56] has now become synonymous with failure. And yes, tragedy in Rochester spells economic opportunity elsewhere, particularly for West Coast entrepreneurs like Jeff Bezos, who has made Christensen's *Innovator's Dilemma* required reading for all Amazon executives.[57]

"Maybe a fire is what's needed for a vigorous new growth, but that's the long view," Paul Simon said to me about the Internet's disruptive impact on creative industries like recorded music and photography. "In the short term, all that's apparent is the devastation." But what happens if the *devastation* is not only permanent, but also the defining feature of our now twenty-five-year-old digital economy? What happens if the tragedy in Rochester is actually a sneak preview of our collective future—a more universal perfect storm of technological, social, and economic change?

Welcome to what Joshua Cooper Ramo, the former executive editor of *Time* magazine, calls "the age of the unthinkable." It's a networked age, Ramo says, in which "conformity to old ideas is lethal"[58] and predictability and linearity have been replaced by what he calls an "epidemic" of self-organization where no central leadership is required. This is an age so destructively *unthinkable*, in fact, that Clayton Christensen's theory of the "Innovator's Dilemma," which suggests an orderly cycle of disruptors, each replacing the previous economic incumbent, now has itself been blown up by an even more disruptive theory of early-twenty-first-century digital capitalism.

Christensen's ideas have themselves been reinvented by the bestselling business writers Larry Downes and Paul F. Nunes, who've replaced the "Innovator's Dilemma" with the much bleaker "Innovator's Disaster." "Nearly everything you think you know about strategy and innovation is wrong," Downes and Nunes warn about today's radically disruptive economy.[59] In their 2014 book, *Big Bang Disruption*,[60] they describe an economy in which disruption is devastating rather than creative. It's a world, they say, in which Joseph Schumpeter's "perennial gales of creative destruction" have become Category 5 hurricanes. Upheavals from big-bang disruptors like Google, Uber, Facebook, and Instagram "don't create dilemmas for innovators," Downes and Nunes warn, "they trigger disasters."[61] And Kodak is the textbook example of this kind of disaster—a $31 billion company employing 145,000 people that, as they note, was bankrupted "gradually and then suddenly"[62] by the hurricane from Silicon Valley.

"An entire city," Jason Farago wrote about the impact of the Kodak bankruptcy on Rochester, "has lost its center."[63] But the real disaster of the digital revolution is much more universal than this. In today's networked age, it's our entire society that is having its center destroyed by a "perfect storm" of technological, social, and economic change. The twentieth-century industrial age, while far from ideal in many ways, was distinguished by what George Packer, writing in the *New York Times*, calls the "great leveling" of the "Roosevelt Republic."[64] For hard-line neoliberals like Tom Perkins, Packer's "great leveling" probably raises the specter of a socialist dystopia. But for those not fortunate enough to own a $130 million yacht as long as a football field, this world offered an economic and cultural center, a middle ground where jobs and opportunity were plentiful.

The late industrial age of the second half of the twentieth century was a middle-class world built, Packer notes, by "state universities, progressive taxation, interstate highways, collective bargaining, health insurance for the elderly, credible news organizations."[65] According to the Harvard economists Claudia Goldin and Lawrence Katz, this was a "golden age" of labor in which increasingly skilled workers won the "race between education and technology" and made themselves essential to the industrial economy.[66] And, of course, it was a world of publicly funded institutions like ARPA and NSFNET that provided the investment and opportunities to build valuable new technologies like the Internet.

But this world, Rochester's fate reminds us, is now passing. As Sequoia Capital chairman Michael Moritz reminds us, today's information economy is marked by an ever-increasing inequality between an elite and everyone else. It's a donut-shaped economy without a middle. Moritz thus describes as "brutal" both the drop between 1968 and 2013 in the US minimum wage (when inflation is accounted for) from $10.70 to $7.25 and the flattening of a median household income that, not even accounting for inflation, has crawled up from $43,868 to $52,762 over the same forty-five-year period.[67]

According to the *New York Times* columnist David Brooks, this inequality represents capitalism's "greatest moral crisis since the Great Depression."[68] It's a crisis, Brooks says, that can be captured in two statistics: the $19 billion Facebook acquisition of the fifty-five-person instant messaging Internet app WhatsApp in February 2014, which valued each employee at $345 million; and the equally disturbing fact that the slice of the economic pie for the middle 60 percent of earners in the US economy has dropped from 53 percent to 45 percent since 1970. The Internet economy "produces very valuable companies with very few employees," Brooks says of this crisis, while "the majority of workers are not seeing income gains commensurate with their productivity levels."[69]

In his 2013 National Book Award–winning *The Unwinding*, George Packer mourns the passing of the twentieth-century Great Society. What he calls "New America" has been corrupted, he suggests, by its deepening inequality of wealth and opportunity. And it's not surprising that Packer places Silicon Valley and the multibillionaire Internet entrepreneur and libertarian Peter Thiel at the center of his narrative.

The cofounder, with Elon Musk, of the online payments service PayPal, Thiel became a billionaire as the first outside investor in Facebook, after being introduced to Mark Zuckerberg by Sean Parker, the cofounder of Napster and Facebook's founding president. The San Francisco–based Thiel lives in a "ten thousand square foot white wedding cake of a mansion,"[70] a smaller but no less meretricious building than the Battery. His decadent house and dinner parties are the stuff of San Francisco high-society legend, featuring printed menus, unscheduled Gatsby-like appearances from the great Thiel himself, and waiters wearing nothing except their aprons. The reclusive Thiel has reinvented himself as a semi-mythical figure—a Gatsby meets Howard Hughes meets Bond villain. He's a Ferrari-driving, Stanford-educated moral philosopher, a chess genius and multibillionaire investor who is accompanied everywhere by a "staff of two blond, black-clad female assistants, a white-coated butler and a cook who prepares a daily health drink of celery, beets, kale, and ginger."[71]

It would be easy, of course, to dismiss Peter Thiel as an eccentric with cash. But that's the least interesting part of his story. He is, in fact, an even richer, smarter, and—as a major funder of radical American libertarians like Rand Paul and Ted Cruz—more powerful version of Tom Perkins. Peter Thiel has everything: brains, charm, prescience, intellect, charisma; everything, that is, except compassion for those less successful than him. In the increasingly unequal America described in Packer's *The Unwinding*, Thiel is the supreme unwinder, a hard-hearted follower of Ayn Rand's radical free-market philosophy who unashamedly celebrates the texture of inequality now reshaping America.

"As a Libertarian," Packer notes, "Thiel welcomed an America in which people could no longer rely on old institutions or get by in communities with long-standing sources of security, where they knew where they stood and what they were bound for."[72] Thiel would, therefore, certainly *welcome* today's age of the unthinkable, in which conformity to old ideas is lethal. He would probably *welcome* the sad fate of old industrial towns like Rochester. He might even *welcome* the sadder fate of those fifty thousand retirees at Kodak who lost their pensions because of the company's bankruptcy.

So what? Thiel might say about these impoverished old people who spent their entire lives working for Kodak and who no longer even own their pensions. *So what?* the multibillionaire with the black-clad female assistants, the white-coated butler, and the cook might say about today's libertarian age, in which a twenty-first-century networked capitalism is collapsing the center of twentieth-century economic life.

You Better Watch Out

To pin all the blame for society's broken center on the Internet would, of course, be absurd. However, Internet economics are now compounding the growing silicon chasm in society. Robert Franks and Philip Cook's 1995 *The Winner-Take-All Society* was one of the first books to recognize the corrosive impact of information technology on economic equality. Up till then, it was assumed that technological innovation was beneficial for society. Vannevar Bush, in the "Science, the Endless Frontier" report he wrote for Roosevelt in 1945, took it for granted that constant scientific and technological progress would inevitably lead to both more jobs and general prosperity. And this optimism was reflected in the work of the MIT economist Robert Solow, whose 1987 Nobel Prize in Economics was awarded for his research showing that over the long term, labor and capital maintained their share of rewards in a growing economy. But even Solow, whose research was mostly based on productivity improvements from the 1940s, '50s, and '60s, later became more skeptical of labor's ability to maintain its parity with capital in terms of reaping the rewards of more economic productivity. In a 1987 *New York Times* Book Review piece titled "We'd Better Watch Out," he acknowledged that what he called "Programmable Automation" hadn't increased labor productivity. "You can see the computer age everywhere," he memorably put it, "but in the productivity statistics."[73]

Timothy Noah, the author of *The Great Divergence*, a well-received book on America's growing inequality crisis, admits that computer technology does create jobs. But these, he says, are "for highly skilled, affluent workers," whereas the digital revolution is destroying the jobs of "moderately skilled middle class workers."[74] The influential University of California, Berkeley economist and blogger J. Bradford DeLong has suggested that the more central a role information technology plays in traditionally skillful professions like law or medicine, the fewer jobs there might be.[75] Loukas Karabarbounis and Brent Neiman, two economists from the University of Chicago's business school, have found that since the mid-1970s, the relative amount of income going to workers has been in decline around the world.[76] Meanwhile the research of three Canadian economists, Paul Beaudry, David Green, and Benjamin Sand, found a similarly steep decline of midlevel jobs—a depressing development that MIT's David Autor, Northeastern University's Andrew Sum, and the president of the Economic Policy Institute, Larry Mishel, have also discovered with their research.[77]

Many others share this concern about the destructive impact of technology on the "golden age" of labor. The George Mason University economist Tyler Cowen, in his 2013 book, *Average Is Over*, concurs, arguing that today's big economic "divide" is between those whose skills "complement the computer" and those whose don't. Cowen underlines the "stunning truth" that wages for men, over the last forty years, have fallen by 28%.[78] He describes the divide in what he calls this new "hyper-meritocracy" as being between "billionaires" like the Battery member Sean

Parker and the homeless "beggars" on the streets of San Francisco, and sees an economy in which "10 to 15 percent of the citizenry is extremely wealthy and has fantastically comfortable and stimulating lives."[79] Supporting many of Frank and Cook's theses in their *Winner-Take-All Society*, Cowen suggests that the network lends itself to a superstar economy of "charismatic" teachers, lawyers, doctors, and other "prodigies" who will have feudal retinues of followers working for them.[80] But, Cowen reassures us, there will be lots of jobs for "maids, chauffeurs and gardeners" who can "serve" wealthy entrepreneurs like his fellow chess enthusiast Peter Thiel.

The feudal aspect of this new economy isn't just metaphorical. The Chapman University geographer Joel Kotkin has broken down what he calls this "new feudalism" into different classes, including "oligarch" billionaires like Thiel and Uber's Travis Kalanick, the "clerisy" of media commentators like Kevin Kelly, the "new serfs" of the working poor and the unemployed, and the "yeomanry" of the old "private sector middle class," the professionals and skilled workers in towns like Rochester who are victims of the new winner-take-all networked economy.[81]

The respected MIT economists Erik Brynjolfsson and Andrew McAfee, who are cautiously optimistic about what they call "the brilliant technologies" of "the Second Machine Age," acknowledge that our networked society is creating a world of "stars and superstars" in a "winner-take-all" economy. It's the network effect, Brynjolfsson and McAfee admit, reflecting the arguments of Frank and Cook—a consequence, they say, of the "vast improvements in telecommunications" and the "digitalization of more and more information, goods and services."

The Nobel Prize–winning Princeton economist Paul Krugman also sees a "much darker picture" of "the effects of technology on labor." Throughout the second half of the twentieth century, Krugman says, workers competed against other workers for resources. Since "around 2000," Krugman notes, "labor's share of the pie has fallen sharply" both in the United States and the rest of the world, with workers being the victims of "disruptive" new technology.[82] This has happened before, Krugman reminds us. In a June 2013 *New York Times* column titled "Sympathy for the Luddites," he describes the late-eighteenth-century struggle of the cloth workers of Leeds, the Yorkshire city that was then the center of the English woolen industry, against the "scribbing" machines that were replacing skilled human labor. Krugman is sympathetic to this struggle, which, he says, was a defense of a middle-class life under mortal threat from machines.

Some will accuse Krugman of a Luddite nostalgia for a world that cannot be re-created. But this is exactly where they are wrong. Nostalgia isn't just for Luddites. And that, I'm afraid, is one more reason to mourn the end of the Kodak Moment.

CHAPTER FOUR

THE PERSONAL REVOLUTION

The Instagram Moment

In the summer of 2010, Kevin Systrom, a six-foot-seven Silicon Valley entrepreneur, took a trip with his girlfriend, Nicole Schuetz, to a hippie colony on the Baja peninsula in Mexico. It was one of those retro artistic communities on the Pacific coast still bathed in the fuzzy glow of the sixties counterculture—an appropriately laid-back place to reinvent oneself. Despite graduating from Stanford University with an engineering degree and having worked at Google for three years, the twenty-seven-year-old Systrom considered himself a failure.

Systrom had come out west to Silicon Valley from New England to, as he delicately put it, "get rich really quickly."[1] But he'd yet to make the kind of "fuck you" money that would have given him the ostentatious mansions, the Bombardier private jets, and the UberCHOPPER rides that some of his contemporaries, churned out of what *Forbes* magazine calls Stanford's "billionaire machine,"[2] already took for granted. Worse still, he'd gotten agonizingly close to two epic deals: first turning down an invitation in 2005 by a Harvard dropout named Mark Zuckerberg to develop a photo-sharing service for a social media startup known as "TheFacebook,"[3] and second, eschewing an internship with Jack Dorsey at Odeo, the San Francisco–based startup that would later hatch into Twitter.

"It was like . . . Great. I missed the Twitter boat. I missed the Facebook boat," he later admitted.[4]

Systrom had come down to Baja to figure out not only how to avoid missing any more boats, but how to launch a big boat of his own. He had a startup called Burbn, an online check-in service backed by Andreessen Horowitz. But there was little about Burbn in the summer of 2010 that distinguished it from market leaders like Foursquare—a well-funded check-in service that enabled its millions of users to broadcast their exact location to their network. And so, to fall back on that well-worn Silicon Valley cliché, Systrom needed a "radical pivot." Burbn really had failed. His me-too startup needed to be blown up and rebooted as a big bang kind of disruption.

So Systrom went into the picture business. Even as a high school student at the exclusive Middlesex School in Massachusetts, where he'd been president of the photography club, Systrom had loved taking pictures. As a Stanford undergraduate, Systrom had even spent a semester studying photography in the Italian city of Florence, where he'd become interested in filtering technology that gave photos a warm and fuzzy glow—a retro aesthetic reminiscent of the hippie colony on the Baja peninsula.

Systrom's pivot was to reinvent Burbn as a social photography-sharing app—a kind of Flickr meets Foursquare meets Facebook app designed exclusively for mobile devices. And it was on a Mexican beach in the summer of 2010 that he made his great breakthrough. As they walked hand in hand together beside the Pacific Ocean, Systrom—ever the consummate salesman—was pitching Nicole on the idea of a social network built around photographs taken from smartphone cameras. But she had pushed back, saying that she didn't have sufficient faith in her creative skills to share her mobile photos with friends. It was then that Kevin Systrom had his "aha" moment, the kind of alchemic epiphany that transformed a serial failure who'd missed both the Facebook and Twitter boats into the next Marc Andreessen.

What if this app featured filters? Systrom thought. What if it enabled its users to create photos that had a warm and fuzzy glow, the sort of sepia-tinged snaps that appeared so retro, so comfortably familiar that even the most untalented photographer wouldn't be ashamed to show them off to their friends? And what if this personalized technology was engineered to operate so intimately on mobile devices that users not only intuitively trusted the social app but also believed that they somehow owned it?

Systrom—all six feet, seven inches of him—was inspired. *Forbes* describes a scene that sounds like a Silicon Valley remix of Jimmy Buffett's hit song "Margaritaville": "He spent the rest of the day lying on a hammock, a bottle of Modelo beer sweating by his side, as he typed away on his laptop researching and designing the first Instagram filter."

And so Instagram and its photos—what Systrom, shamelessly appropriating Kodak's phrase, calls "Instagram moments"—were born. With fuzzily named filters like X-Pro II, Hefe, and Toaster, this free mobile network became an instant viral hit. The scale and speed of its success was astonishing. Twenty-five thousand iPhone users downloaded the app when it launched on October 6, 2010. A month later, Systrom's startup had a million members. By early 2012, as the writing on the Eastman House wall reminds us, it had 14 million users and hosted a billion Instagram moments. In April of that year, after a bidding war between then Twitter CEO Jack Dorsey and Mark Zuckerberg, Kevin Systrom agreed to a billion-dollar acquisition offer from Facebook, even though his eighteen-month-old startup had neither revenue nor even a business model for making money.[5] No matter. Just six months later, Instagram users had skyrocketed to 100 million, with the app hosting 5 billion photos. Over the Thanksgiving holiday in late November 2012, more than 200 Instagram moments were being posted in the United States every second.[6] By the spring of 2013, just as a shrunken Kodak was limping out of bankruptcy, Systrom's mobile network hosted 16 billion photographs, with over 55 million daily uploads by its 150 million members.[7] And by the end of 2013, Instagram—with Facebook, LinkedIn, Pinterest, and Twitter—had, according to the Pew Research Center, emerged as one of the five most popular social media websites in the United States.[8] Most remarkably, usage on Instagram and Facebook combined to make up 26% of all time spent on mobile networks in 2013,[9] with Instagram's 23% growth making it not only the fastest-growing app of the year but also the world's fastest-growing social network.[10]

It was a cultural revolution. The London *Observer*'s Eva Wiseman describes how sepia-tinged Instagram moments have established themselves as a parallel reality for the network generation: "We eat, we sleep, we chat, we eat. But all the time, there's a second plotline, unraveling on our phones. My friends preface any conversation with a brow-raised phrase: *Meanwhile on Instagram* . . ."

Kevin Systrom's boat had come in. He could no longer claim to be a failure. He'd become a star of the "winner-takes-all" economy, a founding member of the Battery. He personally pocketed around half a billion dollars from the Facebook sale, giving him the instant wealth of a Gilded Age tycoon such as Kodak's George Eastman. And like Eastman's late-nineteenth-century startup, Systrom's early-twenty-first-century photo network has imprinted itself on our everyday lives. The Instagram moment has replaced the Kodak moment. Not a bad return-on-investment from a day spent swinging in a hammock on a Mexican beach.

An Untruthful Mirror

But the benefits of Instagram for the rest of us are about as foggy as one of Instagram's Hefe or Toaster filters. "Instagram is focused on capturing the world's moments,"[11] Systrom likes to say. But that's a fiction—just like Instagram itself. In contrast with Kodachrome, a film stock dedicated to sharp-detailed, grain-free images, Instagram's value is its graininess—designed, as the *New York Times*' Alex Williams explains, to make "everyone look a little younger, a bit prettier, more cover-worthy."[12]

Whoever first said that "the camera never lies" had obviously never used Instagram. If Kodachrome was designed as an unsparingly honest window, then Instagram is its reverse, a complimentary mirror "where," as Sarah Nicole Prickett, writing in the *New York Times*, observes, "the grass looks greener."[13] That's its greatest seduction. So rather than accurately capturing the world's moments in all their colorful complexity, Instagram—"the highest achievement in Internet voyeurism," according to Alex Williams, and "the app built to make you covet your neighbor's life,"[14] as Prickett puts it—is actually creating what Williams, citing the title of a 1959 work by Norman Mailer, calls "Advertisements for Myself."[15]

"Advertisements for Myself" have become the unavoidable medium and the message of what Sequoia Capital chairman Michael Moritz calls the personal revolution. It's a world that, Tim Wu caustically notes, is defined by a "race" among social media users to build the most ubiquitous personal brands.[16] Online narcissism is therefore, as Keith Campbell, the coauthor of the bestselling *The Narcissism Epidemic*, explains, a "logical outgrowth of DIY capitalism—the capitalism in which we all have our own "branding business" and we are our "own agent" and "marketing department"[17] No wonder *Time* made "YOU" Person of the Year for 2006. "Yes, you," the magazine announced. "You control the Information Age. Welcome to your world."[18]

Meanwhile, on Instagram . . . it appears as if we've all returned to the Dark Ages in Wu's "branding race" and Campbell's "DIY capitalism." The billions of advertisements for ourselves that we post on Kevin Systrom's creation are making us as ignorantly self-important as our most primitive ancestors. Indeed, the only thing more retro than Instagram's filters is the pre-Copernican belief, encouraged by social networks like Instagram, Facebook, and Twitter, that the new digital universe somehow revolves around us. Fuzzy technology leads to an even fuzzier sense of our place in the cosmos. In today's culture of Instagram moments, celebrity, or at least the illusion of celebrity, appears to have been radically democratized.

Instagram actually represents the reverse side of Silicon Valley's cult of failure. In the Valley, the rich and famous claim to be failures; on social networks like Instagram, millions of failures claim to be rich and famous.

"Our age is lousy with celebrities," says George Packer, who sees our contemporary obsession with celebrity as an important cultural piece of our increasing economic inequality. "They loom larger in times like now," he thus notes, "when inequality is soaring and trust in institutions—governments, corporations, schools, the press—is failing."[19]

Packer is right. The truth about networks like Instagram, Twitter, or Facebook is that their easy-to-use, free tools delude us into thinking we are celebrities. Yet, in the Internet's winner-take-all economy, attention remains a monopoly of superstars. Average is over, particularly for celebrities. In early 2014, for example, Kim Kardashian had 10 million Instagram followers, but only followed 85 people. Justin Bieber, the most popular person of all on Instagram, had almost 11 million followers and followed nobody at all. Rather than cultural democracy, what we are seeing is another spin on Joel Kotkin's new feudalism, in which narcissistic aristocrats like Kardashian and Bieber are able to wield massive armies of loyal voyeurs.

Hello This Is Us

Social networks like Instagram can't, of course, be entirely blamed for this epidemic of narcissism and voyeurism now afflicting our culture. As the work of prominent American psychologists like Jean Twenge, Keith Campbell, and Elias Aboujaoude indicates, our contemporary obsession with public self-expression has complex cultural, technological, and psychological origins that can't be exclusively traced to the digital revolution.[20] Indeed, Twenge and Campbell's *Narcissism Epidemic* was published in 2009, before Systrom even had his "aha" moment on that Mexican beach.

As David Brooks notes, our current fashion for vulgar immodesty represents another fundamental break with the Great Society, which, in contrast with today, was represented by a culture of understatement, abnegation, and modesty. "When you look from today back to 1945," Brooks notes about the "expressive individualism" of our networked age, "you are looking into a different cultural epoch, across a sort of narcissism line."[21]

Nor is Instagram alone in crossing this narcissism line. There's also Twitter and Tumblr and Facebook and the rest of a seemingly endless mirrored hall of social networks, apps, and platforms stoking our selfie-centered delusions. Indeed, in an economy driven by innovator's disasters, new social apps such as WhatsApp, WeChat, and Snapchat—a photo-sharing site that, in November 2013, turned down an all-cash acquisition offer of more than $3 billion from Facebook—are already challenging Instagram's dominance.[22] And by the time you read this, there will, no doubt, be even more destructive new products and companies undermining 2014 disruptors like Snapchat, WhatsApp, and WeChat.

For us, however, Instagram—whether or not it remains the "second plotline" of the networked generation—is a useful symbol of everything that has gone wrong with our digital culture over the last quarter of a century. "I update, therefore I am," I once wrote, half jokingly, about the existential dilemma created by our obsession with social media.[23] Unfortunately, however, the idea that our existence is proven by our tweets or our Instagram moments is no longer very funny. As the *Financial Times*' Gautam Malkani warns about our selfie-centric culture, "if we have no thought to Tweet or photo to post, we basically cease to exist."[24] No wonder that what the *New York Times* columnist Charles Blow calls "the Self(ie) Generation" of millennial 18–33-year-olds has so much lower levels of trust than previous generations—with a 2014 Pew Research Center report showing that only 19% of millennials trust others, compared with 31% of Gen Xers and 40% of boomers.[25] After all, if we can't even trust our own existence without Instagramming it, then *who* can we trust?

"In our age of social networking, the selfie is the new way to look someone right in the eye and say, 'Hello this is me,'" the American movie star and self-confessed Instagram "addict" James Franco confessed in the *New York Times*.[26] And so—from the tasteless Rich Kids of Instagram with their "they have much more money than you and this is what they do" tagline to the craze for selfies at funerals[27] to the hookup app photos of men at the Holocaust Memorial in Berlin[28] to the inevitable "Auschwitz selfies,"[29] to the "Bridge girl," the young woman who casually snapped a selfie in front of somebody committing suicide off New York's Brooklyn Bridge[30] to Franco himself, who in 2014 was accused of heavily flirting with underage girls on Instagram[31]—the shameless self-portrait has emerged as a dominant mode of expression, perhaps even the proof of our existence, in the digital age. Presidents, prime ministers, and even pontiffs have published self-portraits snapped by their mobile phones—with Pope Francis publishing what the *Guardian* called a "badass selfie" inside St. Peter's Basilica.[32]

No wonder the "selfie"—defined as "a photograph that one has taken of oneself, typically one taken with a smartphone or webcam and uploaded to a social media site"—was the *Oxford English Dictionary*'s word of the year in 2013, its use increasing by 17,000% over the year.[33] And no wonder that almost 50% of the photos taken on Instagram in the United Kingdom by 14–21-year-olds are selfies, many of whom use this medium to reify their existence.[34]

"All too often, selfies involve shooting yourself in the foot," Gautam Malkani noted about Barack Obama and David Cameron's selfie debacle at Nelson Mandela's memorial service in December 2013. But the unfortunate truth is that we are all—from Barack Obama to James Franco to the other 150 million selfie addicts on Kevin Systrom's social network—collectively shooting ourselves in more than just our feet with our battery of *Hello this is me* snaps. These "Advertisements for Myself" are actually embarrassing commercials both for ourselves and for our species. They represent the logical conclusion of a "Personal Revolution" over the last twenty-five years in which everything has degenerated into the immediate, the intimate, and, above all, the self-obsessed.

Hello this is us, Instagram is saying about our species. And I, for one, don't like what I'm seeing.

It wasn't supposed to turn out this way. The Internet, we were promised—by entrepreneurs like Kevin Systrom and relentlessly cheerful futurists like Steven Johnson[35]—was going to "capture the world's moments" and create a global village, thereby making us all more open-minded, progressive, and intelligent. One particularly nostalgic futurist, the *Economist*'s erudite digital editor Tom Standage, even believes that the Web is making us more like our civic-minded ancestors from Roman antiquity. In his provocative 2013 book, *Writing on the Wall*,[36] Standage argues that "history is retweeting itself" and that social networks like Facebook, Twitter, and Instagram are transforming us into inheritors of what he calls "Cicero's web."[37] But what is even faintly Ciceronian about Instagram's "unadulterated voyeurism," which, the *Times*' Alex Williams notes, encourages us to "create art-directed magazine layouts of their lives, as if everyone is suddenly Diana Vreeland"?[38] And what, I wonder, would Cicero, that stoical republican, think about the Rich Kids of Instagram, with their snaps of a teenager's "this is how the pimps roll" Ferrari and "reptile" shoe collection, or the photo of a wealthy young woman's head lost in an ocean of her Chanel and Hermès bags?[39]

Standage may be right about the writing being on the wall. But if antiquity really is retweeting itself, it's in the form of the Greek myth of Narcissus. Nicholas Carr famously argued in his 2011 book *The Shallows*, a finalist for the Pulitzer Prize, that the Web is shortening our attention spans and making our minds less focused and more superficial.[40] Probably. But the personal revolution is certainly making us more parochial and unworldly. Just as Instagram enables us to take photos that are dishonest advertisements for ourselves, so search engines like Google provide us with links to sites tailored to confirm our own mostly ill-informed views about the world. Eli Pariser, the former president of MoveOn.org, describes the echo-chamber effect of personalized algorithms as "The Filter Bubble."[41] The Internet might be a village, Pariser says, but there's nothing global about it. This is confirmed by a 2013 study by the Massachusetts Institute of Technology showing that the vast majority of Internet and cell phone communication takes place inside a hundred-mile radius of our homes and by a 2014 Pew Research and Rutgers University report revealing that social media actually stifles debate between people of differnet opinions.[42] But the reality of the Web is probably even more selfie-centric than the MIT report suggests. With more than a quarter of all smartphone use taking place on Facebook and Instagram, most Web communication these days actually takes place inside that intimate hundred-*millimeter* radius between our faces and our mobile devices. The real *myth* is that we are communicating at all. The truth, of course, is that we are mostly just talking to ourselves on these supposedly "social" networks. In her bestselling 2011 book, the MIT professor Sherry Turkle describes this condition as being "alone together." It's a brilliantly terse description of an Internet in which the more social we become, the more we connect and communicate and collaborate, the lonelier we become.

And yet, for all its sad narcissistic inanity and even sadder existential angst, it would be a mistake to see Instagram's problems in primarily cultural terms. Selfie culture is a big enough lie, but it's actually billions of dollars and hundreds of thousands of jobs less dishonest than the economics of selfie culture. And it's here—in the quantifiable realm of jobs, wages, and profit—that we can find the most disturbing implications of the shift from the Kodak to the Instagram moment.

Original Sin

"The personal is the political," was a liberation cry of the sixties countercultural revolution. But, rather than being political, today's personal revolution is all about money and wealth. In our digital age, the personal is the economic. And there's nothing liberating about it at all.

Just as the Kodak tragedy decimated the economic heart of Rochester, so the Internet is destroying our old industrial economy—transforming what was once a relatively egalitarian system into a winner-take-all economy of what Tyler Cowen calls "billionaires and beggars." Rather than just a city, it's a whole economy that is losing its center. For all Silicon Valley's claims that the Internet has created more equal opportunity and distribution of wealth, the new economy actually resembles a donut—with a gaping hole in the middle where, in the old industrial system, millions of workers were once paid to manufacture valuable products.

This economic inequality mirrors the feudal arrangement on Instagram in which Justin Bieber has 11 million followers and follows nobody at all. It's creating what the MIT economists

Andrew McAfee and Eric Brynjolfsson call an economy of "stars and superstars." This new digital economy is a primary reason why life has become so much tougher for many of us over the last twenty-five years. And it's why the Internet—or, at least, the business model of Internet companies like Instagram, Google, Twitter, Yelp, and Facebook—isn't the ideal platform for building an equitable economy in the networked twenty-first century.

In contrast with the dishonesty of selfie economics, the rules of the industrial Kodak economy were as crystalline as the images delivered on Kodachrome film. As Michael Moritz noted about what he called the "second phase" of the industrial revolution in northeastern US cities like Detroit, Pittsburgh, and Rochester, factories were "isolated" from consumers.[43] And just as there were clear walls separating workers and consumers, their economic roles were also clearly demarcated: workers were paid cash in exchange for their labor and consumers paid cash in exchange for Kodak's products. "You press the button, we do the rest"—which involved the development and manufacture of their physical products, which were then shipped, via retail channels, to consumers. But "the rest" required significant investment in both capital and labor. That was the center of the old industrial economy—where Kodak created enormous value and was thus worth $31 billion a quarter century ago. So, back in 1989, those 145,000 unionized Kodak workers in the many research facilities, photo labs, and factories dotting the entire Rochester area were employed to invent and manufacture products that were then sold to consumers. Just as Instagram is the anti-Kodachrome product, so it's also the anti-Kodak company building an anti-Kodak economy. At first glance, Instagram appears to offer a much better deal for everyone than Kodak. The gray Rochester factory has been upgraded to a Mexican hippie resort. A tall dude lies in a hammock on a Pacific beach and, inspired by his girlfriend, invents an awesome photo-sharing app. Two months later, that free app is available for instant download. Three years later, the billion-dollar app has become "a second plotline" for its 150 million users with *Meanwhile on Instagram* being the preface for a whole generation of Internet users. "Software," as Marc Andreessen likes to boast, "is eating the world."[44]

Everybody wins. One hundred and fifty million people can't be wrong? Right?

Wrong. "There's a catch though," as James Surowiecki warns in a 2013 *New Yorker* piece titled "Gross Domestic Freebie," about the Instagram economy. And it's a very big catch indeed. "Digitalization doesn't require a lot of workers: you can come up with an idea, write a piece of software and distribute it to hundreds of millions of people with ease," Surowiecki explains. "That's fundamentally different from physical products, which require much more labor to produce and distribute."[45]

Instagram is a perfect example of Surowiecki's catch. Software might be eating the world, but it's ravenously consuming our jobs, too. When Kevin Systrom had his "aha" idea on that Mexican beach he had one partner at Burbn, another Stanford graduate, a Brazilian-born engineer named Mike Krieger. Together, Systrom and Krieger wrote the initial software and used the Apple app store to distribute the app. And even when they sold Instagram to Facebook for a billion dollars in April 2012, Instagram still only had thirteen full-time employees working out of a small office in downtown San Francisco.

No, that's not a typo. Instagram really did have just *thirteen full-time employees* when Facebook paid a billion dollars for the startup. Meanwhile, in Rochester, Kodak was closing 13 factories and 130 photo labs and laying off 47,000 workers. And these thousands of Kodak employees weren't the only professional victims of selfie economics. Professional photographers have been badly hit, too. Between 2000 and 2012, the number of professional photographers, artists, and photographers working on American newspapers fell from 6.171 to 3,493—a 43% drop at a time when pictures have become "more sexy" than words and we are taking trillions of photos a year.[46]

So who, exactly, is doing the work, providing all the labor, in a billion-dollar startup that employed only thirteen people?

We are. All 150 million of us are members of the new Snap Nation. Kevin Systrom's creation is the quintessential data factory of our new digital economy. In contrast with the old industrial factory—that former skyscraper, on the corner of Factory and State in downtown Rochester—these twenty-first-century factories are as ubiquitous as selfies, existing wherever there is a networked device. You may be reading this on one right now. You almost certainly have one in your pocket or on your desk. And it's our labor on these little devices—our incessant tweeting, posting, searching, updating, reviewing, commenting, and snapping—that is creating all the value in the networked economy.

It's not just Instagram, of course, that has been able to build a massive business with the tiniest of workforces. There's WhatsApp, the San Francisco–based instant-messaging platform that was acquired by Facebook for $19 billion in February 2014. In December 2013, WhatsApp handled 54 billion messages from its 450 million users, yet it only employs fifty-five people to manage its service. "WhatsApp is everything wrong with the U.S. economy," argues Robert Reich, who served as secretary of labor in the Clinton administration, about a service that's not providing any jobs and is compounding the winner-take-all economics of the digital marketplace.[47]

It's one of the greatest ironies of our supposedly technology-rich digital age. In contrast with the industrial economy, the quality of the technology is secondary. When Facebook and Twitter fought a bidding war to acquire Instagram, they weren't competing for Kevin Systrom's cheap, off-the-shelf photography filters or the code he and Mike Krieger slapped together in a few months. What they were paying for was you and me. They wanted us—our labor, our productivity, our network, our supposed creativity. It's the same reason Yahoo acquired the microblogging network Tumblr, with its 300 million users and just 178 employees, for $1.1 billion in May 2013, or why in November 2013 Facebook made its $3 billion cash offering for the photography-sharing app Snapchat with its mere twenty employees.[48]

And that's why Evan Spiegel, Snapchat's twenty-three-year-old, Stanford-educated CEO, turned down Facebook's $3 billion offer for his twenty-person startup. Yes, that's right—he actually *turned down* $3 billion in cash for his two-year-old startup. But, you see, Spiegel's minuscule app company—which, six months after rejecting Facebook's $3 billion deal, was negotiating a new round of financing with the Chinese Internet giant Alibaba at a rumored $10 billion valuation[49]—isn't really as tiny as it seems. Its "workers" actually include around 25% of all cell phone users in the United Kingdom and 50% of all cell phone users in Norway, who, according to Spiegel, "actively" use the Snapchat app.[50]

Data factories are eating the world. But while this has created a coterie of boy plutocrats like Evan Spiegel, Kevin Systrom, and Tumblr's twenty-seven-year-old CEO, David Karp, it certainly isn't making the rest of us rich. You see, for the labor we invest in adding intelligence to Google, or content to Facebook, or photos to Snapchat, we are paid zero. Nothing at all, except the right to use the software for free.

"It wasn't always like this," *TechCrunch* reports about our new data factory economy. "To earn a profit, companies used to have to do the dirty work themselves. They hired huge staffs in real factories to sew textiles or build cars. People worked for wages and bought products. But technology changed all that."[51]

Yes, technology has, indeed, changed *all that.* Some argue that while this might be bad for the old industrial working class, it is actually beneficial for consumers, who, while not being paid for their labor, nonetheless get to enjoy free products like Google's search engine, Twitter's timeline, Yelp's restaurant reviews, and YouTube's videos. In our so-called attention economy, they argue, these services also provide us with the platforms to be visible and enable us to build what Fordham University professor Alice Marwick calls our "micro celebrity" in the social media age.[52]

"Wikipedia is great for readers. It's awful for the people who make encyclopedias." Thus suggests the *New Yorker*'s Surowiecki.[53] But is this really correct? Take Instagram, for example. While Systrom's free photo app is certainly "awful" for Kodak workers and professional photographers, is it really "great" for the rest of us?

Instagram sits in the center of today's perfect storm of technological, social, and economic change. It enables "addicts" like James Franco to broadcast his *Hello this is me* photos to his 1.5 million followers. It's the ideal fix for our narcissistic and voyeuristic age—a personalized, customized, and easy-to-use app that encourages us to tell lies about ourselves. But, along with being a tool that misrepresents the world, Instagram is pitching us a gigantic lie, too. It is selling us the seductive idea that we own this technology. That it's ours.

But the problem is that we don't own any of it—the technology, the profit, maybe not even "our" billions of photographs. We work for free in the data factory and Instagram takes not only all the revenue from their business, but the fruits of our labor, too. In December 2012, after some controversial changes to the wording of Instagram's terms of service, Kevin Systrom had to vociferously deny that Instagram intended to sell users' photos or their data to third parties.[54] Yet the question of who actually owns Instagram's content remains as fuzzy as its photos. As a July 2013 white paper by the American Society of Media Photographers (ASMP) noted, most Instagram users don't "understand the extent of the rights that they are giving away." The company's "onerous" terms of use, the ASMP white paper reported, "gives Instagram perpetual use of photos and video as well as the nearly unlimited right to license the images to any and all third parties."[55]

Whether or not Instagram wants to own our photos, it certainly wants to own us. The personal is, indeed, the economic. Backed by millions of dollars of investment from Silicon Valley venture capitalists, the whole point of the free Instagram app is to make money by mining its users' data. And Instagram's business model—like those of Google, Facebook, Yahoo, Twitter, Snapchat, and most other successful Internet companies—is based upon advertising, a strategy it formally introduced in November 2013.

In "exchange" for using its app, our photos reveal to Instagram more and more about our tastes, our movements, and our friends. The app reverses the camera lens. That's why Facebook paid a billion dollars for Systrom's creation. The *Hello this is me* economy is actually more selfie-centric than even James Franco imagined. We think we are using Instagram to look at the world, but actually we are the ones who are being watched. And the more we reveal about ourselves, the more valuable we become to advertisers. So, for example, had I posted those snaps of Kodak's Rochester world headquarters up on Instagram, the app, by taking advantage of the location data on my iPhone, would have fed me back advertisements with special deals for hotels or, perhaps more appropriately, given the city's dire economic situation, employment agencies in Rochester. As its parent company, Facebook, is already doing, Instagram might even eventually integrate my photo into an advertisement and use it as an endorsement for a product or service featured in my post. All without my permission or even my knowledge.

And it's here that we find the most disturbing flaw in the data factory economy. "Free," you see, is anything but free. Instagram's greatest deceit is taking our self-love to its darkest and most twisted economic end—a nightmarish conclusion that, in homage to Alfred Hitchcock's 1958 classic movie about a private eye who is the victim of an elaborately staged murder, I dubbed, in my last book, *Digital Vertigo*. It creates a surreal economy in which we are not only the creator of the networked product, but also the product itself. The personal revolution, then, is way more *personal* than most of us would like. Hitchcock himself, the master of the "second plotline," couldn't have come up with a better subtext to the selfie economy. The data factory's core economic value is all the personal information extracted from its free laborers. As in one of Hitchcock's dark movies, it's *you*—the innocent bystander, the everyman—who is the victim of something that we neither understand nor control.

From social media networks like Twitter and Facebook to the world's second most valuable company, Google, the exploitation of our personal information is the engine of the "big data" economy. All these companies want to know us so intimately that they can package us up and then, *without our consent*, sell us back to advertisers. This greed for personal data is what Ethan Zuckerman, the director of the MIT Center for Civic Media and one of the inventors of pop-up online ads, describes as the World Wide Web's "original sin"—a "fiasco," Zuckerman says, which forces Internet startups that give away their product for free to move "deeper into the world of surveillance." "*It's obvious now that what we did was a fiasco*," he writes acidly about the "good intentions" of Internet pioneers like himself, "*so let me remind you that what we wanted to do was something brave and noble.*"[56]

Zuckerman's biblical metaphor is an apt description of the Internet's fall from grace. Facebook, for example, a company that was supposedly designed to unite the world, is so guilty of taking advantage of children's images in their ads that a number of US privacy, consumer-rights, and children's nonprofits, as well as parents of exploited teenagers, like the filmmaker Annie Leonard, are involved in a bitter legal dispute to shield kids from this disgraceful exploitation. "You probably won't even know when your family is suddenly starring in a commercial. Neither will your kid, unless she enjoys fine print more than status updates," Leonard wrote in 2014. "But contrary to what Mark Zuckerberg would have you believe, there's not a fine line between a selfie and a sponsored post."[57]

Speaking of *fine lines* and *original sin*, Google, with its suite of free products such as Search, Gmail, its Google+ social network, and YouTube, is the most sophisticated of these big data companies at marketing itself as a selfless nonprofit while simultaneously grossly exploiting its innocent users. Google is already integrating our posts and our photos into advertisements that are then viewed by the billion people who access the two million sites on its display advertising network. Google, whose intentions, like those of Facebook, were no doubt good, is now quite literally transforming us into display ads for their advertising business. We are not only the unpaid product in this economy, but also are becoming the billboards for displaying Google's advertising. Once upon a time, companies paid people to walk up and down the street wearing so-called sandwich boards that displayed advertising. Now we all do it for free.

As Google's then CEO Eric Schmidt confessed to the *Financial Times* back in 2007, Google wants to know us better than we know ourselves so that it can tell us not only what jobs we should take but also how we want to spend our day.[58] "We know where you are. We know where you've been," Schmidt told the *Atlantic*'s editor James Bennet in September 2010. "We can more or less know what you're thinking about."[59] This is the real reason why Google spent $500 million in 2014 on the artificial intelligence startup DeepMind—a technology that, according to *The Information*'s Amir Efrati, wants to "make computers think like humans."[60]

By thinking like us, by being able to join the dots in our mind, Google will own us. And by owning us—our desires, our intentions, our career goals, above all our buying habits—Google will own the networked future.

The Silicon Valley insider and technology critic Jaron Lanier argues "the future should be *our* theater."[61] But the problem with the data factory economy is that we have become the show that is being played in somebody else's theater. And unlike professional actors, we aren't even being paid for our labor. No wonder Lanier is nostalgic for a time when we were optimistic about the future.

I miss the future, too. And to rediscover my enthusiasm for it, I need to go back a quarter century, to a place called Berwick Street in Soho, London.

CHAPTER FIVE

THE CATASTROPHE OF ABUNDANCE

The Narrow Stump

I grew up in England. No, not the England of Winston Churchill's exclusive gentleman's clubs or *Downton Abbey*'s bucolic aristocracy and their unnaturally cheerful servants. Rather than a nostalgic costume drama, my England was London. And my London was Soho—the square-mile district in London's West End that is not only the historic center of the city's fashion business, but also the heart of its independent movie and music industries.

As a kid growing up in the swinging London of the late sixties and seventies, I got to see a much more entertaining show in Soho than anything a *Downton Abbey*–style TV drama could muster. My family was in the rag trade and owned a store on the edge of Soho, so I had the good fortune to spend much of my adolescence wandering around its abundant clubs, cafés, and records stores, and its other, more adult attractions. They were the glory years of the English recorded music industry—a period of remarkable creative fecundity in which London in general and Soho in particular appeared, to me at least, to be the center of the creative universe. The Beatles, the Stones, Jimi Hendrix, Queen, Elton John, and David Bowie all played at Soho clubs like the Marquee and recorded albums in Soho's Trident Studios. Eric Clapton and the Sex Pistols lived there for a while, while the Kinks's 1970 hit "Lola" was set in a particularly adventurous Soho sex club.

My family owned a store called Falbers Fabrics, on the corner of Oxford Street, Europe's busiest shopping street, and Berwick Street, a narrow stump of a street that ran down into the strip clubs and massage parlors of what is euphemistically known as "Old Soho." Berwick Street had a special place in my family's history. It was the street on which my great-grandfather, Victor Falber, an immigrant entrepreneur from the Polish town of Plock, first set up shop in the early twentieth century—a time when almost everyone, from aristocrats to servants, made their own clothes. He was a woolens and silk market trader, carting his goods every day from London's East End to Berwick Street market and selling to dressmakers who would then invest their labor in creating finished clothing. Later, my great-grandfather's business would graduate to a physical store, first at the bottom of Berwick Street and then as "Falbers Fabrics," one of London's best-known fabric retailers, on Oxford Street. And even today, the name Victor Falber remains imprinted on a Berwick Street wall. Outside 12 Berwick Street, there is a marble plinth above the offices of the building's current tenant, a creative agency that produces viral online videos. V. FALBER & SONS, it still says, the ghostlike reminder of a makers' economy in which clothing was self-made rather than mass-produced in a factory.

In comparison with the vertiginous ups and downs of San Francisco's Battery Street and Rochester's Factory Street over the last twenty-five years, the fortunes of Soho's Berwick Street haven't dramatically changed since 1989. Had you strolled down Berwick Street in 1989 and then, having fallen asleep for a quarter of a century, taken that same half-mile stroll once again in 2014, things wouldn't have appeared, on first glance at least, to be much different from before. You'd still find a traffic-clogged street packed with stores, clubs, pubs, and restaurants popular with both tourists and the workers employed by Soho's many media and fashion companies. And you'd still find a vibrant open-air market at the south end of the street, with tradesmen loudly hawking their fruit and vegetables, flowers, and cheap household goods.

But, if you looked carefully enough, there are some things on Berwick Street that have indeed changed over the last twenty-five years. In 1989, the year that Tim Berners-Lee invented the Web, Berwick Street was known as the "Golden Mile of Vinyl." The street was then famous for its more than twenty specialty record stores, covering every genre of music—from bluegrass, reggae, and electronic and house to soul, funk, jazz, and classical. These stores had all been opened after the introduction of Sony and Philips's compact disc format in the early eighties—beginning in 1984 with Reckless Records, a store that became so popular that five years later, it opened a sister branch in Chicago.

It was a golden age of media. Back in 1989, Berwick Street not only hosted what the *Independent* newspaper called the "greatest concentration of record shops in Britain";[1] it was also the center of independent musical life in London. Abbey Road, the St. Johns Wood street a few miles north of Soho immortalized on the cover of the eponymous 1969 Beatles record, might be the most famous musical street in London, but Berwick Street isn't too far behind. An *Abbey Road*– style photograph of the street was even featured on the cover of Oasis's album *(What's the Story) Morning Glory?*, one of the most successful records in British music history, which, after its release in October 1995, was selling two copies a minute in the HMV superstore on Oxford Street.[2] Today, however, neither the HMV superstore nor the Golden Mile of Vinyl exists. Reckless Records—where a cover of *(What's the*

Story) Morning Glory? is nostalgically displayed in its window—is still there. But in 2014, there were only four or five other record stores left on Berwick Street. The glory years are over. Like Victor Falber and his makers' clothing economy, the Golden Mile of Vinyl is now history.

As an avid music collector, I spent many happy hours wandering up and down Berwick Street in the eighties. BUY SELL TRADE, all the stores advertised on their windows. It was my introduction to the "buy, sell, trade" economics of scarce creative goods. Just as my great-grandfather sold valuable woolens or silk in Berwick Street market, so the merchants on the Golden Mile of Vinyl sold valuable musical recordings like the LP version of *(What's the Story) Morning Glory?* or the seven-inch single of the Kinks's "Lola." Price was determined by demand. The scarcer the product, the more demand from buyers, the higher the price. And if you didn't think the price was right, then you could always go next door and buy there. It was a perfect market.

It was a perfect cultural experience, too. The former *Wired* editor in chief Chris Anderson invented the idea of the "long tail" to describe the supposed cornucopia of self-produced cultural goods available on the Web. But Berwick Street, that narrow stump of a Soho street, was the real long tail of musical diversity—existing years before Anderson came out with his theory. If you searched hard enough on the Golden Mile of Vinyl and in Soho's many other independent record shops, you could dig up the most obscure recordings. And if you couldn't find what you were looking for, or weren't sure, then the stores employed real human beings, rather than algorithms, to answer questions and give recommendations of what to sample and buy. These human beings weren't infallible, but they were much more likely to come up with serendipitous recommendations than algorithms that know our entire purchasing history and thus just tell us what we already know.

Back in 1989, I would often come to Soho, not only to buy and sell music but also to meet with friends who were founding record labels, running clubs, spotting talent, or managing young artists. Like so many other people in my generation, my ambition was to get into the music business. Jaron Lanier describes the future as a theater. But twenty-five years ago, the future looked to me like a concert hall. And I wanted a seat in its front row.

Twenty-five years ago, the future of the recorded music industry appeared as richly abundant as Soho's cultural economy. "Perfect Sound Forever," Philips and Sony boasted about their new CD format. And this digital audio technology had indeed triggered a golden age of new labels, genres, artists, and audiences. Technology, it seemed, was a force both for the creative and economic good. Everyone was replacing their vinyl records with the more convenient and cleaner-sounding CDs and the eighties were extremely profitable years for the recorded music industry, creating many thousands of new jobs and investment opportunities. HMV had even invested in the largest music store in the world on Oxford Street, a three-story, 60,000-square-foot building that had been opened by Bob Geldof in a October 1986 ceremony that not only attracted "tens of thousands of people" but also shut down Europe's major shopping street.[3]

Back then, the economic promise of the music business certainly offered a vivid contrast to the sad fate of my family's fashion fabric business. It had gone bankrupt in the mideighties, a victim of rapidly changing technology and fashion. An off-the-rack dress shop had replaced Falbers Fabrics on Oxford Street. Women, it appeared, no longer had the time or interest to make their own clothes—especially given the wide availability of cheap, ready-to-wear clothing now flooding the market. My mom, who never really recovered from the loss of her grandfather's business, went to work as a lowly sales assistant in a department store. And my dad became a cabdriver, before finding clerical work with a family friend.

In 1989, the writing was on the wall. Both for the music and fashion industries. Or so it seemed back then, anyway.

Business 0.02

My Internet career began in the summer of 1996. It was about a year after the Netscape IPO. I was living in San Francisco and had a job as an advertising salesman at a publication called *Fi: The Magazine of Music and Sound*. Founded and published by Larry Kay, a wealthy music lover and the former chairman of IHOP (the International House of Pancakes restaurant chain), *Fi* had hired illustrious music writers like Gary Giddins, Allan Kozinn, Fred Kaplan, and Robert Christgau to build what Kay hoped would become the *New Yorker* of music commentary.

But when Kay called me into his office one afternoon in the summer of 1996, it wasn't to talk about music. He was an old-fashioned corporate type, a suit-and-tie kind of businessman, who today would be persona non grata in the Battery. Back then, Kay barely knew how to use a computer, let alone Netscape's Web browser. He even had his secretary type up his emails when he wanted to communicate electronically with *Fi*'s hip writers. But that didn't mean he couldn't talk about the Internet, as everyone in San Francisco was doing by mid-1996.

Kay waved a newspaper article at me. Titled "Business 2.0," it was one of those breathlessly evangelical, *new-rules-for-the-new-economy*-style midnineties pieces that presented the Internet as a magical place, a promised land in which the old economic rules of buying, selling, and trading no longer applied. With its infinite storage space, infinite opening hours, and infinite global reach, the Web offered *infinite* potential to change everything, the article claimed. By borrowing the same "2.0"-style language that software developers used to describe their products, this article presented economics as if it were software. It imagined that business was akin to an online app and could thus be understood as a cycle of perpetual upgrades, new versions, and fresh releases.

But this interpretation of digital progress was foreign to a seasoned businessman like Larry Kay. "Business 2.0," he said, shaking his old head wearily at me. "What the *hell* does that mean?"

In the summer of 1996, everybody in San Francisco—with the exception of a few "Business 1.0" dinosaurs like Larry Kay—believed in the future of a networked economy. None of us really understood what evangelical terms like "Business 2.0" meant, but we were all seduced by their seemingly infinite promise. Especially me. So, in answer to Kay's question, I pitched him all the standard clichés of the time about the economic potential of the Web. I explained how it was an "interactive" and "frictionless" medium for distributing content in which large media companies would be "distintermediated" by agile Web startups. Quoting Web idealists like John Perry Barlow, I promised the magazine publisher that "information wants to be free," although I had no evidence that information had volition and could demand its own emancipation. Most of all, I presented the Web as a virtual Soho. The Web would create an "abundant" cultural economy, I promised, a cornucopia of music, photographs, writing, and movies where everyone would eventually be able to see, watch, and read anything they chose.

The pitch launched my Internet career. Larry Kay put me in charge of establishing a Web strategy for *Fi*. A few days later, he called me back into his office. Kay had made his fortune selling scrambled eggs and buttermilk pancakes to hungry Americans, so he remained perplexed by the Web's slippery economics.

"This Business 2.0 thing," he asked, looking at me quizzically, as if there was something blatantly obvious that he'd somehow missed. "How do we make money out of it?"

By now, I'd become an expert on the economics of the Internet. At least in theory. "Advertising," I explained, forgetting the *buy, sell, trade* principles I'd learned in Soho. "All the revenue, Larry, is in advertising."

It wasn't hard to be an Internet expert back then. Especially in theory. In the first Web gold rush of the midnineties, nobody—except Amazon—was selling anything online. Even advertising. The traditional *buy, sell, trade* principles of conventional business had been replaced by a "giveaway" economy. The point was to get your content online and give people everything that they wanted. "Eyeballs," as everyone described audience, were the holy grail; the more eyeballs, everyone assumed, the more revenue. It was taken for granted, treated as a matter of faith, like believing in Santa Claus or Webvan, that the advertising revenue would eventually flow from eyeballs. And we were all doing our best imitations of Santa Claus back then. Every website—from Netscape and the *New York Times* to Yahoo—was giving away its online product to "consumers" for free. It was a gift economy—all gift and no economics. As if every day were Christmas.

Chris Anderson later wrote a book in support of this "economy." *Free: The Future of a Radical Price*, it was called, even though Anderson's publisher did have the good sense to charge $26.99 for the book. And, it almost goes without saying, Anderson himself was well compensated for writing this seductive nonsense—getting a reputed $500,000 advance on future sales of a book that advised fellow writers they could build their "brands" by giving away their creative work for nothing on the Internet.

After a few months, I caught the full startup virus and left *Fi* to launch my own Internet company, AudioCafe. It was an easy virus to catch, especially given all the investment money suddenly sloshing around San Francisco. Back then, it really did seem as if the Internet was the answer. The Web "changed everything" about the music industry, I promised my investors. It created a global distribution platform for music, it empowered bands to record and distribute their own creative work, and it revolutionized the physics of merchandizing, I explained. Above all, by turning atoms into bits, the Web did away with scarcity and made music infinite, limitless, and abundant. Whereas those music stores on Berwick Street were physically constrained in how many CDs or vinyl records they could carry, a website could, in theory, carry all the music in the world. And so AudioCafe was designed as an online combination of a Soho club and store, a place to read reviews, listen to music, and interact with musicians. We hardly had any revenue. But we did have eyeballs.

"Advertising," I promised all my investors, when asked about the source of future revenue. Ironically, having escaped my print advertising salesman job at *Fi*, I was now back to being an online advertising salesman as the CEO of an Internet startup. The only difference was that it was much more challenging to sell online than in print. Rather than Business 2.0, the Internet of the late nineties was actually Business 0.02. As Jeff Zucker, then CEO of NBC Universal, said, selling online advertising was like "trading analog dollars for digital pennies."[4]

And that was on a good day, when pennies could be extracted from advertisers still unconvinced of the value of the new medium.

The Catastrophe of Abundance

One afternoon in the fall of 1999, I got a phone call from a journalist at a new magazine called, appropriately enough, *Business 2.0*. "What do you know about Napster?" she asked. "Is it a game changer?"

More than a "game changer," Napster was a game breaker. It represented the logical conclusion to the Web's Santa Claus economics, the Internet's original sin, where "consumers" were treated as spoiled children and indulged with an infinite supply of free goodies in what the *New York Times*' media columnist David Carr calls the "Something for Nothing" economy.[5] Founded by

Shawn Fanning and Sean Parker in 1999, Napster enabled what is euphemistically known as the peer-to-peer sharing of music. Fanning and Parker took Chris Anderson's advice about the *radical* value of "free" to its most ridiculous conclusion. Not merely content to give their own stuff away for nothing, Napster gave away everybody else's as well. Along with other peer-to-peer networks like Travis Kalanick's Scour and later pirate businesses such as Megaupload, Rapidshare, and Pirate Bay, Napster created a networked kleptocracy, masquerading as the "sharing economy," in which the only real abundance was the ubiquitous availability of online stolen content, particularly recorded music.

Over the last fifteen years, online piracy has become an epidemic. In a 2011 report sponsored by the U.S. Chamber of Commerce, it was estimated that piracy sites attracted 53 billion visits each year.[6] In January 2013 alone, the analyst firm NetNames estimated that 432 million unique Web users actively searched for content that infringes copyright.[7] A 2010 Nielsen report estimated that 25% of all European Internet users visit pirate sites each month,[8] while a 2012 study funded by the United Kingdom's Intellectual Property Office found that 1 in 6 of all British Web users regularly accessed illegally streamed or downloaded content.[9]

Such "abundance" has had a particularly catastrophic economic impact on the music industry. Back in the late nineties, just before Fanning and Parker created Napster, the global revenue from the sale of music CDs, records, and tapes reached $38 billion, with US sales being almost $15 billion. Today, in spite of the appearance of legal online sales networks like iTunes and streaming services like Spotify, the music industry's global revenues have more than halved, to just over $16 billion, with American sales shriveling to around $6 billion.[10] Digital sales have made little difference to this decline. In fact, even digital sales fell by 6% in 2013.[11]

No wonder that 75% of the record stores on Berwick Street's Vinyl Mile have closed since 1990. Or that the world's largest music store, HMV's retail outlet on London's Oxford Street, finally shut its doors in 2014, giving us one more reason not to celebrate the twenty-fifth anniversary of the Web.[12]

But it's not just the music industry that is mortally threatened by piracy. Two thousand fourteen saw the launch of Popcorn Time, a Napster for movies that offers a decentralized peer-to-peer service for illegal streaming. Cloned to appear like Netflix, Popcorn Time has already been translated into thirty-two languages and offers what one analyst described as a "nightmare scenario" for the movie industry.[13] The Buenos Aires–based makers of Popcorn Time claim to have invented the service for the convenience of consumers. But the more subscribers Popcorn Time steals from Hulu and Netflix, the fewer resources moviemakers will have to invest in their products. And, of course, the more we use peer-to-peer technologies like Popcorn Time, the emptier movie theaters will become. In 2013, there was a 21% drop in the number of what *Variety* calls the "all important" 18–24 age group buying tickets to watch movies.[14] With the popularity of products like Popcorn Time, expect that number to plummet even more dramatically in the future.

The real cost, both in terms of jobs and economic growth, of online piracy is astonishingly high. According to a 2011 report by the London-based International Federation of the Phonographic Industry (IFPI), an estimated 1.2 million European jobs would be destroyed by 2015 in the Continent's recorded music, movie, publishing, and photography industries because of online piracy, adding up to $240 billion in lost revenues between 2008 and 2015.[15] Less open to speculation is the number of jobs already lost due to this mass larceny. In its study of the impact of piracy on the European creative economy in 2008, for example, the French research group TERA Consultants found that it destroyed 185,000 jobs and caused a loss in sales revenue of 10 billion euros.[16] And that's just for Europe. Just in 2008. And things haven't improved since then. Between 2002 and 2012, for example, the US Bureau of Labor Statistics reported a 45% drop in the number of professional working musicians—falling from over 50,000 to around 30,000.[17]

One of the most misleading myths about online piracy is that it's a bit of harmless fun—an online rave organized by delusional idealists, like Electronic Frontier Foundation founder John Perry Barlow, who just want information to be free. But nothing could be further from the truth.[18] Today, online piracy is the big business of peer-to-peer and BitTorrent portals that profit, mostly in advertising revenue, from the availability of stolen content. A report, for example, by the Digital Citizen Alliance, which closely examined the "business models" of over five hundred illegal sites peddling stolen intellectual goods, found that these websites brought in $227 million in ad revenues in 2013, with the average annual advertising sales of the largest thirty of these sites being $4.4 million.[19]

The most obvious beneficiaries of this economic rape of the creative community are the criminals themselves—thieves like the New Zealand–based Kim Dotcom, the mastermind behind Megaupload, which, at its height, had 180 million registered users and accounted for 4% of all Internet traffic. Emancipating other people's information has made Dotcom a rich man. "I'm not a pirate, I'm an innovator," the six-foot-seven, 280-pound Dotcom claimed in 2014, without ever explaining how his "free" Megaupload platform, which enabled the sharing of stolen property, generated the legal revenue to enable him to buy his £15 million *Downton Abbey*–style mansion in the New Zealand countryside.[20]

But while uberpirates like Kim Dotcom hold much of the responsibility for the decimation of the recorded music industry, not everything can be blamed on these criminals. The problem is the Internet remains a gift economy in which content remains either free or so cheap that it is destroying the livelihood of more and more of today's musicians, writers, photographers, and filmmakers. As Robert Levine, *Billboard*'s former executive editor and author of the meticulously researched 2011 book *Free Ride*, argues, "The real conflict online is between the media companies that fund much of the entertainment we read, see and hear and the technology firms that want to distribute their content—legally or otherwise."[21] And it's this struggle between an entertainment industry that, to survive, needs to be paid for its expensive content and an Internet built around the utopian idea that "information wants to be free," Levine argues, that is "breaking" the Internet.[22]

Many of today's multibillion-dollar Internet companies are complicit in the piracy epidemic. "Free" social networks like Facebook, Twitter, Tumblr, and Instagram, for example, have spurred the growth of the distribution of unlicensed content. What is left of the photography industry is particularly vulnerable to this kind of "sharing" economy. Because much of the content on these social networks isn't accessible to the general public and instead is shared only between individuals, photographers find it nearly impossible to stop this form of unlicensed content use or even to accurately measure the extent of the illegal activity. As the American Society of Media Photographers notes, this problem has been compounded because networks like Instagram, Tumblr, and Facebook make very little effort to warn their members against the illegal sharing of images.[23]

Then there's the Google problem. It's no coincidence that the beginning of the piracy epidemic coincides with the emergence of Google as the Internet's dominant search and advertising company. Nor is there any doubt that Google generates untold millions, even billions of dollars annually from piracy—either directly, by Google's running ads on infringing sites, or indirectly, by its placing pirated content high in its search results. In the United States, for example, a 2013 study sponsored by the Motion

Picture Association of America found that Google was responsible for 82% of all search requests for infringing content[24]—a number even outweighing the 67.5% of the search market that, in March 2014, Google controlled in the United States.[25] And in Britain, where Google is a monopolist with control of an astounding 91% of the search market,[26] things got so bad in 2011 that the British culture secretary, Jeremy Hunt, warned Google that unless it worked on demoting illegal sites in its search results, the government itself would introduce new laws forcing it to do so.[27] But even Google's 2013 reform of its search algorithm, explicitly designed to downgrade or remove pirate sites, hasn't made much difference—with both the Recording Industry Association of America and *Billboard* reporting that these changes have, if anything, made the problem even worse.[28]

For all its self-proclaimed promises of doing no evil, the transformation of Google from a 1998 startup to the world's most powerful company in 2014 has been a catastrophe for most professional creative artists. As the owner of YouTube, Google has been sued by Viacom for "brazen" copyright infringement. It has been investigated by European Commission officials for illegally "scraping" proprietary content from rival search sites. It has been subject to class-action lawsuits by both authors and photographers claiming willful copyright infringement by Google Books.[29] Even German chancellor Angela Merkel publicly condemned Google's attempt to create a massive digital library, saying that the Internet shouldn't be exempt from copyright laws.[30]

Yes, Google has invested in YouTube, the world's dominant user-generated video platform, which, with Netflix, gobbles up half of US Internet traffic. But YouTube isn't the answer. Certainly not for the independent musical artists like Adele, Arctic Monkeys, and Jack White, who, in June 2014, were threatened with being thrown off YouTube unless they signed up to the website's new subscription music service.[31] Nor is it the answer for the millions of professional video producers who are "partnering" with the Google-owned company for advertising revenue. The problem is that Google demands 45% of all this "partnership," making it a struggle for these companies to make any money at all—particularly since YouTube's advertising rates are going down, dropping, for example, from $9.35 per thousand ad views in 2012 to $7.60 in 2013.[32] Meanwhile, YouTube's privileged partners, the one hundred production companies that, in 2012, were given $1 million apiece to polish up their videos, are rebelling against Google's greed. One of these partners, the Los Angeles–based media entrepreneur Jason Calacanis, even wrote a blog post titled "I Ain't Gonna Work on YouTube's Farm No More," explaining why what he calls "the absurd 45% YouTube tax" a kind of digital tithe that grants YouTube 45% of all advertising revenue from independently produced content, inevitably leads to the "demise" of independent producers.[33]

The "free" Google search engine might be getting rich on the massive taxes it extracts from the Internet, but the online "free" economy simply isn't working as a viable economic model for independent content companies. "The outbreak of free is being felt all over the economy," warns the *New York Times*' David Carr.[34] Jeff Zucker's trade of print dollars for Web pennies remains the online rule, with even the most popular websites being caught in what the media and advertising pundit Michael Wolff calls "the CPM vice"—the ever-downward spiral of the cost-per-thousand page views afflicting even the most popular sites like *Business Insider*, *Buzzfeed*, and *Gawker*. Wolff notes that more traffic isn't resulting in equivalent rises in advertising revenue and believes that the "digital conundrum" for prominent online content brands is that "it costs more to get traffic than what you can sell it for."[35] It's a fatally flawed model, Wolff concludes, and can only be circumvented by websites like the *Huffington Post* or *Forbes* that use free user-generated content or by Internet businesses able to subsidize unprofitable online content with offline conferences and subscriptions.

Certainly online eyes remain much less valuable than offline ones, with average advertising rates of the printed edition of a major newspaper being around ten times its online cost.[36] The same is true of the value of offline versus online readers, with the Newspaper Association of America estimating that the average print reader is worth around $539 versus the $26 value of the online reader.[37] And free certainly isn't working as an economic model for online newspapers. Take, for example, the world's third most frequently visited news website, the London *Guardian*. In spite of breaking the *News of the World* phone hacking scandal and the Edward Snowden and WikiLeaks stories, the *Guardian* has reported operating losses of more than £100 million since 2010, with a stunning £50 million lost just between 2012 and 2013.[38] No wonder the *Guardian* is experimenting with a robot-generated print edition called #Open001, which replaces editors with algorithms to select relevant stories for publication.[39]

But robots can't write the kind of high-quality journalism that distinguishes the *Guardian* from most of its rivals. So the newspaper's response to its mounting losses has been to double down on its advertising strategy. In February 2014, the paper announced it was starting a new "branded content and innovation agency" in partnership with Unilever that would, essentially, sell sponsored content to advertisers. As the blogger Andrew Sullivan warned about this "native advertising" strategy, it's actually a public relations campaign "disguised as journalism in order to promote Unilever's image as a green company."[40] So the next time you read something complimentary about Unilever on the *Guardian* website, make sure you check the fine print. The article might have been "supported" by Unilever's marketing department.

The carnage of job losses has been particularly bloody in the news industry, with full-time professional reporters' and writers' jobs at US newspapers falling from 25,593 to 17,422 between 2003 and 2013, a drop of 31% in newsroom staffing to go alongside the 55% fall in advertising sales, 47% drop in weekday print circulation, 35% fall in aggregate revenue, and 37% drop in pretax profits.[41] The same period also saw a drop of 27% in newspaper editorial jobs and a hideous 43% fall in positions for photographers and videographers.[42] Things haven't improved in 2013, with Microsoft's online network MSN laying off all its editors and Bloomberg and the London *Independent* canning their entire staffs of cultural writers. Things are equally bad outside the United States and Britain, with 15% of all Australian journalists losing their jobs in 2013[43] and 25% of Spanish journalists being made redundant since the recession[44]—making them, according to the *Christian Science Monitor*, one of the "biggest casualties" of the crisis.[45] And the future will be no less depressing for journalists everywhere. The perspicacious New York University media scholar Clay Shirky—who describes today's threatened loss of journalistic talent as "catastrophic"—predicts that in the short future "many newspapers will go bankrupt" in Kodak style: "gradually and then suddenly." Shirky entitles his obituary *Last Call*: "The End of the Printed Newspaper."[46]

Most of all, however, what the *Guardian* calls Silicon Valley's "most striking mantra," its "culture of failure," has come to the recorded music business.[47] The latest attempts by Silicon Valley to reinvent the industry are legal streamed subscription services like Pandora, Rhapsody, and Silicon Valley's current darling, Spotify. Backed not only by Sean Parker but also by Peter Thiel's Founders Fund, Spotify, which has raised over $500 million and was valued in late 2013 at $4 billion,[48] is a virtual Berwick Street. It has aggregated most of the world's music into a single service, offering more than 20 million songs as either a free advertising-supported service or for a $5 or $10 monthly all-you-can-eat rate. But while Spotify may be Santa Claus 2.0 for its over 40 million mostly nonpaying users, the still unprofitable subscription service (at least in mid-2014)[49] is an absolute disaster for musicians.

As with YouTube, the problem is that Spotify exploits creative talent to spoil consumers with either free or unnaturally low-priced content. The company may have raised more than half a billion dollars and have amassed 10 million paid subscribers, but very little of that cash is going back to artists, with only an average of 0.6 cents per stream being paid to the musician. Former Talking Heads guitarist David Byrne, who believes that Internet companies are sucking all creative content out of the world, notes that for a four-person band to each make the US minimum wage of $15,080, they would need to get a quarter of a trillion plays for their music on Spotify.[50] Radiohead star Thom Yorke put it more crudely. "New artists get paid fuck all with this model," he complained, as his pulled his solo songs and all his Atoms for Peace music from Spotify.[51] Byrne and Yorke are far from alone in rejecting the Spotify model. Other notable artists who have openly spoken out against the exploitative streaming service include Aimee Mann, Beck, the Black Keys, Amanda Palmer, will.i.am, Zoe Keating, and Pink Floyd.[52]

It's not just Spotify that is the problem. Similar streamed subscription services like Pandora are equally exploitative. For example, in November 2012, the Grammy–nominated hit songwriter Ellen Shipley reported that one of her most popular tracks got played 3,112,300 times on Pandora and she got paid a measly $39.61. "Pandora talks a great deal about their need to make a profit and to survive . . . but they couldn't care less about the fate of those creators who already are hurting so badly, they are dropping out of music," Shipley wrote, noting the 45% drop in the number of professional songwriters since 2000.[53]

Like the newspaper industry example, free or radically underpriced streamed music forces artists to rely more and more heavily on advertising business models to survive. As David Carr explains,

"In a streamed world where music itself has every little value, selling out is far from looked down upon, it's the goal." At the 2014 South by Southwest (SXSW) music festival, Carr noted that while labels were invisible, "big brands owned the joint," sponsoring all the top performers.[54] Everyone at SXSW was singing for their supper. Jay-Z and Kanye West performed on behalf of Samsung, Coldplay shilled for Apple iTunes, and the Dorito-sponsored Lady Gaga was "smeared in barbeque sauce and mock-roasted like a pig and then . . . bit the tortilla chip that fed her."[55] But we can't blame Lady Gaga or Doritos for this sad state of affairs, Carr says. It's a consequence of what he satirically calls a "perfect world" in which "the consumer wants all the music that he or she desires—on demand, at a cost of zero or close to it."[56]

In 1989, I was profoundly wrong about the rosy future of the music business. David Byrne is right. Over the last twenty-five years, the Internet has indeed sucked much of the musical creativity out of the world. In 2008 alone, there were 39,000 jobs lost in the British creative economy.[57] Today, in 2014, the prospects of young musicians or entrepreneurs breaking into the industry are dramatically worse than they were twenty-five years ago. Back in 1989, we all wanted to work in the music business; but today, in 2014, the new new thing is multibillion-dollar companies like Spotify and Pandora that are destroying the livelihoods of independent musicians.

Yes, the Internet did change *everything* in the music industry. Music is, indeed, now abundant. And that's been the catastrophe of the last quarter century.

CHAPTER SIX

THE ONE PERCENT ECONOMY

An Abundance of Stupidity

My own epiphany about the Internet's disastrous impact on culture is well documented. In the fall of 2005, I was invited to a weekend event called FOO Camp. FOO, as I mentioned earlier, is an acronym for "Friends of O'Reilly" and it refers to that same Tim "How I Failed" O'Reilly who owned and operated the profitable Web 2.0 meme and is now, according to his modest Twitter profile, "helping the future unfold." FOO Camp is O'Reilly Media's annual slumber party in which the media mogul invites a couple of hundred illustrious geeks—Silicon Valley's antiestablishment establishment—to spend a weekend on the idyllic grounds of his Sonoma, California, wine country headquarters to celebrate how the Internet is radically disrupting the world.

Just as Michael Birch presented the Battery as an unclub, FOO Camp described itself as an "unconference conference"—the ideal event, of course, for the Web's unestablishment. In practice, this meant that the camp was an entirely unstructured event whose monotonously repetitive agenda was set by its self-aggrandizing participants. Like the Internet itself, the only FOO Camp rule was that there were no rules. Anyone could give talks about anything they liked. And, mirroring the Internet's own echo chamber culture, this resulted in a cacophonous uniformity of opinion.

The real abundance at FOO Camp were of the words *media* and *democracy*. Phrases like "media democracy," "the democratization of media," and "democratic media" were chanted ad nauseam by the young white male FOO Campers. The speeches—or the "conversation," to use the digitally correct term—were all variations upon a single theme. *What can help us create a better world in the digital age?* everyone at FOO Camp asked. The Internet was the answer, they all agreed, because it "democratized" media, giving a voice to everyone, thereby making it more diverse. By "disintermediating" traditional media, FOO Campers all agreed, Web 2.0 companies like YouTube, Flickr, Blogger, and Wikipedia circumvented what they pejoratively called "the gatekeepers"—those guys like Larry Kay, my old boss at *Fi*, who had historically controlled the printing presses, recording studios, and movie studios.

What was particularly annoying about FOO Camp was how all the powerful, wealthy campers—from Silicon Valley investors to entrepreneurs to technologists—assumed that their self-interest in transforming the Web into a platform for user-generated content automatically squared with the general interest of everybody else in the world. Like most revolutionaries, they had appointed themselves as the emancipators of the people, without bothering to check with the people first. There was no real conversation at FOO Camp. Irrespective of the question, the Internet was always the answer.

FOO Camp was my wake-up call to the absurdity and hypocrisy of the Silicon Valley unestablishment. It triggered my 2007 book, *The Cult of the Amateur: How Today's Internet Is Killing Our Culture*, in which I argued that this supposed "democratization" of media had benefited a small minority of technology insiders rather than the majority of people. A thriving twentieth-century music, video, and publishing economy, I argued, was being replaced by multibillion-dollar monopolists like YouTube, which charged creators an impossibly high 45% feudal tithe for the right to advertise on its platform. *The Cult of the Amateur* was a defense of the golden age of media—an economy in which there were paid jobs for everyone from editors, cameramen, fact checkers, and sound engineers to musicians, writers, and photographers.

Some critics accused me of being an elitist, claiming that I was defending a privileged class of professional journalists, publishers, and filmmakers. But if defending skilled labor is "elitist," then I wear that badge with honor. Besides, these critics conveniently forgot that the old media economy is critical to the prosperity of millions of middle-class workers. They overlooked the fact that in the European Union, copyright-intensive industries account for nearly 9.4 million direct and indirect jobs and contribute nearly 510 billion euros a year to the European GDP.[1] They failed to take into account the fact that the US television and movie industries in 2011 supported 1.9 million jobs that generated $104 billion in wages.[2] Above all, these critics conveniently forgot that, as President Obama's commerce secretary Penny Pritzker told a roomful of Nashville music executives in 2013, "instead of viewing a new album as an expense to our economy, we now view it as an asset because it supports jobs and generates revenue for years to come."[3]

You'll remember that Paul Simon described Web 2.0 as a "fire . . . for vigorous new growth."[4] Today, in 2014, almost a decade after I attended FOO Camp, the smoke has begun to clear from this fire. But what Simon identified as the "devastation" of this digital conflagration remains all around us. We are going backward now rather than forward. Instead of "new growth," what we are seeing is the resurrection of a pre-industrial cultural economy of patronage determined by the whims of a narrow economic and cultural elite rather than by the democracy of the marketplace.

Just as the digital revolution destroyed Berwick Street's Golden Mile of Vinyl and the Kodak offices and factories in downtown Rochester, so it's also knocking out the heart of a creative economy that once employed many thousands of professional, middle-class workers. It's the same winner-take-all, donut-shaped economy that is reshaping the rest of twenty-first-century society. Average is over in media. The digital revolution, with its abundance of online access and content, has been presented by Silicon Valley as enabling our great emancipation from a media supposedly run by a clique of privileged white men. But the Internet is actually compounding this inequality and deepening the chasm between this handful of wealthy guys and everyone else.

The One Percent Rule

Web 2.0 was supposed to democratize media and empower those historically without a voice. So, yes, anyone can now post on Twitter, Tumblr, and Pinterest. Some of us may even win the lottery and get retweeted or friended by what George Packer memorably described as one of the "celebrity monuments of our age."[5] And, yes, we can post our ideas on the *Huffington Post*, our videos on YouTube, our photos on Instagram, and our music on Facebook. But there's no money in any of this for the vast majority of young writers, musicians, photographers, journalists, or filmmakers. It's mostly a gift economy where the only profits are being made by a tiny group of increasingly monopolistic Internet companies.

Yes, there remain successful digital publishing networks that actually pay their contributors—such as Buzzfeed, the listicle-dominated, highly trafficked "news" site that raised $50 million from Andreessen Horowitz in August 2014 and that the writer Heather Havrilesky describes as the "apotheosis of American trivia-focused escapism, served up with an overabundant garnish of 'trashy' and 'cute' and 'yaaass.'"[6] And yes, there still are creative superstars—Malcolm Gladwell and J. K. Rowling in books, Lady Gaga and Eminem in music, Glenn Greenwald and Andrew Sullivan in investigative journalism—who are able to greatly profit from their talent. But in our networked economy of abundance, there is a growing chasm between this tiny group of global superstars and everybody else. Harvard Business School professor Anita Elberse defines this as a "blockbuster" economy, which, she says, is exaggerated by the Internet's abundance of content. "In today's markets where, thanks to the Internet, buyers have easy access to millions and millions of titles," she argues, "the principle of the blockbuster strategy may be more applicable than ever before."[7]

"Winners take all," mourns Robert Frank about a world dominated by a tiny aristocracy of creative artists.[8] It's the opposite of Chris Anderson's profoundly flawed theory of the long tail, with its nostalgic guff of a cottage industry of middle-class cultural producers all making a reasonable living from the digital economy. The more abundant the online content, the more dramatic the contrast between the massive success of a few hits and the utter obscurity of everything else. Elberse notes, for example, that of the 8 million tracks in the iTunes store during 2011, 94%—that's 7.5 million songs—sold fewer than a hundred units, with 32% selling just a single copy. "The recorded-music tail is getting thinner and thinner over time," Elberse concludes about a music industry dominated by fewer and fewer artists.[9]

In 2013, the top 1% of music artists accounted for 77% of all artist-recorded music income while 99% of artists were hidden under what one 2014 industry report, titled "The Death of the Long Tail," called "a pervasive shroud of obscurity."[10] This has been caused in part by the increasing monopoly of online music retail stores like iTunes and Amazon and partly by consumers being subjected to the tyranny of an overabundance of choice. This income inequality in the industry is reflected in live music, too, where, between 1982 and 2003, the revenue share of the top 1% of touring acts more than doubled, while the revenue share of the bottom 95% of artists fell in the same period by more than half. As the *Guardian*'s Helienne Lindvall concludes about these trends, "not only is the wider middle class in society shrinking, so is the musician middle class."[11]

The most serious casualty of the digital revolution is diversity. This one percent rule is now the dominant economic feature of every cultural sector. According to Jonny Geller, the CEO of a prominent British literary talent agency, the old Pareto law of 80 percent of sales coming from 20 percent of writers is now "more like 96 to four."[12] Meanwhile, a 2014 British study revealed that 54% of conventionally published writers and almost 80% of self-published authors make less than a $1,000 a year from their written work.[13] The most serious casualty of the one percent economy in publishing is the disappearance of the "midlist," which, according to Colin Robinson, the co-publisher of the New York–based print-on-demand publisher OR Books, "comprise[s] pretty much all new titles that are not potential blockbusters."[14] What this means, Robinson warns, is that publishers can no longer afford to gamble on "obscure" or "offbeat" titles—thereby, once again, narrowing rather than broadening the variety of young or new writers in whom they invest.

It's affecting the e-learning industry, too, where superstar teachers, with instant access to audiences of millions of students, are establishing a two-tiered economy in one of the historically most egalitarian of professions. For example, in *The Smartest Kids in the World*, Amanda Ripley describes a new breed of "rock-star teachers" in Korea like Andrew Kim, who earns $4 million a year from an annual online audience of over 150,000. "The Internet,"

Ripley explains about Kim's success, "had turned his classes into commodities."[15] Today's hysteria around massive online open courses (MOOCs) threatens to do the same to university education, which is one reason why, in 2013, the philosophy department at San Jose State University balked at including materials from the Harvard academic superstar Michael Sandel in their online courses.[16] One star academic, the Princeton sociologist Mitchell Duneier, even cut ties with the Silicon Valley–based MOOC provider Coursera because of his fear that these kind of winner-take-all classes would undermine public higher education.[17]

As the educationalist William Deresiewicz notes, MOOCs are "not about democratizing education. That is just their cover story." The truth, Deresiewicz argues, is exactly the reverse. "They're about reinforcing existing hierarchies and monetizing institutional prestige," he warns. "The kids at Harvard get to interact with their professors. The kids at San Jose State get to watch the kids at Harvard interact with their professors. San Jose looks worse than before; Harvard looks even better."[18]

These inequalities are also reflected in the type of students taking MOOCs. Researchers at the University of Pennsylvania who looked at 400,000 Coursera students found that most people enrolled in taking these MOOCs were men. "So much for the borderless, gender-blind, class-blind and bank account–blind MOOCs," notes the technology writer Jessica McKenzie. "If anything, this shows that MOOCs are widening the educational divide, not leveling the playing field."[19]

This unequal economy is particularly pronounced in online journalism, where, amid the massive layoffs at regional newspapers, highly paid American reporters like Nate Silver, Ezra Klein, Matt Taibbi, and Glenn Greenwald represent what Emily Bell, the director of the Tow Center for Digital Journalism at Columbia University, calls "a one percent economy."[20] Ironically, for all the talk of how the Internet was supposed to diversify the news industry, the end result of the combination of a one percent economy and massive layoffs is less diversity in the newsroom, with minority employment for American journalists down almost 6% between 2006 and 2012.[21] And as Bell also notes, the most recent wave of venture-capital-funded "personal brand" journalist startups are almost all supporting white male superstars like Greenwald, Taibbi, Silver, and Klein.[22]

But the most damaging discrimination is against paid work. Apart from a few highly paid superstars and winner-take-all venture capital–backed websites like Buzzfeed and Vice, everybody else is participating in what *Guardian* columnist Suzanne Moore describes as a "kind of sophisticated X Factor," in which we all post our online content for free and hope it will be the next viral success story.[23] On the Internet, most of us are perpetual interns. As the author Tim Kreider notes, this lottery is a consequence of an information economy "in which 'paying for things' is a quaint discredited old twentieth-century custom, like calling people after having sex with them."[24] This one percent economy forces aspiring artists like the young singer Alina Simone to become startup entrepreneurs of the self and focus on the promotion of their own personal brand rather than their creative work. "What I missed most about not having a label wasn't the monetary investment, but the right to be quiet, the insulation provided from incessant self-promotion," Simone writes. "I was a singer, not a saleswoman. Not everyone wants to be an entrepreneur."[25]

None of this impacts Silicon Valley's gilded class. Some—like Google's Eric Schmidt, Facebook's Sheryl Sandberg, and LinkedIn founder Reid Hoffman—are also part of that tiny elite of best-selling celebrity authors. Indeed, Hoffman's 2012 bestseller was titled *The Start-up of You* and advised everyone to think about their professional life as if it were an entrepreneurial project. But for those insiders who didn't get multimillion-dollar book contracts to write about their own success, there's always the *Huffington*

Post—a platform designed for celebrities to post free content that peddles their own agendas, personal brands, or companies.

If there's a single online media outlet that captures all the hypocrisy of the digital revolution, it's Arianna Huffington's online creation—a publication that, like its self-promotional proprietress, dresses itself up as a crusading newspaper, but actually just offers social media hotshots, superstar marketing consultants, and other one percent friends of Arianna a free platform to shamelessly promote themselves. As Peter Goodman, the former global editor of the *Huffington Post*, wrote to Arianna Huffington before very publicly quitting his job in March 2014, "there is a widespread sense on the team that the HuffPost is no longer fully committed to original reporting; that in a system governed largely by metrics, deep reporting and quality writing weigh in as a lack of productivity."[26] What Goodman calls "original reporting" has, according to the media reporter Joe Pompeo, been replaced by a Buzzfeed-like focus on social and mobile platforms where "people love sharing stories about health and meditation and exercise and sleep."[27]

"The unfortunate fact is that online journalism can't survive without a wealthy benefactor,"[28] mourns the GigaOm columnist Mathew Ingram. And I'm afraid the same is increasingly becoming true of many unprofitable bookstores, too, which are desperately relying on crowdfunding sites like Indiegogo or Kickstarter to raise money from benefactors.[29] And, of course, there is no lack of rich benefactors from Silicon Valley who are buying up the very old media that their revolution has destroyed. The poachers are now the gamekeepers. There is Mark Zuckerberg's Harvard roommate, Chris Hughes, a cofounder of Facebook, who bought the venerable *New Republic* magazine in 2012. Then there's Amazon right-libertarian CEO Jeff Bezos, who acquired the equally venerable *Washington Post* newspaper in 2013, no doubt giving all its reporters a required reading list including *The Innovator's Dilemma* and *The Black Swan*. Meanwhile, multibillionaire eBay founder and chairman Pierre Omidyar has set up his own new Internet publishing empire, First Look Media, and used his massive wealth to hire superstar investigative journalists like Glenn Greenwald and Matt Taibbi to peddle Omidyar's own left-libertarian agenda.

For the last quarter of a century, we've been told ad nauseam by tenured professors of journalism like New York University's Jay Rosen that the Internet's destruction of old media is a good thing because it democratizes the information economy. Making a lucrative career from peddling the idea of the online information consumer as "the People Formerly Known as the Audience," Rosen has become a cheerleader for the decimation of the curated twentieth-century news industry. But Rosen—who was Arianna Huffington's partner at a failed citizen journalism initiative called "OffTheBus" and who is now an "advisor" to Omidyar's First Look Media—is wrong about the Internet's democratization of media. "The people formerly known as the audience" are still the audience—only now they are angrier and mostly more ill-informed than ever. And "the people who used to be the media owners" remain the media owners. Only now they are called Bezos or Omidyar rather than Sulzberger, Graham, or Hearst. And rather than millionaires, they are now billionaires.

The People Formerly Known as the Audience

The people formerly known as the audience—the online commentators, tweeters, and posters, the lurkers and that quintessential inhabitant of the Internet, the "troll" (a purposeful sower of discord)—are angry. Very angry. According to a 2013 study of the Chinese social media site Weibo made by Beihang University in Beijing, the emotion that spreads most quickly on social media is anger, with joy coming in a very distant second. According to one academic psychologist, professor Ryan Martin from the University of Wisconsin, the reason anger is so viral online is that we are more prone to share our rage with strangers than our happiness.[30] "They want to hear that others share it," Martin says about social neediness of people's individual anger. "Because they feel they're vindicated and a little less lonely and isolated in their belief."

Just as the business of online content is returning to a pre-modern patronage system, its culture is going backward, too. "You do wonder sometimes whether you're in 2014 or 1814. People telling me they're going to turn up on my doorstep and murder me, photos of lynchings, racist abuse, anti-Semitism, homophobic abuse," the English sports broadcaster Stan Collymore, who had been blitzed with angry insults on Twitter after expressing a mildly controversial opinion about the Uruguayan soccer star Luis Suarez, told the BBC.[31] This online hatred isn't just an English disease. In Spain, eighteen thousand people used Twitter in May 2014 to post tweets with a hateful anti-Semitic hashtag after a Madrid team was beaten by Maccabi Tel Aviv in the final of the European basketball tournament.[32]

It wasn't, of course, supposed to turn out this way. According to Internet evangelists like Jay Rosen, Tim O'Reilly, and the FOO Camp unestablishment, the Internet's so-called disintermediation of media gatekeepers would inspire a democratic enlightenment in which anyone could voice their opinion online through free networks like Reddit, Twitter, or Facebook. The old media, they said, was parochial, self-interested, and sexist; new media, in contrast, would reflect a broad diversity of opinion outside the stuffy old elites at the *New York Times*, the BBC, and CNN. Old media represented power and privilege, they claimed; new media would empower the weak, the unfortunate, those traditionally without a voice.

But just as the Internet has added to economic inequality, so it has also compounded hatred toward the very defenseless people it was supposed to empower. Today's network, of course, didn't invent hatred. And much of the rage articulated on the Internet would have existed whether or not Tim Berners-Lee had invented the Web. But the Internet has nonetheless become a platform for amplifying the views of what media critic Jeff Jarvis calls the "plague of trolls, abusers, harassers, lunatics, imposters, and assholes online.".[33] And things are only getting worse. "The Internet," the *New York Times'* Farhad Manjoo warns, "may be losing the war against trolls" because the speed and chaos of social media provides these anonymous hooligans with the cover to distribute their poisonous messages.[34] "The faster that the whole media system goes, the more trolls have a foothold to stand on," explains Whitney Phillips, an academic expert on online bad behavior. "They are perfectly calibrated to exploit the way media is disseminated these days."[35]

According to the feminist writer and journalist Amanda Hess, women are no longer welcome on the Internet.[36] As evidence, she points to the rageful tweets she has received, like "Happy to say we live in the same state. I'm looking you up, and when I find you, I'm going to rape you and remove your head," from men who've disagreed with her writing. Hess is far from alone in being stalked online by male psychopaths. When the political campaigner Caroline Criado-Perez petitioned the Bank of England to add Jane Austen's face to its banknotes, she received an avalanche of rape and death threats on Twitter, including such messages as "All aboard the rape train" and "I will rape you tomorrow at 9 p.m. . . . Shall we meet near your house?"[37] When the technology blogger Kathy Sierra received death threats in 2007, she shut down her blog and withdrew from public life.[38] While the Hess, Criado-Perez, and Sierra stories have been well publicized, many thousands of other women are victims of a less well-known misogyny on blogs and other online forums.

Indeed, a 2005 Pew Research report found that the proportion of Internet users who participated in online chat groups "dropped from 28% in 2000 to as low as 17% in 2005, entirely because of women's fall off in participation. The drop-off that occurred during the last few years coincided with increased awareness of and sensitivity to worrisome behavior in chat rooms."[39] This "pervasive misogyny" has led some former Internet evangelists, such as the British author Charles Leadbeater, to believe that the Internet is failing to realize its potential.[40] "It's outrageous we've got an Internet where women are regularly abused simply for appearing on television or appearing on Twitter," Leadbeater said. "If that were to happen in a public space, it would cause outrage."[41]

Hatred is ubiquitous on the Internet. "Big hatred meets big data," writes the Google data scientist Seth Stephens-Davidowitz about the growth of online Nazi and racist forums that attract up to four hundred thousand Americans per month.[42] Then there are the haters of the haters—the digital vigilantes, such as the group OpAntiBully, who track down Internet bullies and bully them.[43] Worst of all are the anonymous online bullies themselves. In August 2013, a fourteen-year-old girl from Leicestershire in England named Hannah Smith hanged herself after she had been savagely bullied on the anonymous teen network Ask.fm. Comments left on Smith's Ask.fm profile include "go die, evry1 wuld be happy," "do us all a favour n kill ur self," and "no1 would care if ya died u cretin."[44] Tragically, there have been a rash of other child suicides on Ask.fm. In late 2012, two Irish girls, fifteen-year-old Ciara Pugsley and thirteen-year-old Erin Gallagher, and Florida teenager Jessica Laney, sixteen, all killed themselves after being anonymously bullied on the site. And in the first half of 2013, two English boys from Lancashire, fifteen-year old Josh Unsworth and sixteen-year-old Anthony Stubbs, both committed suicide after being subjected to hideous abuse on Ask.fm. Unfortunately, Ask.fm—which was acquired in August 2014 by media mogul Barry Diller's IAC family of websites—is far from the only source of cyberbullying. In September 2013, Rebecca

Ann Sedwick, a twelve-year-old Florida girl, jumped to her death from an abandoned cement factory after experiencing a year of bullying[45] on Facebook. Then there's the January 2013 suicide of a fourteen-year-old Italian girl, Carolina Picchio, after she was bullied on Facebook and on WhatsApp, where she received 2,600 abusive messages before her death.[46]

Most troubling of all, anonymous networks and apps are now among the hottest investments in Silicon Valley, with venture capitalists pouring tens of millions of dollars into startups like Secret, Whisper, Wut, Confide, Yik Yak, and Sneeky. While Michael Moritz's Sequoia Capital and John Doerr's KPCB are investors in Secret and Whisper, Andreessen Horowitz—to its great credit—has stayed out of the frenzy to profit from online anonymity. "As designers, investors, commentators, we need to seriously ask ourselves whether some of these systems are legitimate and worthy," Marc Andresseen tweeted in March 2014. ". . . not from an investment return point of view, but from an ethical and moral point of view."[47]

Anonymous or not, the people formerly known as the audience are not only angry; some of them are also propagandists of terror and genocide. After the 2010–11 Arab Spring, many Internet evangelists—such as the Google executive and author of *Revolution 2.0* Wael Ghonim—argued that social media networks like Facebook and Twitter were undermining the old autocracies in the Middle East and empowering the people. But as the Arab Spring has degenerated into brutal religious and ethnic civil wars in Syria and Iraq, and the reestablishment of military dictatorship in Ghonim's own Egypt, social media has been leveraged in a much more corrosive way. "By a geopolitical fluke," notes the *Financial Times'* David Gardner, "the cold war ended just as technology developed unique power to encourage global tribes."[48] Twitter and Facebook are thus being used by both Sunni and Shiite radicals to spread their doctrinal message and find recruits in what the *Financial Times* calls "Jihad by social media."[49] In June 2014, for example, the Islamic State in Iraq and Syria (ISIS) hijacked the soccer World Cup hashtags, used its Facebook accounts as "a death-threat generator," and broadcast its atrocities on YouTube and Twitter, where it posted a video of a beheading with the message: "This is our ball. It's made of skin #WorldCup."[50] Researchers at King's College London have also shown how two Sunni preachers are using Facebook to recruit foreign fighters in the war against Bashar al-Assad in Syria. One of the radical preachers, Musa Cerantonio, this 2014 study shows, has received twelve thousand "likes" on his Facebook page.[51]

ISIS's effective use of social media highlights the core problem with the Internet. When the gatekeeper is removed and anyone can publish anything online, much of that "content" will be either propaganda or plain lies. In the July 2014 war between Israel and Hamas, for example, both sides deployed large teams on Twitter, Facebook, and YouTube to distribute their own deeply subjective versions of the struggle. Israel deployed four hundred students to run five Facebook pages in five different languages to present its version of the war. Meanwhile, Hamas's military wing, al-Qassam, was posting tweets in Arabic, English, and Hebrew to its nearly twelve thousand Twitter followers about what it described as Israeli "genocidal aggression" and Palestinian "martyrs."[52] The complex truth about the war, on the other hand, to quote Winston Churchill, hasn't had time to put on its pants. Indeed, given the power and popularity of social media, particularly among digital natives, one of the most serious consequences of digital age wars like the 2014 Israel-Hamas conflict is the truth itself, which is lost amid the Facebook photos of beheadings and mass executions.

The people formerly known as the audience are being tricked and misled by much of the content on the Internet, which is about as accurate as an Instagram photo. We were promised that user-generated-content review sites like Yelp and Amazon would create a more honest media. But information without gatekeepers is almost always either inaccurate or corrupt or both. On Amazon, for example, top reviewers get sent a ton of free merchandise, which inevitably affects their reviews.[53] In September 2013, New York regulators cracked down on deceptive Internet reviews on nineteen Internet companies including Yelp, Google, CitySearch, and Yahoo, and fined them $350,000.[54] Then there are the "click farms" outsourced in low-wage countries like Bangladesh, which are used to produce hundreds of thousands of fake Facebook "likes" and Twitter followers.[55] "Individually none of these little lies are ruinous," notes Tim Wu about what he calls the "little lies the Internet told me" on consumer review sites, "but they add up, and they take both an economic and cultural toll."[56]

Trust is the greatest casualty here. It's no wonder that the Internet generation is suffering such a scarcity of trust in an age when traditional authority and institutions are in crisis. Even the world's sixth most popular website, Wikipedia—the most noble and promising of all the user-generated content networks—isn't really trustworthy. Yes, some of the entries are really very good and it's hard not to be impressed and not a little bemused by the altruism of its unpaid contributors. But as US scientists found in a 2014 study published by the American Osteopathic Association, 9 out of 10 of Wikipedia's health entries contain mistakes, with most of these entries containing "many errors."[57] But the main problem with Wikipedia is its cultural biases. Given that it is essentially authored and edited by the Internet, it reflects the libertarian values and interests of its digital natives. And so, as Tom Simonite notes in a comprehensive 2013 article ominously titled "The Decline of Wikipedia," in the *MIT Technology Review*, Wikipedia is undermined by its "skewed coverage." There are too many entries about Pokémon and female porn stars, Simonite argues, and "sketchy" coverage of women novelists and places in sub-Saharan Africa.[58]

"The main source of those problems is not mysterious," Simonite writes of the problems with the lacunae of editorial authority on Wikipedia. "The loose collective running the site today, estimated to be 90% males, operates a crushing bureaucracy with an often abrasive atmosphere that deters newcomers who might increase participation in Wikipedia and broaden its coverage."[59] Writing about Wikimedia Foundation, the San Francisco–based organization that runs Wikipedia, the *Guardian*'s Anne Perkins concurs with Simonite. "The fact remains that what you get in Wikimedia," Perkins notes, "is the world according to the young white western male with a slight personality defect."[60]

Simonite and Perkins might have been describing the Internet itself, where there are too many abrasive young men with personality defects and not enough accountable experts. It's Robert Merton's Law of Unintended Consequences once again. Web 2.0's cult of transparency and openness, its faith in the wisdom of the crowd, has ironically spawned opaque bureaucracies controlled by anonymous elites. Without paid curators fully accountable for their work, the Internet is degenerating into propaganda, lies, and a surfeit of information about Pokémon and porn.

Fashion 3.0

Back in 1989, not only had I been wrong in my optimism about the future of the music industry, but I got the future of the fabric business wrong, too. Twenty-five years ago, the maker economy appeared as dead as my family's fashion fabric store on Oxford Street. But the Internet has even changed this. Today, in 2014, this maker movement is a much smarter investment than the music business. Indeed, the networked fabric business is one of the newest new things in today's digital economy.

Every decade there's a major revolution in Silicon Valley. In the mid-1990s, it was the original Web 1.0 revolution of free websites like Netscape, Yahoo, and Craigslist. In 2005, it was Tim O'Reilly's Web 2.0 user-generated-content revolution of Google, Wikipedia, and YouTube. And today, in 2014, it's the "Internet of Things" revolution of 3-D printing, wearable computing, driverless cars, and intelligent drones.

To learn more about today's revolution, I had returned to the scene of my original disenchantment with the Internet. I'd once again come to the O'Reilly Media offices in Sebastopol, the little town up in Sonoma County, California, some fifty miles north of San Francisco. But rather than spending another annoying weekend at FOO Camp, I had come to meet with Dale Dougherty, the guy who first came up with the "Web 2.0" term. And Dougherty's current venture is Maker Media, a company that he spun out of O'Reilly Media in 2013 but that's still based at the O'Reilly headquarters in Sebastopol.

Dougherty is once again pioneering the future with Maker Media. The "maker movement," which brings a do-it-yourself mentality to technology, is becoming all the rage in Silicon Valley. This frenzy is being fueled by the commercial development of 3-D printers—desktop-sized devices that automate the manufacture of everything from intricate industrial parts such as airplane wings[61] to the replacement parts of human bodies. These 3-D printers are like portable factories. By automating the transformation of bytes into atoms, they enable any Internet user to become a manufacturer. It's a revolution being pioneered by companies like MakerBot, the manufacturer of the popular Replicator 2 3-D printer. Although we are still in the early, hobbyist stages of this revolution, there is already a small army of do-it-yourself tech enthusiasts using printers like the Replicator 2 to reproduce 3-D images of unborn babies in the womb, 3-D representations of selfies, and the world's first ready-to-wear, completely 3-D-printed article of clothing—a bikini snapped together with plastic pieces.[62]

It might be 1995 all over again. Back then, you'll remember, it was believed that networked technology could enable anyone to become the owner of a vast record store. Now, with 3-D printers, we can supposedly set up factories in our own homes and, with the appropriate software, create anything we like. Technology is once again the great liberator. And, inevitably, Chris Anderson has written a book hyping a revolution that supposedly "empowers" us to "disintermediate" the industrial factory and manufacture our own products. In his 2012 manifesto, *Makers*, Anderson, spouting an unholy mashup of libertarianism and Marxism, argues that this "new industrial revolution" democratizes the tools of invention and production. Now that the digital revolution has "reached the workshop, the lair of Real Stuff," Anderson breathlessly promises us, it will have "its greatest impact yet."[63]

Makers of the world unite!

We've heard this kind of nonsense before. We heard it from Anderson's first two books, *The Long Tail* and *Free*, which got our abundant future entirely wrong. We heard it from Web 1.0 revolutionaries like Kevin Kelly, who promised us that the Internet would reinvent the traditional rules of business by giving away everything for free. We heard it in Dougherty's Web 2.0 revolution, too, when we were promised that everybody could become an online writer or musician. But, of course, rather than democracy and diversity, all we've got from the digital revolution so far is fewer jobs, an overabundance of content, an infestation of piracy, a coterie of Internet monopolists, and a radical narrowing of our economic and cultural elite.

After Dougherty had showed me around the Maker Media office with its collection of cutting-edge 3-D printers spewing out their fully finished products, we sat down to talk. The jobs question was foremost on my mind. After all, if everyone in the future has a manufacturing facility on their desktop, then what happens to the tens of millions of people around the world already employed in industrial factories?

"So, Dale, what about employment?" I asked Dougherty, who, in contrast with many Silicon Valley entrepreneurs, is willing to acknowledge the darker side of the networked revolution. "If these machines make everything we need, then what will everyone do all day?"

The founder and CEO of Maker Media shuffled nervously in his chair. He was far too honest and intelligent to feed me some nonsense about a long tail of networked digital makers all trading 3-D selfies or unborn babies with each other in an idyllic global village. His silence was illuminating. Yes, Dougherty has once again seen the future before everyone else. But is this a future that any of us—especially Dale Dougherty—really wants?

Take, for example, the impact of the maker's 3-D printing revolution on the fashion industry. Back in the early twentieth century, my great-grandfather, Victor Falber, bought fabric from the woolen mills that he then sold in Berwick Street market to people who made their own clothes. This Maker 1.0 economy was replaced in the mid-twentieth century by the Maker 2.0 model of mass-produced, off-the-rack clothing—the Oxford Street of retailers like the Gap, American Apparel, Esprit, and Next. And over the next quarter of a century, as the Maker 3.0 revolution of 3-D printing begins to popularize the manufacturing of personalized clothing, these stores may—like Oxford Street's 60,000-square-foot HMV music emporium—become redundant.

The Silicon Valley hype machine is beginning to identify the world's fashion industry as the source of the next great disruption. "Why 3D printing will work in fashion," one *TechCrunch* writer glibly reveals.[64] "3D-printed fashion: off the printer, rather than off the peg," is how the *Guardian*'s Alice Fisher describes the so-called democratization of fashion in which we can all design our own personalized clothing. "It could revolutionize garment sizing and product development in mass production," Fisher promises. "It could also allow startup labels to produce small orders to avoid unsold stock, and allow easy customization."[65]

But weren't we promised this same customized, personalized, democratized cornucopia in the nineties about the music industry? And didn't this dream degenerate into the sour reality of a blockbuster-dominated, advertising-saturated industry that has been cut in half by the free and pirated content of Internet startups like Napster?

"Will 3-D printing upend fashion like Napster crippled the music industry?" asked Mashable's Rebecca Hiscott.[66] Yes, it will, I'm afraid. Like recorded music, all the economic value of fashion lies in its intellectual property. So when the design of new clothing is readily available, legally or otherwise, on the Internet and anyone can make personalized dresses or shirts on their 3-D printer, how will professional designers and clothing companies be rewarded for their creative labor? If the case of the demise of the recorded music industry is anything to go by, they won't. Perhaps fashion designers will have to fall back on Lady Gaga's Dorito business model of finding sponsors to pay for her performances. Or perhaps in today's selfie-centric culture, fashion designers will give out their work for free in exchange for us freely advertising them online. In 2014, the hip online clothing retailer ASOS introduced the #AsSeenOnMe promotion, which posts Instagram or Twitter selfies of ourselves wearing ASOS clothing. "Monetize me," Contagious's Katrina Dodd characterizes this strategy that does, quite literally, turn us into a free models for ASOS fashions.[67]

In May 2014, I spoke alongside the science fiction writer Bruce Sterling at a *Wired* magazine conference in Milan, the center of Italy's high-end fashion industry. Sterling, who is refreshingly critical of big data Internet companies like Facebook and Google, advised the audience of local designers to explore what he called "open source luxury" as a way of circumventing Silicon Valley toll booths. But while I'm a great admirer of Sterling's sparkling imagination, it's hard to see the business model of open-source luxury. Unlike software, design and creativity can't be viable given out as a free license. Luxury will, by definition, always be a closed system. Once Fendi, Gucci, or Armani give out their source code for free, they become commodities with the same lack of value as the Internet's cornucopia of online content.

Silicon Valley will, no doubt, profit from this Makers 3.0 revolution. As the investor Fred Wilson predicts, there will inevitably be a winner-take-all YouTube or Uber-style platform—something like the website Etsy, which is already aggregating buyers and sellers of handmade goods and taking a cut of every transaction. But, to paraphrase Robert Levine, the real conflict in the networked maker's economy is likely to be between the fashion companies that design our clothes and the technology firms that want to distribute their designs—"legally or otherwise."

"We are at the dawn of the age of sharing where, even if you try to sell things, the world is going to share it anyway," argues Bre Pettis, the CEO of MakerBot, about the maker's "sharing" economy.[68] But Pettis's notion of "sharing" is a euphemism for theft and the consequences of his maker's revolution threaten to be even more damaging than those that decimated the music industry. After all, if anyone can copy any design and make their personalized clothing on home 3-D printers, then what becomes of the millions of workers who are employed in garment factories around the world? Some Western liberals might celebrate the end of the sweatshop. But I'm not sure the millions of people who work in the garment industry would agree.

The "age of sharing" evangelists such as Pettis would, no doubt, accuse me of being a Luddite. But there is no shame in sometimes questioning the economic impact of technology on society. As Paul Krugman reminds us in "Sympathy for the Luddites," twenty-first-century digital technology is, like it or not, displacing and devaluing educated workers.[69] Krugman uses the example of the eighteenth-century woolworkers of Leeds, who questioned the destructive impact of mechanized technology on their jobs, as being an inspiration to us today. As the economic historian Eric Hobsbawn notes, it was at these textile mills in the north of England that the global industrial revolution was born. These were the same mills that produced the cloth that my great-grandfather sold in Berwick Street market in the early twentieth century. And they are the same kind of mills that will be radically "disintermediated" in the makers' 3.0 economy.

Victor Falber had a nephew named Reuben Falber. I always knew him as Uncle Reuben, but the world remembers him quite differently. Reuben Falber was the longtime assistant secretary of the Communist Party of Great Britain, who was exposed after the fall of the Berlin Wall and the collapse of the Soviet Union as the official responsible for laundering large amounts of Soviet cash into Britain to finance the communist revolution.[70] But my own memories of Reuben Falber were of a scholarly man who would use quotes from Marx to explain to me why the collapse of capitalism was inevitable.

One of his favorite quotes was from Marx's *18th Brumaire of Louis Bonaparte*. "Men make their own history, but they do not make it just as they please," my uncle Reuben liked to remind me about the supposedly greater historical forces controlling our destiny. But with 3-D printing, I fear, we will eventually be able to *make* anything that we *please*. Everything, that is, except the illusion of our own histories.

CHAPTER SEVEN

CRYSTAL MAN

The Ministry of Surveillance

If we really do make our own histories, then who exactly *made* the Internet? Technology historian John Naughton claims it was the RAND telecom engineer Paul Baran. TCP/IP inventors Bob Kahn and Vint Cerf say they created it. Others award the honor to "As We May Think" author Vannevar Bush or to J. C. R. Licklider, the "Man-Computer Symbiosis" visionary who dreamed up the Intergalactic Computer Network. More literary types even suggest that the Argentine writer Jorge Luis Borges, the author of stories like "The Library of Babel" and "Funes the Memorious," about "infinite libraries and unforgetting men,"[1] imagined the Internet before anyone else.

Then, of course, there is Albert Arnold "Al" Gore Jr. "During my service in the United States Congress, I took the initiative in creating the Internet," Gore told CNN's Wolf Blitzer in March 1999. And if I had a dollar for every bad Al-Gore-invented-the-Internet joke, I could probably afford to be Trevor Traina's neighbor up on Billionaire Row. But, of course, Gore didn't invent the Internet, consciously or otherwise, even though the former American vice president has personally profited so massively from what he called the "information superhighway" as an Apple board member, Google advisor, partner of John Doerr and Tom Perkins at KPCB, and cofounder of CurrentTV, that he could, no doubt, afford a $37 million house or two of his own up in San Francisco's ritziest neighborhood.

But there is one politician who, in contrast with Al Gore, could really claim to have stumbled upon the idea of the Internet almost before anyone else. This politician pioneered a computer network that aggregated all of his country's educational, medical, financial, and other personal records into a single database. Like big data companies such as Google and Facebook, the goal of this unforgetting politician was to amass so much information about us that he would know us all better than we know ourselves. And like Tim Berners-Lee, this politician was developing his revolutionary idea in 1989.

His name is Erich Mielke and, between 1957 and 1989, he was the head of the East German secret police, the Stasi. I'm half joking, of course, about it being Mielke, rather than Al Gore, who invented the Internet. Although, unlike the amusingly self-important Gore, there's nothing even vaguely funny about this East German communist politician whose ubiquitous secret police transformed an advanced industrial country into a surveillance camp.

In 2010, Google CEO Eric Schmidt boasted that Google was so familiar with all our habits that it automatically knew where we are and what we've been doing. But twenty-five years before Schmidt boasted about Google's data omniscience, Mielke began to develop a similarly ambitious project for a comprehensive database of human intentions. The idea was born in the spring of 1985. Erich Honecker, the head of the East German Communist Party, who liked to think of his country as more technically advanced than the capitalist West, even though its main business model and source of foreign currency was selling its citizens to West Germany, wanted to "start collating computerized files and reports" on all sixteen and a half million people in East Germany.[2] The historian Victor Sebestyen describes this as a "computerized snooping system." Its intention was to digitize the 39 million index cards and 125 miles of documents containing more than 2 billion sheets of paper.[3] The goal was a computer system that knew everything about everyone in the country.

By the mideighties, Mielke's Stasi had become the largest company in East Germany, employing around 100,000 full-time snoops and at least another half a million active informers. According to *Stasiland* author Anna Funder, Mielke's organization might have turned as many as 15% of all East Germans into one kind of data thief or another.[4] Known as "the Firm" to East Germans, Stasi was attempting to transform the whole of East Germany into a real-time set of *Rear Window*. The country was, as *Big Data* authors Viktor Mayer-Schönberger and Kenneth Cukier note, "one of the most comprehensive surveillance states ever seen."[5] Like Ted Nelson's Xanadu project to develop hypertext, Mielke's East Germany eliminated the concept of deletion.

"We had lived like behind glass," explained the novelist Stefan Heym. Mielke organized his society around the same kind of brightly lit principles that the architect Frank Gehry is now using to build Facebook's new open-plan office in Silicon Valley. Mark Zuckerberg—who once described Facebook as a "well-lit dorm room" in which "wherever you go online you see your friends"[6]—describes this multimillion-dollar Gehry creation as "the largest open office space in the world." Gehry's "radically transparent" building will be without internal walls, floors, or private offices, even for senior Facebook executives. Its purpose, Zuckerberg explains, is to make "the perfect engineering space."[7] But Gehry's office is an architectural metaphor for Zuckerberg's cult of the social: a *well-lit* place where not only can you *see* your friends, but your friends—especially, of course, the autistic Facebook founder—can *see* you.

Mielke amassed personal data with the same relentlessness that Google's Street View car collected the emails, photos, and passwords of online German citizens between 2008 and 2010—a privacy breach that Johannes Caspar, the German regulator in charge of the investigation into Google's behavior, described as "one of the biggest data-protection rules violations known."[8] But, as a violator of our online data, Google faces stiff competition from its rival Facebook. *TechCrunch*'s Natasha Lomas suggests that Facebook's "creepy data-grabbing ways," such as the 2013 harvesting of the personal contact information of 6 million of its users, or that secret 2012 study to control the emotions of 689,000 of its users,[9] make it the "Borg of the digital world."[10] WikiLeaks founder Julian Assange, who knows a thing or two about spying himself, even accuses Facebook of being the "greatest spying machine the world has ever seen."[11]

So is Facebook really the *greatest* spying machine in world history—greater than either the Stasi, the CIA, or Google? Citing Google's Street View car privacy violations, the German privacy regulator Johannes Caspar might doubt Assange's assertion, as probably would privacy watchdogs in the United Kingdom, Germany, and Italy who collectively told Google in the summer of 2013 that the company would face legal sanctions unless it changed its 2012 policy of unifying personal data collected from all its different services.[12] Others would also award this dubious honor to Google. Such as those plaintiffs who, in a July 2013 California court case, claimed that "Google uses Gmail as its own secret data-mining machine, which intercepts, warehouses, and uses, without consent, the private thoughts and ideas of millions of unsuspecting Americans who transmit e-mail messages through Gmail."[13] Or the millions of students whose mail messages were allegedly surreptitiously captured by Google to build advertising profiles of them—a "potentially explosive" lawsuit, according to *Education Week* magazine, that is also currently being heard in US federal court.[14]

In any case, before Facebook and Google, there was Erich Mielke's twentieth-century Stasi. Mielke was originally against Honecker's vision of digitizing all the Stasi's analog records. But by August 1989, as protests against the communist regime intensified, he gave the order to begin the digital collation of information of every East German citizen. Officially known as the "Regulation for the Use of Stored Data," it sought to collect all personal data from the country's legal institutions, banks, insurance agencies, post offices, hospitals, libraries, and radio and television companies. According to the East Germany historian Stefan Wolle, Mielke was particularly enthusiastic about the "complete interconnectedness" of this data project.[15] Rather than socialist man, Wolle says, Mielke wanted to create crystal man ("der gläserne Mensch"). Mielke's goal was to build a place where everyone lived "behind glass" and nobody could escape his electronic gaze.

In contrast, however, with the Internet, Erich Mielke's "Regulation for the Use of Stored Data" project was never realized. The Wall fell in November 1989 and he was arrested in 1990, imprisoned in 1993, and died in 2000. But Mielke's work has been memorialized in the old Berlin headquarters of the Stasi, which has been transformed into a museum displaying the technologies of surveillance that he used to snoop on the East German people.

The former East German Ministry for State Security is located on a particularly gray, nondescript street near the Magdalenenstrasse U-Bahn station, a few subway stops away from the center of Berlin. It's not too far from the US embassy on Pariser Platz, where, the American whistle-blower Edward Snowden revealed, the NSA had a spy hub that monitored the cell phone calls of German chancellor Angela Merkel[16]—a privacy breach so angering Merkel that the chancellor, who grew up in East Germany, compared the snooping practices of the NSA to the Stasi's.[17] Nor is it a great distance from the British embassy beside the Brandenburg Gate, where, according to documents leaked by

Snowden, the British intelligence agency GCHQ was running its own separate spying operation on the German government.[18]

The gray old Stasi headquarters in Berlin, permanently frozen now in its 1989 appearance, is defiantly analog. The Stasiplex certainly is no Googleplex. There's nothing high-tech about either the office's dingy, cramped rooms or the electric typewriters, rotary telephones, and primitive switchboards on all of its desks. In spite of Mielke's order to network its information, much of Stasi's data in 1989 was still confined to handwritten or typed index cards. The museum even has an index card on display written by Mielke's secretary explaining what the Stasi chief liked to eat for breakfast.

But for all its millions of meticulously transcribed index cards, East Germany's former ministry of surveillance is as much an introduction to the digital future as it is a look back at the analog past. As a museum displaying how technology was used to acquire other people's data, the Stasi museum—in our age of data-hungry multinationals like Google and Facebook and big data agencies like NSA and GCHQ—has contemporary relevance. Like the seemingly insatiable thirst of both contemporary government intelligence organizations and Internet companies for our most intimate information, the Stasi's appetite for data was astonishing. The museum's exhibits include such data-gathering technologies as miniature cameras hidden in pens, tie pins, and neckties. It has several rooms dedicated to showing off locally made Zeiss-Jena cameras concealed in handbags, briefcases, purses, and thermos. One exhibit even features a watering can with a hidden camera near its spout.

Yet there is one thing about the Firm that distinguishes it from Internet companies like Google or Facebook. To borrow a popular Silicon Valley term, Erich Mielke's operation didn't "scale." Mielke was a twentieth-century information thief who may have transformed East Germany into a data kleptocracy.

But compared with twenty-first-century data barons, he still was thinking too small, too locally about his information empire. It never occurred to him that billions of people globally might freely give up their most personal data. And he didn't understand that there were much more scalable strategies for aggregating people's photos than by disguising cameras inside watering cans.

No, to create a truly global crystal man, it wasn't enough to put a hundred thousand spies on your payroll and have 39 million handwritten index cards. On the Internet, an electronic world of increasingly intelligent connected machines that Nicholas Carr calls a "Glass Cage," there are billions of "gläserne Menschen." And, it seems, they are all willing to work for free.

The Eyes of the Venetian

In Las Vegas, there isn't a casino built around the theme of either East Germany or the Berlin Wall, surprisingly enough. But Las Vegas does possess one entertainment complex that pays homage to another of history's great spying machines—the Venetian Republic, which, in its fifteenth- and sixteenth-century heyday, was notorious for its dense network of spies working for the State Inquisitors, a panel of judges that was a late medieval version of the Stasi. So it was serendipitous that a part of the 2014 Consumer Electronics Show (CES), the world's largest event dedicated to networked consumer devices, was held in Las Vegas's version of Venice—the Venetian Resort Hotel Casino. Situated on Las Vegas's strip, the Venetian, with its gaudily inauthentic piazzas and canals, represents a version of the Italian city-state that might be charitably described as augmented reality.

At CES 2014, surveillance technologies were, so to speak, on show throughout the Venetian. Companies were demonstrating networked cameras that could do everything from peeping under walls and peering around corners to peeking through clothing. It was like being at a conference for spooks. At the Indiegogo-sponsored section of the show, hidden in the bowels of the Venetian, one crowd-financed startup from Berlin named Panono was showing off what it called a "panoramic ball camera," an 11 cm electronic ball with thirty-six tiny cameras attached to it, that took panoramic photos whenever the ball was thrown in the air and then, of course, distributed them on the network. Another Indiegogo company, an Italian startup called GlassUP, was demonstrating fashionably designed glasses that—like Google Glass—recorded everything they saw and provided what it called a "second screen" to check emails and read online breaking news. There were even "Eyes-On" X-ray style glasses, from a company called Evena Medical, that allowed nurses to see through a patient's skin and spy the veins underneath. Just about the only thing I didn't see in the Venetian were cameras hidden inside watering cans.

There were electronic eyes everywhere one looked. There was even an entire exhibition dedicated to intelligent eyeglasses. This "Retrospective Exhibition: 35 Years of Augmented Reality Eyewear," a kind of history of the future, was held inside the "Augmented Reality Pavilion" in the Venetian. It featured row upon row of plastic heads, all wearing augmented glasses that had been developed over the last thirty-five years. The exhibition was sponsored by two of today's leading developers of augmented glasses—an Israeli firm called OrCam, and Vuzix, whose $1,000 Smart Glasses M100 model, the world's first commercially available networked eyewear, feature a hands-free camera that can record everything it sees. "Unforgettable" or "Public Eye" might have been more appropriate names for Vuzix's creepy surveillance glasses.

"Welcome to Infinite Possibilities," one banner hanging at the Venetian proclaimed in welcoming CES attendees. "Living in Digital Times: Connecting Life's Dots," another announced about a networked world in which the volume of data produced between 2012 and 2013 made up 90% of all the data produced in human history.[19] In 2012, we produced 2.8 zettabytes of data, "a number that's as gigantic as it sounds," according to data expert Patrick Tucker, and by 2015 that number is expected to double to over 5.5 zettabytes. To put this into perspective, in 2009 all the content on the World Wide Web was estimated to have added up to about half a zettabyte of data.[20]

But, rather than *infinite*, the possibilities of most of the new electronic hardware at CES 2014 were really all the same. They were all devices greedy for the collection of networked data. These devices, some of which were being crowdfunded by networks like Indiegogo and Kickstarter, were designed to *connect our dots*—to know our movements, our taste, our physical fitness, our driving skills, our facial characteristics, above all where we've been, where we are, and where we are going.

Wearable technology—what the Intel CEO Brian Krzanich in his keynote speech at the show called a "broad ecosystem of wearables"—dominated CES 2014. Sony, Samsung, and many, many startups were all demonstrating products that wouldn't have been out of place at that old East German Ministry for State Security in Berlin. Two of the most hyped companies producing so-called quantified self products at CES were Fitbit, the maker of a wrist device that tracks physical activity and sleep patterns, and Swedish-based Narrative, the manufacturer of a wearable tiny camera clip designed to be worn on a lapel that automatically takes photos every thirty seconds and is known as a "lifelogging" device for recording everything it sees.

"What's interesting about both companies is they make the invisible part of our lives visible, in an ambient ongoing fashion," explained one venture capitalist who'd invested in Fitbit and Narrative.[21] Thirty years ago, Mielke would have likely bought

Narrative devices for the entire East German population. But today, the only bulk orders are likely to come from North Korea.

But it wasn't just Fitbit and Narrative that were making the invisible visible. Everywhere at CES, companies were introducing surveillance products designed to spew our personal data. I judged a CES "hackathon" in which entrants innocently developed "innovative" new surveillance products, including hats and hoodies outfitted with sensor chips that instantly revealed the location of their wearer. A Canadian company, OMSignal, was demonstrating spandex clothing that wirelessly measured heart rate and other health data. Another smart clothing company, Heapsylon, even had a sports bra made of textile electrodes designed to monitor its wearer's vital statistics.[22]

While Google wasn't officially represented in the Augmented Reality Pavilion, there were plenty of early adopters wandering around the Venetian's fake piazzas and canals wearing demonstration models of Google Glass, Google's networked electronic eyeglasses. Michael Chertoff, the former US secretary of homeland security, described these glasses, which have been designed to take both continuous video and photos of everything they see, as inaugurating an age of "ubiquitous surveillance."[23] Chertoff is far from alone in being creeped out by Google Glass. Several San Francisco bars have banned Google Glass wearers—known locally as "Glassholes"—from entry. The US Congress has already launched an inquiry into their impact on privacy. And in June 2013, privacy and data officials from seven countries, including Canada, Australia, Mexico, and Switzerland, sent Google CEO Larry Page a letter expressing their discomfort about the impact on privacy of these glasses. Like Chertoff's, their country's fears were of a "ubiquitous surveillance"—a world in which everyone was being watched all the time by devices that are collecting massive amounts of our most personal health, location, and financial data.[24]

But it wasn't only wearables that were on show at CES. To borrow the corporate language of Intel CEO Krzanich, it was the "broad ecosystem of life" that was being networked by all these new electronic devices spewing out those zettabytes of data that, according to Patrick Tucker, are now making anonymity impossible.[25] The Internet of Things had arrived in Las Vegas. Quite literally, *everything* at CES was becoming networked, *everything* was being reinvented as a smart, connected device. There were smart ovens, smart clothing, smart thermostats, smart air conditioners, smart lighting systems, and smartphones, of course, all designed to capture data and distribute it on the network. One part of the show was dedicated to smart televisions—devices much more intelligent than most TV shows themselves. Indeed, South Korean electronics giant LG's connected televisions are so intelligent that they are already logging our viewing habits in order to serve us up targeted ads.[26]

Another part of CES was dedicated to the connected car—automobiles that are so all-seeing they know our speed, our location, and whether or not we are wearing our seat belt. According to the consultancy Booz, the market for connected cars is about to explode, with demand expected to quadruple between 2015 and 2020 and generate revenues of $113 billion by 2020.[27] But even today's connected car is a data machine, with the onboard cameras from Mercedes-Benz's new S-Class saloon already generating 300 gigabytes of data per hour about the car's location and speed and the driver's habits.[28]

And then there's Google's driverless car, an artificially intelligent, networked car that is driven by software called Google Chauffeur. The idea of driverless cars might sound as science fictional as the idea of augmented reality glasses—but Nevada and Florida have already passed laws permitting their operation and the sight of trial versions of Google's automated cars driving themselves up and down Route 101 between San Jose and San

Francisco is not an uncommon one. While there's no doubt that driverless cars do have enormous potential benefits, particularly in terms of safety and convenience, not to mention the potential environmental benefits of much lighter and thus more energy-efficient vehicles, Google's pioneering role in them is deeply problematic. The software that powers their cars, Google Chauffeur, is essentially the automotive version of Google Glass, a "free" product designed to track everywhere we go and to feed all that data back to the main Google database so that it can *connect the dots* of our lives. As the *Wall Street Journal* columnist Holman Jenkins notes about these so-called autonomous driverless vehicles, "they won't be autonomous at all," and they may "pose a bigger threat to privacy than the NSA ever will."[29] After all, if Google links the data collected from its driverless cars with data amassed from the rest of its ubiquitous products and platforms—such as the smartphone it is developing that uses 3-D sensors to automatically map our physical surroundings so that Google always knows where we are[30]—then you have a surveillance architecture that exceeds even anything that Erich Mielke, in his wildest imagination, ever dreamed up.

Tim Berners-Lee invented the Web in order to help him remember his colleagues at CERN. "The Web is more a social creation than a technical one," he explains. "I designed it for a social effect—to help people work together—and not as a technical toy. The ultimate goal of the Web is to support and improve our weblike existence in the world. We clump into families, associations, and companies. We develop trust across the miles and distrust around the corner."[31]

But when Berners-Lee invented the Web in 1989, he never imagined that this "social creation" could be used so repressively, both by private companies and governments. It was George Orwell who, in *1984*, invented the term "Big Brother" to describe secret policemen like Erich Mielke. And as the Internet of Things transforms every object into a connected device—50 billion of them by 2020 if we are to believe Patrik Cerwall's researchers at Ericsson, with five and a half zettabytes of data being produced by 2015—more and more observers are worrying that twentieth-century Big Brother is back in a twenty-first-century networked guise—dressed in a broad ecosystem of wearables. They fear a world resembling that exhibition at the Venetian in which row after row of nameless, faceless data gatherers wearing all-seeing electronic glasses watch our every move.

Big Brother seemed ubiquitous at the Venetian. Reporting about CES, the *Guardian*'s Dan Gillmor warned that networked televisions that "watch us" are "closing in on Orwell's nightmarish Big Brother vision."[32] Even industry executives are fearful of the Internet of Things's impact on privacy, with Martin Winterkorn, the CEO of Volkswagen, warning in March 2014 that the connected car of the future "must not become a data monster."[33]

But there is one fundamental difference between the Internet of Things and Erich Mielke's twentieth-century Big Brother surveillance state, one thing distinguishing today's networked society from Orwell's *1984*. Mielke wanted to create crystal man against our will; in today's world of Google Glass and Facebook updates, however, we are *choosing* to live in a crystal republic where our networked cars, cell phones, refrigerators, and televisions watch us.

The Panopticon

"On Tuesday I woke up to find myself on page 3 of the *Daily Mail*," wrote a young Englishwoman named Sophie Gadd in December 2013. "That may be one of the worst ways to start the day, after falling out of bed or realizing you've run out of milk. My appearance was not the result of taking my clothes off, but the consequence of a 'Twitter Storm.'"[34]

A final-year history and politics undergraduate at the University of York, Gadd had inadvertently become part of a Twitter storm when, while on vacation in Berlin, she tweeted a painting of the eighteenth-century Russian czarina Catherine the Great from the Deutsches Historisches Museum in Berlin. In her tweet, Gadd suggested that the face in the painting, completed in 1794 by the portrait painter Johann Baptist Lampi, had an uncanny resemblance to that of the British prime minister David Cameron.

"Within hours," Gadd explains, "it had been retweeted thousands of times," with the tweet eventually becoming a major news story in both the *Daily Mail* and the *Daily Telegraph*. "This experience has certainly taught me a few things about viral social media," Gadd says, including the observations—which have already been made by many other critics, including Dave Eggers in *The Circle*, his 2013 fictional satire of data factories like Google and Facebook—that "the Internet is very cynical" and "nothing is private."[35]

Gadd's experience was actually extremely mild. Unlike other innocents caught up in an all-too-public tweet storm, she didn't lose her job or have her reputation destroyed by a vengeful online mob or land up in jail. The same month, for example, that Sophie Gadd woke up to find herself on page 3 of the *Daily Mail*, a PR executive named Justine Sacco tweeted: "Going to Africa. Hope I don't get AIDS. Just Kidding. I'm white!" Sacco published it as she was about to board a twelve-hour flight from London to Cape Town. By the time Sacco arrived in South Africa, she had only been retweeted three thousand times but had become such a source of global news that the paparazzi were there to snap her image as she stumbled innocently off her plane. Labeled the Internet's public enemy number one for her stupid tweet, Sacco lost her job and was even accused of being a "f****** idiot" by her own father.[36] Sacco will now forever be associated with this insensitive but hardly criminal tweet. Such is the nature and power of the Internet.

"When you only have a small number of followers, Twitter can feel like an intimate group of pub friends," Sophie Gadd notes about a social Web that is both unforgetting and unforgiving.[37] "But it's not. It's no more private than shouting your conversations through a megaphone in the high street."

The dangers of the crystal republic predate George Orwell's *1984* and twentieth-century totalitarianism. They go back to the enlightened despotism of Catherine II of Russia, the subject of Johann Baptist Lampi's portrait hanging in Berlin's Deutsches Historisches Museum, the David Cameron look-alike painting that had landed Sophie Gadd on page 3 of the *Daily Mail*.

The Italian-born Lampi hadn't been the only late-eighteenth-century European to go to Russia to enjoy Catherine the Great's largesse. Two English brothers, Samuel and Jeremy Bentham, also spent time there gainfully employed by Catherine's autocratic regime. Samuel worked for Count Grigory Potemkin, one of Catherine's many lovers, whose name has been immortalized for his "Potemkin villages" of fake industrialization he built to impress her. Potemkin gave Bentham the job of managing Krichev, his hundred-square-mile estate on the Polish border that boasted fourteen thousand male serfs.[38] And it was here that Samuel and his brother Jeremy, who joined him in 1786 in Krichev and is best known today as the father of the "greatest happiness" principle, invented the idea of what they called the "Panopticon," or the "Inspection House."

While Jeremy Bentham—who happened to have graduated from the same Oxford college as Tim Berners-Lee—is now considered the author of the Panopticon, he credits his brother Samuel with its invention. "Morals reformed—health preserved—industry invigorated—instruction diffused—public burthens lightened—Economy seated, as it were, upon a rock—the Gordian knot of the poor law not cut, but untied—all by a simple idea in Architecture!" Jeremy Bentham wrote triumphantly in a letter from Krichev to describe this new idea.

What Jeremy Bentham called a "simple idea in Architecture" reflected his brother's interest in disciplining the serfs on Potemkin's Krichev estate. Borrowing from the Greek myth of Panoptes, a giant with a hundred eyes, the Panopticon—intended to house a large institution like a prison, a school, or a hospital—was a circular structure designed to house a single watchman to observe everyone in the building. This threat of being watched, Jeremy Bentham believed, represented "a new mode of obtaining power of mind over mind." The Panopticon was a "vividly imaginative" fusion of architectural form with social purpose," the architectural historian Robin Evans explains. And this purpose was discipline. The more we imagined we were being watched, Jeremy and Samuel Bentham imagined, the harder we would work and the fewer rules we would break. Michel Foucault thus described the Panopticon as a "cruel, ingenious cage." It was "a microcosm of Benthamite society," according to one historian, and "an existential realization of Philosophical Radicalism," according to another.[39]

As the founder of Philosophical Radicalism, a philosophical school better known today as utilitarianism, Jeremy Bentham saw human beings as calculating machines driven by measurable pleasure and pain. Society could be best managed, Bentham believed, by aggregating all these pleasures and pains in order to determine the greatest collective happiness. In the words of the British legal philosopher H. L. A. Hart, Bentham was a "cost-benefit expert on the grand scale."[40] And the nineteenth-century Scottish thinker Thomas Carlyle criticized Bentham as a philosopher focused on "counting up and estimating men's motives." Half a century before his compatriot Charles Babbage invented the first programmable computer, Bentham was already thinking about human beings as calculating machines. And the Panopticon—which he spent much of his life futilely trying to build—is a "simple idea in Architecture" that enables everything and everyone to be watched and measured.

The establishment of a Bentham-style electronic panopticon, fused with his utilitarian faith in the quantification of society, is what is so terrifying about twenty-first-century networked society. We are drifting into a Benthamite world in which everything—from our fitness to what we eat to our driving habits to how long and how hard we work—can be profitably quantified by companies like Google's smart home device manufacturer Nest, which is already building a lucrative business managing the electricity consumption of consumers on behalf of energy utilities.[41] And with its Gross National Happiness Index and its secret experiments to control our moods, Facebook is even resurrecting Bentham's attempt to quantify our pleasure and pain.

In an electronic panopticon of 50 billion intelligent devices, a networked world where privacy has become a privilege of the wealthy, it won't just be our televisions, our smartphones, or our cars that will be watching us. This is John Lanchester's "new kind of human society," a place where everything we do and every place we go can be watched and turned into personal data—a commodity that EU consumer commissioner Meglena Kuneva describe as the "new oil of the Internet and the new currency of the digital world."[42]

"Is the Internet now just one big human experiment?"[43] asked the *Guardian*'s Dan Gillmor in response to July 2014 revelations about emotion-manipulation experiments conducted by Facebook and by the dating site OkCupid. In the future, I'm afraid, the answer to Gillmor's question will be yes. As the sociologist Zeynep Tufekci warns about this infinitely creepy networked world, big data companies like Facebook and OkCupid "now have new tools and stealth methods to quietly model our personality, our vulnerabilities, identify our networks, and effectively nudge and shape our ideas, desires and dreams."[44]

Such nudging and shaping—particularly for dating—isn't necessarily new, argues the *Financial Times*' Christopher Caldwell. But in the pre-Internet past, he notes, this has been done by outside authorities—particularly parents, communities, and religious bodies. "The difference," Caldwell notes, between OkCupid's experiment and parent and religious groups, "is that these groups actually loved the young people they were counselling, had a stake in ensuring things did not go wrong, would help as best they could if things did, and were not using the young lovers strictly as a means of making money."[45]

We will be observed by every unloving institution of the new digital surveillance state—from Silicon Valley's big data companies and the government to insurance companies, health-care providers, the police, and ruthlessly Benthamite employers like Jeff Bezos's Amazon, with its scientifically managed fulfillment centers where the company watches over its nonunionized workforce. Big data companies will know what we did yesterday, today, and, with the help of increasingly accurate predictive technology, what we will do tomorrow. And—as in what Christopher Caldwell calls OkCupid's "venal" experiment—the goal of these big data companies will be strictly to make money from our personal data rather than use it as a public service.

Our Crystal Future

Imaginary dystopias about a future dominated by monstrously powerful technology companies tend to be presented as updated versions of the Orwellian totalitarian state. One example is Ridley Scott's *Prometheus*, a 2012 movie about a future in which a tech company called the Weyland Corporation has become so powerful that its CEO is able to boast, "We are the gods now." The assumption is these companies will replace the government. That they will become Big Brother.

Such a dramatic scenario works well in movies, but is an overly Manichaean take on the future. In our libertarian age of hostility to the state, Google doesn't really need to actually become the government to give it more power over us. So Eric Schmidt, when asked if Google wanted to operate like a government, said that his company didn't want to have the responsibilities of being a country. "We're not becoming a state," he explained. "We don't want to be because states have a lot of complicated problems."[46] But, of course, Google doesn't need to become an old-fashioned state—with all those "complicated problems" of tax collection and welfare and educational policy—to increase its power and wealth. Google can, instead, partner with the government to create a more efficient and profitable surveillance society.

"Who should we fear more with our data: the government or companies?" asks *Guardian* columnist Ana Marie Cox.[47] Unfortunately, however, it's not an either/or question. In today's networked world, we should fear both the government and private big data companies like Facebook and Google.

We got a preview of this terrifying new world in the summer of 2013 with the National Security Agency data-mining Prism scandal revealed by the former NSA analyst Edward Snowden. "If Big Brother came back, he'd be a public-private partnership," explained the British historian Timothy Garton Ash. And it's exactly this kind of partnership between big data companies like Google and the NSA—both the government *and* private companies—that we should most fear.

According to a June 2013 report in the *New York Times*, the Prism program "grew out of the National Security Agency's desire several years ago to begin addressing the agency's need to keep up with the explosive growth of social media."[48] Prism showed the backdoor access to the data of their customers that Microsoft,

Yahoo, Google, Facebook, PalTalk, AOL, Skype, YouTube, and Apple all gave—or were legally required to give, according to these companies—to the government. As the Internet historian John Naughton notes, Prism uncovered the "hidden wiring of our networked world"[49] and revealed the fact "that Google, Facebook, Yahoo, Amazon, Apple and Microsoft are all integral components of the US cyber-surveillance system."[50]

The Prism scandal reveals what the *New York Times*' James Risen and Nick Wingfield call the "complex reality" of data mining as "an industry and a crucial intelligence tool" that "binds N.S.A and Silicon Valley leaders."[51] The *Atlantic*'s Michael Hirsh argues that "the government's massive data collection and surveillance system was largely built not by professional spies or Washington bureaucrats but by Silicon Valley and private defense contractors."[52] As the *New York Times*' Claire Cain Miller adds, some Internet companies, notably Twitter, "declined to make it easy for the government" to collect personal data. But most were compliant and "many cooperated at least a bit"[53] with the government. Google, for example, complied with government requests during the second half of 2012 for information 88% of the time.[54]

Unfortunately, the NSA Prism scandal is not the only example of data collusion between Internet companies and the US government. One of the creepiest online data companies is Acxiom, an information broker that, according to the technology writer Sue Halpern, has "profiles of 75% of all Americans, each around five thousand data points that can be constructed and deconstructed" to find supposedly suspicious people. "It should come as no surprise," Halpern says, "that the NSA and the Departments of Defense and Homeland Security buy this material from Acxiom."[55]

Competing with Acxiom as the Internet's creepiest public-private partnership is Peter Thiel's 2004 data intelligence startup

Palantir, "the go-to company mining massive data sets for intelligence and law enforcement applications."[56] Funded in part by a $2 million investment from the CIA's venture arm Q-Tel, with the CIA being its only client between 2005 and 2008, Palantir now boasts a client list that includes the FBI, CIA, Army, Marines, Air Force, and Defense Department and was valued at $9 billion when the private company raised $107.5 million in 2013. According to Mark Bowden, the author of a popular book about the killing of Osama bin Laden, Palantir "actually deserves the popular designation Killer App."[57] One Special Forces member based in Afghanistan who has extensively used Palantir compares its intelligence to a God-like force. "It's like plugging into the Matrix," he told *Bloomberg*'s Ashlee Vance and Brad Stone. "The first time I saw it, I was like, 'Holy crap. Holy crap. Holy crap.'"[58]

Since the Snowden leak, Internet companies have scrambled to distance themselves from the NSA and the US government or any association with creepy data collectors like Acxiom. There have also been calls from both Google and Twitter for more encryption of Web traffic[59] and the publication of an open letter to Congress and Barack Obama for the American government to "take the lead" and put an end to digital surveillance.[60] But as a December 2013 editorial in *Bloomberg* argued, the effort of Silicon Valley's retrospective critique of the NSA is "richly hypocritical" because "collecting, packaging and selling personal information, often without users' full knowledge and sometimes without their informed consent, is generally what these companies do for a living."[61]

The *Bloomberg* editorial is right. "The primary business model of the Internet is built on mass surveillance," notes Bruce Schneier, a leading computer security expert, "and our government's intelligence-gathering agencies have become addicted to this data."[62]

So rather than an aberration, Silicon Valley's involvement with the NSA's Prism surveillance program conforms with the

Internet's core identity. Data, as the EU's Meglena Kuneva reminds us, is the new oil of the digital economy. So whether it's Google's attempt to embed tiny cameras in networked contact lenses[63] or the networked home with its detailed knowledge of our comings and goings,[64] or smart cities that track everything from our driving to our shopping habits,[65] surveillance remains the Internet's main business model.

"Cities are our paradises of anonymity, a place for self-erasure and self-invention," the veteran technology reporter Quentin Hardy reminds us.[66] So what becomes of self-erasure and self-invention in today's digital panopticon, with products like the aptly named Panono ball camera that films everything it sees? What is the fate of privacy in an Internet of Everything and Everyone?

Today's "simple idea of Architecture," as Jeremy Bentham put it, is an electronic network in which everything we do is recorded and remembered. Bentham's eighteenth-century Panopticon has been upgraded to a twenty-first-century instrument of mass surveillance. Like Vannevar Bush's Memex, its trails never fade; like Ted Nelson's hypertext, there is no "concept of deletion"; like Erich Mielke's Stasi, its appetite for our personal data is insatiable. The Internet has, indeed, become a crystal republic for crystal man.

We shape our architecture; and thereafter it shapes us.

CHAPTER EIGHT

EPIC FAIL

FailCon

Big Brother might be dead, but one department of the old totalitarian state remains in robust health. Orwell's Ministry of Truth—in fact, of course, the Ministry of Propaganda—was supposed to have gone out of business in 1989 with the fall of the Berlin Wall. But, like other failed twentieth-century institutions, the ministry has relocated its operations to the west coast of America. It has moved to the epicenter of twenty-first-century innovation—to Silicon Valley, a place so radically disruptive that it is even reinventing failure as the new model of success.

On the list of all-time greatest lies, the idea that FAILURE IS SUCCESS doesn't quite match the Orwellian trinity of WAR IS PEACE, FREEDOM IS SLAVERY, or IGNORANCE IS STRENGTH, but it's still an astonishing perfidy, worthy of the best Ministry of Truth propagandist. And yet, in Silicon Valley the "failure is success" lie has become such an accepted truth that there is now even a San Francisco event called FailCon, dedicated to its dissemination.

Along with several hundred other aspiring disruptors, I'd gone to FailCon to learn why, in the Valley at least, failure is considered to be desirable. Held at San Francisco's luxury Kabuki hotel a couple of miles west of the Battery, FailCon was part countercultural remix of the old Protestant work ethic, part classic Californian self-help therapy, and—like most technology events in Silicon Valley—wholly divorced from reality. It's as if Orwell's Ministry of Truth had, to borrow another fashionable Valley word, "pivoted" into the conference business. "Stop being afraid of failure and start embracing it,"[1] the event instructed its audience. And to help us overcome the fear, to make it feel good to fail, FailCon invited some of Big Tech's greatest innovators to outfail each other with tales of their losses.

At FailCon, the F-word was ubiquitous among illustrious Silicon Valley speakers like Airbnb cofounder Joe Gebbia, the billionaire venture capitalist Vinod Khosla, and Eric Ries, the author of a bestselling handbook for Internet success called *The Lean Startup*. Indeed, the more uncannily prescient the investor, the more moneyed the startup entrepreneur, the bigger the influencer, the more boastfully they broadcasted their litany of failures. At FailCon, we heard about failure as the most valuable kind of education, failure as a necessity of innovation, failure as a version of enlightenment, and, most ironically, given the event's self-congratulatory tenor, failure as a lesson in humility.

But the award for the most successful and least humble of FailCon failures went to Travis Kalanick, the cofounder and CEO of the transportation network Uber, whose prematurely graying hair and hyperkinetic manner suggested a life of perpetual radical disruption. Both his appearance and his business "innovations" personified Schumpeter's "perennial hurricane of creative destruction." This self-styled "badass," a pinup for our libertarian age who identifies himself as one of the violent criminals in Quentin Tarantino's movie *Pulp Fiction*,[2] certainly isn't too shy to present himself as a historic risk taker. On Twitter, @travisk even once borrowed the cover of *The Fountainhead*, Ayn Rand's extreme libertarian celebration of free-market capitalism, as his profile photo.[3]

Kalanick's $18 billion venture is certainly a badass company, with customers accusing its drivers of every imaginable crime from kidnapping[4] to sexual harassment.[5] Since its creation, the unregulated Uber has not only been in a constant legal fight with New York City, San Francisco, Chicago, and federal regulators, but has been picketed by its own nonunionized drivers demanding collective bargaining rights and health-care benefits.[6] Things aren't any better overseas. In France, opposition to the networked transportation startup has been so intense that, in early 2014, there were driver strikes and even a series of violent attacks on Uber cars in Paris.[7] While in September 2014, a Frankfurt court banned Uber's budget price UberPop product entirely from the German market, claiming that the massively financed startup unfairly competed with local taxi companies.[8]

Uber drivers don't seem to like Kalanick's anti-union company any more than regulators do. In August 2013, Uber drivers sued the company for failing to remit tips and in September 2014 around a thousand Uber drivers in New York City organized a strike against the company's unfair working conditions. "There's no union. There's no community of drivers," one sixty-five-year-old driver who has been working for Uber for two years complained to the *New York Times* in 2014. "And the only people getting rich are the investors and executives."[9]

The fabulously wealthy Silicon Valley investors, who will ride the startup till its inevitable IPO, love Uber, of course. "Uber is software [that] eats taxis. . . . It's a killer experience," you'll remember Marc Andreessen enthused.[10] Tragically, that's all too true. On New Year's Eve 2013, an Uber driver accidentally ran over and killed a six-year-old girl on the streets of San Francisco. Uber immediately deactivated what they call their "partner's" account, saying that he "was not providing service on the Uber system during the time of the accident."[11]

How generous. And happy 2014 to all our partners, Uber might have added.

So much for shared responsibility in the sharing economy. No wonder Kalanick's own drivers, whom he calls "transportation entrepreneurs," are picketing Uber. And no wonder that the parents of Sofia Liu, the San Francisco girl killed by the Uber driver, are suing Uber itself in a wrongful-death lawsuit.

It's not just drivers and pedestrians who are being killed by Uber. If you don't like it, walk, Uber tells its customers, with Kalanickian tact, about a service that uses "surge" pricing—a euphemism for price gouging—which has resulted in fares being 700–800% above normal on holidays or in bad weather.[12] During a particularly ferocious December 2013 snowstorm in New York City, one unfortunate Uber rider paid $94 for a trip of less than two miles that took just eleven minutes.[13] Even the rich and famous are being outrageously ripped off by the unregulated Uber service, with Jessica Seinfeld, Jerry's wife, being charged $415 during that same December storm to take her kid across Manhattan.[14]

Along with other startups such as Joe Gebbia's Airbnb and the labor network TaskRabbit, Uber's business model is based upon circumventing supposedly archaic twentieth-century regulations to create a "what you want when you want it" twenty-first-century economy. They believe that the Internet, as a hyperefficient and so-called frictionless platform for buyers and sellers, is the solution to what they call the "inefficiencies" of the twentieth-century economy. No matter that much of the business generated at networks like Airbnb is under investigation by US authorities, with many of the fifteen thousand "hosts" in New York not paying tax on their rental income.[15] Nor that TaskRabbit's so-called distributed-workforce model—whose simple goal, according to its CEO, Leah

Busque, is to "revolutionize the world's labor force"[16]—profits from what Brad Stone calls the "backbreaking" and "soul-draining" nature of low-paying menial labor.[17]

"This revolutionary work built out of Silicon Valley convenience is not really about technological innovation," warns the podcaster and writer Sarah Jaffe about the role of labor brokers like TaskRabbit in our increasingly unequal economy. "It's just the next step in a decades-old trend of fragmenting jobs, isolating workers and driving down wages."[18] And with 7.5 million Americans working in part-time jobs in July 2014 because they didn't have full-time jobs, Leah Busque's "revolutionizing" of the world's workforce is, in truth, a reflection of a new poorly paid class of peer-to-peer project workers, dubbed the "precariat" by the labor economist Guy Standing.[19] "With piecemeal gigs easier to obtain than long-term employment," warns the *New York Times*' Natasha Singer, this highly insecure labor model, the dark underbelly of DIY capitalism, is becoming an increasingly important piece of the new networked economy.[20]

But that's all beside the point for these self-styled disrupters who, *without our permission*, are building the distributed capitalist architecture of the early twenty-first century. The market knows best, hard-core libertarians like Travis Kalanick insist. It solves all our problems. "Where lifestyle meets logistics" is how Uber all too innocently describes its mission to become the platform for the way people and things are transported in our electronically networked age. But Uber-style, let-the-market-decide companies are actually building an on-demand superhighway of luxury services and products for members of the new elite. As George Packer argues, companies like Uber have been designed to solve "all the problems of being twenty years old, with cash in hand."[21] Tap your smartphone and these companies deliver whatever you want: an instant limousine, an instant worker, an instant teacher, even an instant currency like Bitcoin. They represent Ayn Rand's free-market fantasy of radical privatization: everybody's private jet, everybody's private hotel room, everybody's private doctor, everybody's private employee, everybody's private charity, everybody's private economy. In short, everybody's private society.

Kalanick is no stranger to controversy. Back in the late nineties, he cofounded a peer-to-peer music-sharing startup called Scour, which, like Napster, helped decimate the recorded music industry by enabling consumers to steal the latter's products. While Kalanick paced relentlessly around the FailCon stage as if he'd just strode out of an Ayn Rand novel, he quantified his own dramatic failure at Scour by explaining that he'd been sued for a quarter of a trillion dollars by some of the world's most powerful entertainment companies.

"Two hundred and fifty billion dollars!" Kalanick exclaimed, jumping around as if even he didn't quite believe such a staggering sum. "That's the GDP of Sweden—the gross national product of a midsized European economy."[22]

Among the FailCon audience, these revelations were greeted reverentially, with a collective nodding of heads. Only in Silicon Valley does getting sued for a quarter of a trillion dollars grant rock star status. A number of amateur paparazzi even waved their iPhones in the air to capture Kalanick's image—the surest sign of approval from a crowd for whom the ontological argument "pix it or it didn't happen" is gospel and an experience isn't considered real until it is publicly posted on Instagram or Twitter.

A young, disheveled, and unshaven fellow seated next to me seemed particularly taken with the enormity of Kalanick's failure. "Awesome," the guy muttered to his friend. "That's so totally awesome."

And his friend, also young, male, and disheveled, was, if anything, even more impressed with Kalanick's losses. "Epic . . .

fucking . . . fail," he added, iterating these three words so slowly that each was designed to sound like a fully formed sentence.

Epic. Fucking. Fail.

The Real Failure

At the FailCon cocktail party later that evening, I ran into Kalanick, whom, as a fellow startup Web entrepreneur, I had known for almost twenty years. Back in the nineties, while he was failing with Scour, I was also failing with my own music startup, AudioCafe. We had shared some of the same investors and appeared on the same panels to argue about the value of disruption. He'd even spoken at an event I'd produced in 2000 about the future of music. But, compared with his, my failure was pathetic. I'd only lost a paltry few million dollars of other people's money. And nobody, I'm ashamed to admit, has ever sued me for the GDP of a midsized European country.

"Hey, Travis, here's to failure," I toasted, raising a glass to the paper billionaire, who, in his hyperkinetic way, was conducting several conversations simultaneously with an entourage of admirers.

"Yo, dude, success is failure," Kalanick said, stopping momentarily and bumping his fist against my glass. "He who fails most—wins."

"Yo, *dude*, doesn't that make you the big winner," I replied, with a thin smile.

No wonder FailCon had been held at the Kabuki. It was bizarre theater. Here we were, at an exclusive San Francisco hotel, surrounded by some of the most successful, the most powerful, and the wealthiest people on earth. And what was this elite doing? They were toasting failure. Yes, the Ministry of Truth really had relocated to Silicon Valley. FailCon is building an entire media company around the failure meme. It has introduced another event called FailChat, which instructs entrepreneurs to "come prepared with your own personal stories of struggle, confusion or doubt."[23] And it is going international, too, holding FailCon conferences in Germany, Singapore, France, Norway, Brazil, India, and, most absurdly, in recession-ravaged Spain—where there's certainly no scarcity of people with *personal stories of struggle, confusion, or doubt*.

But the truth, the real truth about failure, is the opposite of the glossy version choreographed by Silicon Valley's slick apologists of disruption. Real failure is a $36 billion industry that in a decade shrank to $16 billion because libertarian badasses like Travis Kalanick invented products that destroyed its core value. Real failure is the $12.5 billion in annual sales, the more than 71,000 jobs, and the $2.7 billion in annual earnings estimated to have been lost just in the United States' music industry because of "innovative" products like Napster and Scour.[24] Real failure is the 55% drop in Spanish music sales between 2005 and 2010 because of online theft.[25] Real failure is such a decimation of Spanish musical talent that a country that had historically produced international stars like Julio Iglesias hasn't had an artist selling a million copies of an album in Europe since 2008.[26] No wonder FailCon is coming to Spain.

FailCon is coming everywhere soon. While it's amusing to satirize libertarian clowns like Travis Kalanick with their pathetic boasts about $250 billion lawsuits and their adolescent Ayn Rand fetishes, this really is no laughing matter. Behind many of today's hyperefficient network companies like Google, Facebook, Amazon, Airbnb, and Uber—with their assault on traditional market regulations, their "free" business models, their "disintermediation" of paid human labor by artificial algorithms, and their "transparent" big data factories in which we all unknowingly work—there is failure. Traumatic failure. Indeed, the real failure, the thing that nobody at FailCon ever dreamed of associating with failure, is the digital upheaval itself.

Rather than the answer to our contemporary problems, the Internet, that human-computer symbiosis that J. C. R. Licklider believed "would save humanity," is actually diminishing most aspects of our lives. Instead of creating more transparency, we have devices that make the invisible visible. Instead of a globally connected online citizen, we now have the selfie. Instead of the village pub, we have the Battery. Instead of a cultural cornucopia, we have a post–"Golden Mile of Vinyl" Berwick Street. Instead of a thriving economy, we have downtown Rochester, New York.

The Ministry of Truth is back in business. In Silicon Valley, everything is the opposite of what is claimed. The sharing economy is really the selfish economy; social media is, fact, antisocial; the "long tail" of cultural democracy is actually a long tale; "free" content is turning out to be shatteringly expensive; and the success of the Internet is, in truth, a huge failure.

Epic. Fucking. Fail.

At the FailCon cocktail party, I shared a drink with the two disheveled guys who'd been sitting next to me during Kalanick's speech. "So, the Internet, is it working?" I asked them about the intergalactic computer network created by J. C. R. Licklider, Paul Baran, Bob Kahn, and Vint Cerf. "Has it been an unqualified success?"

"A *success*?" one of them repeated, glancing at me as if I'd just been whisked down to earth by an UberCHOPPER.

In a sense, perhaps, I had. It was a question so taken for granted at evangelical events like FailCon that, amid this technology crowd, I might as well have been speaking Sanskrit or Swahili. In Silicon Valley, everyone knows the answer. Their answer is an unregulated, hyperefficient platform like Airbnb for buyers and sellers. Their answer is the distributed system of capitalism being built, unregulated cab by cab, by Travis Kalanick. Their answer is a "lean startup" like WhatsApp that employs fifty-five people and sells for $19 billion. Their answer is data factories that turn us all into human billboards. Their answer is the Internet.

"It's obviously been a success for all of us," I explained, sweeping my hand around the room packed with fabulously wealthy failures. "But is the network the answer for everyone else? Is it making the world a better place?"

My question triggered a couple of lies that, while not quite in the same league as the FAILURE IS SUCCESS whopper, could still have been coined at the Ministry of Truth. Yes, they both affirmed, nodding their heads vigorously, the Internet *is* the answer.

"The Net gives power to the people," one said, smiling broadly. "For the first time in history, anyone can produce, say, or buy anything."

"Yeah, it's the platform for equality," the other added. "It allows everyone an equal share in our new abundance."

The Internet gives *power* to the people? The Internet is the platform for *equality*? Neither of these disheveled guys knew anything about "the people" or "the platforms" outside Silicon Valley. They were the very kind of twenty-year-olds with cash in hand for whom Uber's expensive private black limousine service was designed. Both had recently graduated from Stanford. Both worked at big data startups with insatiable appetites for collecting other people's private information. Both were engineers of an increasingly *unequal* future, in which ordinary people will experience a scarcity, rather than an abundance of economic, political, and cultural power.

"That's not true," I said. "The Internet is a winner-take-all economy. It's creating a two-tiered society."

"Where's the evidence?" one engineer responded. He wasn't smiling anymore.

"Yeah, I'd like to see your data," the other chimed in.

"Open your eyes," I said, pointing at the bustling San Francisco street outside the hotel window. "There's your *data*."

The Alien Overlord Spaceships

Outside the San Francisco hotel, the future had arrived and, to paraphrase William Gibson, it was distributed most unequally. Uber limousines lined up outside the club to whisk Silicon Valley's successful young failures around town. Cars from rival transportation networks hovered hopefully around the hotel, too—companies like Lyft, Sidecar, and the fleet of me-too mobile-ride-hailing startups trying to out-Uber Travis Kalanick's $18 billion market leader. Some of the people scrambling for a living as networked drivers were themselves aspiring entrepreneurs with billion-dollar startup ideas of their own.[27] So even in these unlicensed cabs, it was impossible to get away from the pitches for the next WhatsApp, Airbnb, or Uber, which pitches, sadly, were mostly just a glorified form of begging. "San Francisco," as one observer about the digital gold rush dryly noted, is "full of people walking around with 1.2% of nothing."[28]

The streets of San Francisco were also full of buses. Some were open-topped, red double-deckers filled with tourists snapping their Instagram moments of what appeared, to the naked eye, at least, to be a city with splendidly panoramic views of the Bay. A less romantic but equally vital feature of San Francisco was its public buses. These were the traditional municipal vehicles, with bright orange Muni logos painted on their sides, a service financed by San Francisco's transit authority, which, for a small fee, allows anyone to ride on them. Their windows were entirely transparent. These Muni buses are what Silicon Valley entrepreneurs and investors would probably dismiss as "legacy products." They now seem like a relic of mass labor's "golden age," a halcyon time when paid workers traveled to their jobs on publicly subsidized vehicles.

"I don't know why old people ride Muni. If I were old, I'd just take Uber," the *Los Angeles Times* reports one San Francisco techie saying to his friends after reluctantly giving up his seat to an old lady on a Muni bus.[29] Perhaps old ladies take Muni, I would have explained, because they can afford the $0.75 senior's fare, whereas Travis Kalanick's Uber service, with its surge pricing, could cost them $94 for a two-mile ride.

And then there's what the San Francisco–based writer Rebecca Solnit dubs, collectively, "the Google Bus."[30] These are sleeker and more powerful buses, menacingly anonymous in their absence of any identifying marks, with the same kind of opaque, tinted windows that masked the Battery from the prying eyes of the outside world. Unlike the Muni's legacy buses, the Google Bus isn't for everyone. It is a private bus designed to transport tech workers from their expensive San Francisco homes down to the offices of Google, Facebook, and Apple. Google alone runs more than one hundred of these daily buses, which make 380 trips to its Googleplex office in Mountain View.[31] These luxurious, Wi-Fi-enabled private buses—which, in total, make around four thousand daily scheduled pickups at public Bay Area bus stops—have been superimposed on top of San Francisco's public transit grid by tech companies that have even begun to employ private security guards to protect their worker-passengers from irate local residents.[32]

The Google Bus has sparked such animosity from locals that, in December 2013, protesters in West Oakland attacked one of them, smashing a rear window and so outraging Tom Perkins that he compared the glass breaking to Kristallnacht in Nazi Germany.[33] And, as if to mark the twenty-fifth anniversary of the Web, 2014 is the year that these demonstrations have become more politically organized and coherent. They are even spreading outside the Bay Area, with antigentrification protests taking place in February 2014 in Seattle against private Microsoft buses.[34]

Kristallnacht it certainly isn't. Rather than racial genocide, the Bay Area's problem is the ever-widening economic inequality between tech workers and everyone else. In many ways, failure is as endemic here as it is in Rochester. "After decades in which the country has become less and less equal," mourns the Palo Alto–born-and-bred George Packer, "Silicon Valley is one of the most unequal places on earth."[35] Figures from the Chapman University geographer Joel Kotkin suggest that the Valley has actually hemorrhaged jobs since the dot-com crash of 2000, losing some forty thousand jobs over the last twelve years.[36] A 2013 report by Joint Venture Silicon Valley confirms Kotkin's findings, adding that homelessness in Silicon Valley has increased by 20% between 2011 and 2013 and reliance on food stamps has reached a ten-year high.[37] In Santa Clara County, the geographical heart of Silicon Valley, the poverty rate shot up from 8% in 2001 to 14% in 2013, with the food stamp population jumping from 25,000 in 2001 to 125,000 in 2013.

Even those lucky enough to get jobs at tech startups are likely to lose them again very quickly. According to research by the US Bureau of Labor Statistics, which tracked changes in employment between 2012 and 2013, new companies fired 25% of their staff in their first year. This contrasts with an average annual rate of 6.6% at established companies.[38] This cult of the so-called lean startup[39] created by the FailCon speaker Eric Ries, with its brutal churn of employees, makes it particularly risky for older people with kids to feed and mortgages to pay to work in such a casino-style economy. No wonder, then, that Silicon Valley's demographic is radically different from the rest of America. In a US economy where, according again to the Bureau of Labor Statistics, the overall median age of workers is 42.3 years old, the median age of workers is 28 at Facebook and 29 at Google.[40] And even at supposedly "mature" technology companies like Oracle or Hewlett-Packard, the average age of workers is significantly less than the US average.

Just as Silicon Valley is biased against older workers, it also discriminates against women. "Women are no longer welcome on the Internet," the feminist writer Amanda Hess says. And they certainly don't seem to be welcome, either, in the offices of Silicon Valley's venture capitalists. Even though, as the entrepreneur and academic Vivek Wadhwa reminds us, female-founded startups are more capital-efficient than those founded by men and have lower failure rates and higher annual revenues, women are still radically underrepresented in Silicon Valley.[41] The numbers on this are disturbing. Fewer than one in ten venture-funded startups in Silicon Valley are led by women, with only 3% of that venture money going to all-female teams.[42] An estimated 2–4% of engineers at tech companies are women,[43] and, according to Measure of America, these Silicon Valley women earn less than half of what Silicon Valley men do.[44] Equally troubling, there is a persistent sexist culture among many of the young male programmers, the so-called tech bros, who openly treat women as sexual objects and unashamedly develop pornographic products such as the "Titshare" app introduced at the 2013 TechCrunch Disrupt show in San Francisco,[45] designed to humiliate their female colleagues. This misogynistic culture extends throughout the Valley, with bias claims surging in 2013 against the male-dominated tech industry[46] and even a blue-chip venture capital firm like John Doerr and Tom Perkins's KPCB becoming embroiled in a discrimination suit with a former female investment partner.[47]

The Internet hasn't really benefited most San Franciscans, either. Wave after wave of speculative tech booms have made San Francisco almost as exclusive a private club as Michael and Xochi Birch's Battery, with the city ranking as one of America's four most unequal cities, according to the U.S. Census Bureau.[48] It's a view of the city that the snap-happy tourists on top of those red double-decker buses never get to see. In 2013, San Francisco's median house price of $900,000 and monthly rent of $3,250 had made the city unaffordable to 86% of its residents.[49] Evictions are up, too, an overall 38% increase between 2011 and 2013, in large part due to the 1985 Ellis Act, which allows landlords to evict renters and leave the rental housing business. These evictions are up by 170% over the same period.[50] The Internet's so-called sharing economy has compounded the problem, with the increasing profitability of unregulated Airbnb rentals being one reason for the surge in Ellis Act evictions.[51] One San Francisco tenant even sued his Russian Hill landlords for "unjust eviction" in 2014 because, rather than moving into the apartment themselves, they rented his $1,840-a-month apartment out on Airbnb for up to $145 a night.[52]

"Warning: Two-Tier System." Protesters in San Francisco's Mission District waved such a construction-style sign outside the Google buses.[53] "Public $$$$$$$$ Private Gains," another sign said.[54] Others were less polite about these mysterious buses' whisking their expensive cargo of privileged, mostly young white male workers down to Silicon Valley. "Fuck off Google," came the message from West Oakland.[55]

Rebecca Solnit's drawing attention to the "Google Bus," which rides on public infrastructure and stops at public bus stops but is a private service run by private companies, has become the most public symbol now of this economic division between Silicon Valley and everyone else.

"I think of them as the spaceships," is how Solnit describes this new feudal power structure in Silicon Valley, "on which our alien overlords have landed to rule over us."

Class Warfare

These alien overlords certainly don't have much sympathy for the city's poor and homeless. "San Francisco has some of the craziest homeless people I have ever seen in my life. Stop giving them money, you know they just buy alcohol and drugs with it, right? Next time just hand them a handle of vodka and a pack of cigarettes," one founder of an Internet startup wrote in a notorious post titled "10 Things I Hate About You: San Francisco Edition."[56] Another tech founder and CEO was even more blunt, calling San Francisco's homeless "grotesque . . . degenerate . . . trash."[57]

Equally disturbing are the technorati's solutions to the poverty and hunger afflicting many Bay Area residents. In May 2014, the Google engineer and libertarian activist Justine Tunney, who in 2013 tried to fund a private militia on Kickstarter,[58] came up with the idea of replacing food stamps with Soylent, a "food product" that claims to "provide maximum nutrition with minimum effort."

"Give poor people @soylent so they can be healthy and productive. If you're on food stamps, maybe you're unhealthy and need to eat better," Tunney tweeted, without bothering to check first with people on food stamps to see if they wanted to eat what the technology critic J. R. Hennessy calls "tasteless nutrition sludge."[59] No matter. In a month, Tunney had raised $1 million on Kickstarter for a repellent social experiment that brings to mind *Soylent Green*, the 1974 dystopian movie about a world in which the dominant food product was made of human remains.

This libertarian elite doesn't have much affection for labor unions and the industrial working class, either. When, in 2013, the city's metro system union, the Bay Area Rapid Transit (BART) workers, went on strike over the threats of automation to their jobs and their relatively low pay in one of America's most expensive cities, the technology community erupted in a storm of moral outrage.

"My solution would be to pay whatever the hell they want, get them back to work, and then go figure out how to automate their jobs," the CEO of one tech startup wrote on Facebook.[60] Indeed, much of the "work" being done by Google-acquired robotic companies like Nest, Boston Dynamics, and DeepMind is focused on figuring out how to automate the jobs of traditional workers such as BART drivers. "Coming to an office near you," we've been warned about the automated technology of the future. And, just as Google is developing the self-driving car, there is no doubt some innovative Google engineer is working on an automated train that won't employ either drivers, guards, or ticket takers.

If poor people and unions are the problem for Silicon Valley's tech elite, then technology, and the Internet in particular, is always the answer. And it's this delusional "thinking" that has infected San Francisco, transforming one of the world's most diverse cities—a place that has historically, as Solnit reminds us, been a "refuge for dissidents, queers, pacifists and experimentalists"[61]—into a laboratory for an outsourced, networked economy that wants to feed people Soylent and employ them to wait in lines.

Technology companies, and technology in general, are beginning to replace government in San Francisco. The city is granting massive tax breaks to San Francisco–based Internet companies in exchange for charity and outreach work. And the result is a predictable set of self-interested "charity" projects such as private monthlong dance classes held for Yammer employees by a local ballet company. "Instead of job training, there are cocktail parties," as one technology blog describes the consequences of this outsourcing of political responsibilities to multibillion-dollar private companies like Twitter. "Community engagements equal Yelp reviews written by and for techies. And some of the 'giving back' initiatives conveniently double as employee perks, stretching the definition of charity."[62]

The libertarian fantasy of private companies usurping government is, I'm afraid, becoming a reality. "It's becoming excruciatingly, obviously clear to everyone else that where value is created is no longer in New York, it's no longer in Washington, it's no longer in L.A. It's in San Francisco and the Bay Area," boasted Chamath Palihapitiya, a Silicon Valley venture capitalist whose Social+Capital fund includes Peter Thiel as an investor. "Companies are transcending power now. We are becoming the eminent vehicles for change and influence, and capital structures that matter. If the government shuts down, nothing happens and we all move on, because it just doesn't matter."

The Battery member and Uber investor Shervin Pishevar expressed this same techno-libertarian fantasy in under 140 characters. "Let's just TaskRabbit and Uberize the Government," Pishevar tweeted to his 57,000 followers.[63]

He might as well have said: Let's just TaskRabbit and Uberize the economy. Let's just turn everything into the so-called sharing economy, a hyperefficient and frictionless platform for networked buyers and sellers. Let's outsource labor so that everyone is paid by the day, by the hour, by the minute. Because that's indeed what is happening to the Bay Area economy, with some Oakland residents even crowdfunding their own private police force[64] and Facebook (of course) being the first US private company to pay for a full-time, privately paid "community safety police officer" on its campus.[65]

Pishevar probably believes that unions should be Uberized and TaskRabbited, too. But, of course, with freelance Web service platforms like TaskRabbit—which provide such short-term "jobs" as waiting in line to buy a new iPhone on behalf of one of San Francisco's lazy "meritocrats"—there is no role for unions, no place for anything protecting the rights of the laborer, no collective sense of identity, no dignity of work. TaskRabbit has even managed to offend traditional freelancers, with the executive director of the FreelanceUnion arguing that "the trend of stripping work down to discrete, short-term projects without benefits for workers is troubling."[66]

TaskRabbit calls its iPhone service #SkipTheLine. But actually, the economic system being rigged up is all about the Bay Area's wealthy techies—who, surprise-surprise, tend to be as white, male, and young as those awesome dudes at FailCon—skipping a more fundamental line. It's a two-tier system of overlords and the unemployed, the underemployed and the occasionally employed. An economy in which menial tasks are handled by an outsourced underclass who will do anything for an hourly rate on labor networks like TaskRabbit—from cleaning houses to outsourcing romantic errands. Rather than revolutionizing the world's labor force, TaskRabbit is commodifying life itself so that everything—from buying a rose to waiting in line—can be bought and sold.

Secession

In a May 2013 speech to his company's Internet developers, Larry Page, Google's cofounder and CEO, confessed his fantasy about the future. "We are at maybe 1% of what is possible. We should be focused on building the things that don't exist," he said.[67] "Maybe we could set apart a piece of the world. I like going to Burning Man, for example. An environment where people can try new things." Thus did Page lay out what one critic identified as his "techno-libertarian utopia."[68]

Burning Man, the annual countercultural festival of what it calls "radical self-expression" and "self-reliance"[69] in Nevada's Black Rock Desert, has already established itself as one of the most fashionable events on the Silicon Valley calendar, with tech entrepreneurs bringing their own celebrity chefs, hiring teams of "Sherpas" to treat them like "kings and queens," and erecting air-conditioned yurts in the desert.[70] But Page's vision is to take Burning Man out of the desert. "I think as technologists we should have some safe places where we can try out new things and figure out the effect on society," he explained to his developers. "What's the effect on people, without having to deploy it to the whole world."

But Page—or "Larry," as everyone in Silicon Valley likes to call this member of America's 0.0001% multibillionaire class—may already have the "safe place" for his vision of secession. That laboratory where technologists can experiment with new things on society actually exists. Burning Man has already been liberated from the Nevada desert. It is now called San Francisco.

Today the San Francisco Bay Area has become the vehicle, both literally as a transportation network and otherwise, for a radical experiment in "self-reliance." As the laboratory for the most important social experiment of our age, the Bay Area has come to represent a libertarian *fantasy* about how Internet companies can somehow detach themselves from their wider responsibilities in society and how networked technology can replace government. Never mind Larry Page's hubristic claim about achieving "the 1% of what is possible"; the really relevant one percent are that minority of wealthy Silicon Valley entrepreneurs like Page who are massively profiting from what *New York* magazine's Kevin Roose calls a "regional declaration of independence."[71] It's an experimental fantasy of outsourced labor, hostility to labor unions, a cult of efficiency and automated technology, a mad display of corporate arrogance, and an even crazier celebration of an ever-widening economic and cultural inequality in San Francisco.

The fantasy of secession from the real world, the reinvention of the "New Frontier" myth, has become one of those fashionable memes, like the cult of failure, now sweeping through Silicon Valley. While PayPal cofounder and Tesla and SpaceX CEO Elon Musk is planning to establish an 80,000-person high-tech colony on Mars,[72] others are focused on building their fantasy high-tech colonies within Northern California itself. The third-generation Silicon Valley venture capitalist Tim Draper is launching a 2014 "Six Californias" ballot measure to redraw California into six separate US states, including one called "Silicon Valley."[73] And the venture capitalist Vinod Khosla, who boasted at FailCon about his own failure, has already seceded. Having bought a $37.5 million, 89-acre property in Half Moon Bay, a coastal town just south of San

Francisco, Khosla unilaterally declared independence and blocked all public access to a much-loved local beach beside his property.[74]

Balaji Srinivasan, a Stanford University lecturer and startup entrepreneur, has taken the secession fantasy one crazy step further. At one of Paul Graham's "Failure Central" Y Combinator startup events, Srinivasan pitched the concept of what he called "Silicon Valley's Ultimate Exit," a complete withdrawal of Silicon Valley from the United States. "We need to build opt-in society, outside the US, run by technology," is how he described a ridiculous fantasy that would turn Silicon Valley into a kind of free-floating island that *Wired*'s Bill Wasik satirizes as the "offshore plutocracy of Libertaristan."[75] And one group of "Libertaristanians" at the Peter Thiel–funded, Silicon Valley–based Seasteading Institute, founded by Patri Friedman, a former Google engineer and the grandson of the granddaddy of free-market economics, Milton Friedman, has even begun to plan floating utopias that would drift off the Pacific coast.[76]

Behind all these secession fantasies is the very concrete reality of the secession of the rich from everyone else in Silicon Valley. Forget the floating utopias of Libertaristan. What we are seeing in the San Francisco Bay Area is the actual emergence of two separate and radically unequal worlds: one, a privileged, privatized place for the wealthy tech caste; the other, a shabbier, public one for everyone else. It represents what Joel Kotkin calls "a high-tech version of feudal society"—a type of society in which people may appear to live, travel, and work in the same physical space, but are actually residents of two quite foreign universes. These twin realms are separated by what the *New York Times*' Timothy Egan describes as the "texture of inequality"[77]—a marked chasm in Bay Area quality of life affecting everything from real estate and transportation to work and corporate architecture.

Google, the owner and operator of the world's largest and most profitable data factory, dominates this reinvented feudal landscape. Take flying, for example. When I flew to Rochester from San Francisco via the joyless Chicago O'Hare Airport, I traveled, like 99% of regular travelers do, on scheduled aircraft that were both cramped and almost always delayed. But multi-billionaires like Google's cofounders Larry Page and Sergey Brin and executive chairman Eric Schmidt not only fly on their own private jets, but even have their own private Bay Area airport, at NASA's Ames Research Center. Page, Brin, and Schmidt have six luxury planes: Boeing 757 and 767 intercontinental aircraft, three Gulfstream 5 long-range jets, and a Dassault Alpha light attack jet capable of firing an impressive array of guns, rockets, missiles, and bombs. Best of all, at least from Page, Brin, and Schmidt's point of view, Google has even been subsidized by NASA for cheap fuel, after what the agency's inspector general described as a "misunderstanding" over pricing.[78] So many of their jaunts around the world—from charity events in Africa to their presence at the World Economic Forum in Davos—are actually in part funded by public money.

Google's determination to reinvent reality can be seen in its plans to create a new Googleplex office, a medieval-style walled city called "Bay View"—featuring entirely self-enclosed offices, restaurants, gyms, laundries, crèches, even dormitories—that will, in good feudal fashion, cut off its privileged workers from everything around them. According to *Vanity Fair*, the 1.1-million-square-foot offices will be organized on strict algorithmic principles so that no Google worker will be more than a two-and-a-half-minute walk from any other Googler.[79] Funded, of course, by all of our free labor, the creepy Bay View will be made up of nine identical four-story buildings designed to engineer serendipity by maximizing "casual collisions of the workforce."

While the proposed Bay View office might not quite have the breathtaking panoramas offered from the top of San Francisco's tourist buses, it nonetheless should offer sufficiently good views to allow all the Google workers to see the new high-speed catamarans hired by their company to ferry them around the Bay.[80] On a clear day, they might even catch sight of a four-story Google barge about the size of the Battery, which the company operates as a floating classroom to educate workers as they travel around the Bay.[81]

Boat, barge, airplane, and bus travel are all being reinvented by Google so that its employees can commute to Bay View on fast, luxurious, and exclusively private vehicles that will run on publicly funded highways and seaways. Perhaps Google will even open its own Bay View airport so that it can house a squadron of Dassault jets to repel invaders from Mars or Washington, D.C.

Google is far from alone among tech leviathans in turning contemporary reality into a feudal landscape replete with high-tech castles, moats, and towers. Silicon Valley is transforming itself into a medieval tableau—a jarring landscape of dreadfully impoverished and high-crime communities like East Palo Alto, littered with unemployed people on food stamps, interspersed with fantastically wealthy and entirely self-reliant tech-cities designed by world-famous architects such as Norman Foster and Frank Gehry.

Apple, a company that has been accused of cheating the US government out of $44 billion in tax revenue between 2009 and 2012,[82] is building a Norman Foster–designed $5 billion Silicon Valley headquarters that will feature a 2.8-million-square-foot circular, four-story building containing a 1,000-seat auditorium, a 3,000-seat café, and office space for 13,000 employees.[83] Before he died, Steve Jobs described Foster's design for the new building as looking a "little like a spaceship." Elon Musk should take note. After all, what's the point of colonizing Mars when Martian architecture is already colonizing the Bay Area?

And then there's "the largest open office space in the world,"[84] which Mark Zuckerberg has hired Frank Gehry to build for Facebook's 3,400 employees. Zuckerberg's new office resembles Facebook itself: an intensely opaque, secretive company that has built its multibillion-dollar brand upon the lies of transparency and openness. This building might be internally "open," but—like the new Google or Apple corporate city-states dotting the Silicon Valley landscape—it will be firmly shut off from the outside world. Indeed, Zuckerberg, the high priest of everybody else's personal transparency, revealed his own personal commitment to "openness" and "collaboration" when, in October 2013, he spent more than $30 million buying the four houses surrounding his Palo Alto house to guarantee his absolute privacy from the outside world.[85]

As in the medieval world, Google, Apple, and Facebook have detached themselves from the physical reality of the increasingly impoverished communities around them. These companies provide so many free services to their employees—from gourmet meals, babysitting, and gyms, to dry cleaning, medical services, and even living spaces—that they are destroying businesses that have traditionally relied on the business patronage of local workers. The same is even happening in San Francisco. Twitter's new downtown offices feature an in-house dining area called "The Commons," where gourmet meals are always available. But, as the *New York Times*' Allison Arieff notes, Twitter's free food service, while uncommonly good for Twitter employees, has destroyed the business of local restaurants and cafés.[86] So once again, the end result is more distance, literally and otherwise, in what the *Weekly Standard*'s Charlotte Allen called the new "Silicon chasm" in the Bay Area, between digital billionaires and analog beggars.[87]

"It's the opposite of gentrification,"[88] one local critic noted. Yes. And the opposite of gentrification is the impoverishment of communities that have the misfortune of being located next to buildings that resemble spaceships or artificial algorithms. Forget about regional declarations of independence. Internet companies like Google, Apple, Facebook, and Twitter have actually declared independence—architecturally or otherwise—from everything around them. The digital overlords have seceded from the analog peasants. It's the ultimate exit.

CONCLUSION

THE ANSWER

The Fancy-Dress Affair

I first met Michael Birch, the owner of the Battery social club, at a party in Marin County, the exclusive suburb over San Francisco's Golden Gate Bridge where Tom Perkins has one of his trophy mansions. It was one of those rather tiresome sixties nostalgia affairs at which everyone squeezes into the bell-bottomed trousers, Mary Quant miniskirts, and psychedelic shirts of the fifty-year-old counterculture. As a cultural event, it was about as historically authentic as the Venetian Resort Hotel Casino in Las Vegas. But the slightly built, bespectacled Birch, with his long blond flowing hair, already resembled a hippie, with or without the tight purple shirt and matching headband he was wearing for the party. There was a strangely ethereal quality to the Anglo-American entrepreneur. As if he'd just stepped out of an alien spaceship.

We talked beside the hot tub, which, in good Marin County tradition, was already full of revelers. "Hey brother," I asked, trying, without much success, to capture the party's vibe. "What's goin' on?"

What was going on with Michael Birch was the Battery. As we stood together in the warm California evening, he pitched me his vision for the unclub. He explained how he wanted to bring a diverse community together. "Different-thinking people" is how Birch, in the oddly detached language of a Web programmer, put it. He spoke dispassionately about his "social project," which, he told me, would build community and understanding in San Francisco. With his half-British accent and eccentric air, he might have been Jeremy Bentham detailing, with mathematical precision, the social utility of his greatest happiness principle.

"How do you become a member?" I asked.

"We want diversity. Anyone original will be welcome," he explained in a mid-Atlantic drawl. "Especially people who think outside their traditional silos."

"Sounds like the Internet," I said. "Or a village pub."

"Exactly," he said, without smiling.

"So could I join?"

The social engineer peered at me suspiciously, unconvinced, I suspect, by my ability to think outside any *silo*. "You have to be nominated by a member," he mumbled.

He did, however, invite me to visit the Battery. "Thanks," I replied. "I'll come for lunch."

"Cool," he said.

But *cool*, once the aesthetic of genuine rebellion, is no longer cool. The rebellious, disruptive culture of "cool" has instead become the orthodoxy of our networked age. Thomas Friedman describes the social forces of global upheaval, the so-called new Davos Men, as the "Square People"[1]—but the *real* square people of our networked age are those who see themselves as uniquely disruptive. "If you need to inform the world that you are original," notes the *Financial Times*' Edward Luce dryly, "chances are you are not."[2] Beware "Silicon Valley's cool capitalism," warns the *Observer*'s Nick Cohen about alien overlords like Birch, Kevin Systrom, and Sean Parker, who've become the slickly marketed icons of what Cohen calls networked capitalism's "borderless future." This libertarian worship of the unregulated network and disdain for government destroys jobs "without creating new ones," Cohen explains, and it compounds "the already dizzying chasm between the rich and the rest."[3]

The origins of this infinitely disruptive libertarianism, of the only rule being the absence of rules, can be traced back to the 1960s. According to the Stanford University historian Fred Turner, the Internet's borderless idealism, and its ahistorical disdain for hierarchy and authority, especially the traditional role of government, were inherited from the countercultural ideas of Internet pioneers like WELL founder Stewart Brand and the "Declaration of the Independence of Cyberspace" author John Perry Barlow.[4] Silicon Valley, Turner says, has become an extension of the fancy-dress affair in Marin County where I met Michael Birch. It's a sixties nostalgia fantasy hosted by space cadets like Birch who appear to have seceded from both time and space.

To borrow some of Apple's most familiar marketing language, everybody now is supposed to "think different." Unorthodoxy is the new orthodoxy in a world where the supposedly most *different* kind of thinkers—those who have escaped their traditional silo—are branded as the new rock stars. The only convention is to be unconventional and work for uncompanies, join unclubs, or attend unconferences. But today's technology hipsters aren't quite as cool as they imagine. Steve Jobs, the founding father of Silicon Valley's "reality distortion field" and the original tech hipster, who idolized Bob Dylan and spent a summer in an ashram, also outsourced the manufacturing of Apple products in Foxconn's notorious 430,000-person Shenzhen factory.[5] And Jobs ran an astonishingly profitable company that, according to the US senator Carl Levin, has been cleverly avoiding paying the American government a million dollars of tax revenue *per hour*.[6] Rather than "Think Different," "Think Irresponsibly" might have been the mantra of the Apple accountants who organized this unethical and possibly even illegal scheme to avoid paying American tax.

So how can we really think *differently* about the crisis? What's the most innovative strategy for disrupting the disruptors?

Disrupting the Disruptors

Just as there are many questions about today's networked society, so everyone—from activists to writers to entrepreneurs to academics to governments—has their own answer to the Internet's failure to realize most of its much-trumpeted promise. Some of these answers are more coherent and viable than others. But they all are understandable responses to the wrenching economic and social dislocation of networked society.

For the outraged, the knee-jerk answer is smashing the windows of Google buses and calling for the "dismantling of techno-industrial society."[7] For the more contemplative, the answer is switching off the network through "digital detoxes,"[8] technology Sabbaths, or joining the "slow Web" movement.[9] For idealistic Web pioneers like Tim Berners-Lee, the answer is an online "Magna Carta," a digital Bill of Rights that protects the Web's neutrality and openness against both governments and Internet corporations.[10] For other publicly spirited technologists, the answer is developing anti-Google or anti-Facebook products like the "no tracking" search engine DuckDuckGo, the open-source and nonprofit social network Diaspora, and even an ambitiously decentralized project called Bitcloud that aims to create a new Internet.[11] For curated websites like *Popular Science*, which have tired of the inanity of most user-generated content, the answer is banning anonymous comments.[12] For Germany, the answer is in Chancellor Angela Merkel's 2014 proposal to build a European network where data wouldn't pass through the United States.[13]

The answer for the German government may even lie—irony of ironies—in reverting to the technology of the Stasi and using analog typewriters for secret communications, in an effort to protect itself from foreign snoops.[14]

For cultural theorists like Jaron Lanier, the answer is in reinventing the business model of online content to "multitudinous, diverse, tiny flows of royalties."[15] For political critics like the technology scholar Tim Wu and the *Financial Times* columnist John Gapper, the answer lies in Internet entrepreneurs growing out of their "obsessive adolescence" and taking adult responsibility for disruptions like Bitcoin.[16] For humanists like Nicholas Carr, the answer lies in us shaping our networked tools before they shape us. For Internet skeptics like Talking Heads founder and lyricist David Byrne, the answer is that there isn't an answer. "What will life be like after the Internet?" Byrne asks, with his characteristic dark humor. "I mean nothing lasts forever, right?"[17]

In the European Union, where there is a particular sensitivity about data privacy, one controversial answer lies in establishing a "right to be forgotten" law that bans inaccurate and accurate but unflattering online search engine links. While this law, at least in its mid-2014 form, is slightly impractical,[18] it is nonetheless an important beginning to the legal debate about controlling online misinformation. "Discombobulated geniuses" like the hypertext inventor Ted Nelson might think that the network shouldn't have a "concept of deletion," but for the rest of us—especially those whose reputations have been compromised by vicious online smears—there is clearly a need for some sort of "right to be forgotten" legislation that enables us to delete links to these lies.

And yet if there is just one answer, a single solution, to the Internet's epic failure, it is the opposite of forgetting. That answer is more memory—of the human rather than the computer kind. The answer is history.

It's not just Michael Birch who has seceded from time and space. Fukuyama may have thought that history ended in 1989, but it's that other world-historic 1989 event, Tim Berners-Lee's invention of the World Wide Web, that has unintentionally created another, more troubling version of the end of history.

"I recently took my 16-year-old daughter Adele to see a section of the Berlin Wall that has been preserved as part of a museum devoted to the division of the city, Germany and Europe. It was a bright Berlin morning," writes the *New York Times* columnist Roger Cohen about revisiting the divided Berlin of Erich Mielke and the Stasi. "Adele, born in 1997, with just a toehold in the last century, wandered around. She examined these curious relics. Every now and again she checked her Facebook page on her device. 'This just seems so ancient,' she said, leaning back against the wall. 'I mean, it feels like it comes from the 19th century.'"[19]

At least Adele Cohen has a sense of the past, even if she misidentifies it by a hundred years. But for many of her generation of Internet natives, the only time is the perpetual present. As the *Guardian*'s Jonathan Freedland explains, today's networked generation, in their preoccupation with "trading Instagrams and Vines," has created an intimate, always-on culture that will—like a disappearing Snapchat photograph—vanish forever and leave nothing to posterity. "The point is that a fundamental aspect of human life—memory—is being altered by the digital revolution," Freedland warns.[20] The savage irony is that the more accurately the Internet remembers everything, the more our memories atrophy. The result is an amnesia about everything except the immediate, the instant, the now, and the me. It's the end of history as a shared communal memory, the end of our collective engagement with the past and the future. "Once we had a nostalgia for the future," warns Mark Lilla. "Today we have an amnesia for the present."[21]

"The libertarian age," Lilla argues, "is an illegible age."[22] But this isn't quite right, either. It might be illegible for a traditional historian like Lilla, but not for a seasoned observer of networked society like the American media theorist Douglas Rushkoff. "I had been looking forward to the 21st century," Rushkoff writes at the beginning of his 2014 book, *Present Shock: When Everything Happens Now*.[23] But "looking forward," Rushkoff confesses, has gone out of fashion in our networked age of real-time technology. Twentieth-century futurism, he says, has been replaced with a chaotic twenty-first-century "now-ist" culture that resembles Jonas Lindvist's pointillist graphical image on the wall of the Ericsson's Stockholm office. Rather than futurists, Rushkoff observes, we are all now "presentists" locked in to a mesmerizing loop of tweets, updates, emails, and instant messages. It's this "narrative collapse," he says, that makes sense of our hyperconnected world. It's what makes networked society legible.

And so to rebel against this world, to think differently, to question Silicon Valley's ahistorical confidence, means reviving the authority of our collective narrative. It's particularly through the lens of nineteenth- and twentieth-century history that we can best make sense of the impact of the Internet on twenty-first-century society. The past makes the present legible. It's the most effective antidote to the libertarian utopianism of Internet evangelists like John Perry Barlow, who imagines the Internet as something like a fancy-dress rave in exclusive Marin County, where, perhaps not uncoincidentally, Barlow also happens to live.

"Governments of the Industrial World, you weary giants of flesh and steel, I come from Cyberspace, the new home of mind," Barlow wrote in his Declaration of the Independence of Cyberspace. And this fantasy of imagining the Internet magically floating outside time and space, as an unplace, away from the authority of traditional laws, has become the standard justification for Silicon Valley disruption. No wonder the cult book among multibillionaire libertarian entrepreneurs like Sean Parker and Peter Thiel is Tolkien's fantasy *The Lord of the Rings*. Thiel named Palantir, "the creepiest startup ever," according to one British technology journalist,[24] after the seeing stones in Tolkien's trilogy. And Parker spent $10 million in June 2013 on a shamelessly meretricious *Lord of the Rings*–style wedding in the California forest featuring fake medieval stone castles, gates, bridges, and columns.

"For the first time in history, anyone can produce, say, or buy anything," one of the young engineers I met at FailCon promised, articulating a faith in the Internet so magically redemptive that it resembles a Tolkienesque fantasy. He was, however, wrong. Not for the first (or last) time in history, believers are using dramatic language like *for the first time in history* to tout a revolution that isn't really new. Yes, the decentralized network accidentally created by Cold War scientists like Paul Baran and Robert Kahn is original. Yes, today's data factory economy is, in many ways, different from the factories of the industrial age. Yes, Internet technology is fundamentally changing how we communicate and do business with each other. But while all this technology might be novel, it hasn't transformed the role of either power or wealth in the world. Indeed, when it comes to the importance of money and influence, Silicon Valley is about as traditional as those three thousand bottles of vintage wine in the Battery's illustrious cellar.

History is, in many ways, repeating itself. Today's digital upheaval represents what MIT's Erik Brynjolfsson and Andrew McAfee call the "second industrial revolution." "Badass" entrepreneurs like Travis Kalanick and Peter Thiel have much in common with the capitalist robber barons of the first industrial revolution. Internet monopolists like Google and Amazon increasingly resemble the bloated multinationals of the industrial epoch. The struggle of eighteenth-century Yorkshire cloth workers is little different from today's resistance of organized labor to Amazon, Uber, and Airbnb. Our growing concern with the pollution of "data exhaust" is becoming the equivalent of the environmental movement for the digital age. Web 2.0 companies like Facebook, YouTube, and Instagram have reassembled the Bentham brothers' eighteenth-century Panopticon as data factories. Bentham's utilitarianism, that bizarre project to quantify every aspect of the human condition, has reappeared in the guise of the quantified-self movement. Even the nineteenth-century debate between Bentham's utilitarianism and John Stuart Mill's liberalism over individual rights has reappeared in what Harvard Law School's Cass Sunstein calls "the politics of libertarian paternalism"—a struggle between "Millville" and "Benthamville" about the role of "nudge" in a world where the government, through partnerships with companies like Acxiom and Palantir, has more and more data on us all[25] and Internet companies like Facebook and OkCupid run secretive experiments designed to control our mood.

Nick Cohen describes the "cool capitalism" of the networked age as our "borderless future."[26] But while Paul Baran, Vint Cerf, and Tim Berners-Lee consciously designed the Internet to be without a center, that distributed architecture hasn't been extended to the all-important realms of money or power. Here the future is actually as *bordered* as the past. And its center is in Silicon Valley, the home of Michael Birch and the other alien overlords of our digital age.

The Medium Is Not the Message

In May 2014, I spoke alongside Alec Ross, the former senior advisor for innovation to Hillary Clinton and a particularly smooth-talking Internet evangelist, at the European Parliament in Brussels.[27] In this influential political chamber, where some of the most innovative Internet legislation is being enacted, such as the EU's "right to be forgotten" law, Ross laid out a binary vision of twenty-first-century networked society. Rather than the old difference between left and right ideologies, he predicted, the key distinction in what he called "the shift in power from hierarchies to networks of citizens" would be between the good "open" society and the bad "closed" society.

But, like other Internet evangelists such as John Perry Barlow and *Without Their Permission* author Alexis Ohanian, Ross has mistaken the medium for the message. "We shape our tools and thereafter our tools shape us," McLuhan wrote. And the error these evangelists make is to assume that the Internet's open, decentered technology naturally translates into a less hierarchical or unequal society. But rather than more openness and the destruction of hierarchies, an unregulated network society is breaking the old center, compounding economic and cultural inequality, and creating a digital generation of masters of the universe. This new power may be rooted in a borderless network, but it still translates into massive wealth and power for a tiny handful of companies and individuals.

"In Darwinian terms these new corporate giants are just the latest stage in the evolution of the public corporation," warns the Internet historian and journalist John Naughton about "open" Internet companies like Facebook, Yahoo, Amazon, and Google. "They exist to create wealth—vast quantities of it—for their founders and shareholders. Their imperative is to grow and achieve dominance in their chosen markets—as well as in others which they now deem to be within their reach. They are as hostile to trade unions, taxation, and regulation as John D. Rockefeller, J. P. Morgan and Andrew Carnegie ever were in their day. The only difference is that the new titans employ far fewer people, enjoy higher margins and are less harassed by governments than their predecessors."[28]

In their infatuation with an "open" and "permissionless" future, Internet evangelists like Ross and Ohanian have failed to learn from the past. The first industrial revolution was, for the most part, a success because it blended openness with new laws to regulate its excesses. What George Packer calls "the great leveling" of the Roosevelt Republic and Harvard economists Claudia Goldin and Lawrence Katz describe as the "golden age" of labor was secured through progressive government regulation on labor law, taxation, working conditions, competition, and, above all, antitrust issues. Robber barons like John D. Rockefeller and industrial monopolies like Standard Oil didn't just go away. They were legislated out of existence.

As the distinguished New York University and London School of Economics sociologist Richard Sennett notes, these progressives actually "set great store on the power of technology to build a better society." But unlike "your garden-variety Silicon Valley billionaire," Sennett explains, "the progressives of a century ago believed that once in power, the plutocrat would inevitably stifle talent which threatened his or her domain."[29] And that's why, according to Sennett, "it's time to break up Google." The "problem is simple," he says. "The company is just too powerful, as are Apple and many other big tech groups."

"Were he alive today," Sennett writes about President Theodore Roosevelt, the American president who trust-busted Standard Oil, "I believe Roosevelt would concentrate his firepower on Google, Microsoft and Apple. We need modern politicians who will be similarly bold."[30]

"Imagine that it's 1913 and the post office, the phone company, the public library, printing houses, the U.S. Geological Survey mapping operations, movie houses, and all atlases are largely controlled by a secretive corporation unaccountable to the public," Rebecca Solnit writes in an article about Google's new monopolistic power. "Jump a century and see that in the online world that's more or less where we are."[31]

The answer, the most important solution to the Internet's epic fail, lies in the work of political bodies like the European

Parliament or the United States Congress, which, *with our permission*, controls "secretive" monopolistic corporations like Google. As Mathias Dopfner, the head of Europe's largest newspaper company, Germany's Axel Springer publishing house, and an outspoken critic of Google's attempt to create what he calls a "digital superstate," said in April 2014, "institutions in Brussels have never been as important as they are now."[32]

The answer is shaping what GigaOm columnist Mathew Ingram calls the Internet's "quasi-monopolies"[33] before they shape us. The answer is Richard Sennett's "bold politicians," able to stand up to quasi-monopolists like Google. The answer is an accountable, strong government able to stand up to the "alien forces" of Silicon Valley big data companies.[34] The answer is the aggressive antitrust investigation of Google conducted by EU competition commissioner Joaquín Almunia. The answer is a politician like Margaret Hodge, the chair of the British House of Commons public accounts committee, who, while investigating Google's tax avoidance scheme in the United Kingdom, told a Google executive that his company's tax behavior was "devious, calculated and, in my view, unethical."[35] The answer, as Marc Rotenberg, the executive director of the Electronic Privacy Information Center, argues, is "putting teeth" into privacy fines against "one of the biggest violations in history"—Google's "Street View" mapping program, which secretly aggregated information from private homes and intercepted communications from personal Wi-Fi networks.[36] The answer, as the Italian government has insisted, is to require Google to obey European law and ask permission before creating a profile of Internet users.[37]

It's not just Google that needs to be confronted by the government. The answer also lies in a bold political response to other Internet giants, like Jeff Bezos's Amazon. In July 2014, the *Nation*'s Steve Wasserman asked the right question: "When will the Justice Department take on Amazon?"[38] We should thus celebrate the

2013 efforts of German antitrust watchdog the Bundeskartellamt to investigate Amazon's unfair pricing practices against its third-party partners.[39] We should welcome the July 2014 decision by the US Federal Trade Commission to sue Amazon for allegedly allowing children to make millions of dollars of unauthorized purchases in its app store.[40] We should encourage the efforts of the International Association of Machinists and Aerospace Workers to petition the National Labor Relations Board to enable Amazon workers in US warehouses to form their first labor union.[41] Above all, we should applaud the efforts of small publishers like Melville House's Dennis Loy Johnson to challenge the increasingly monopolistic power of Amazon in the book business. "How is this not extortion?" Johnson asked about Amazon's 2014 decision to delay shipments of books from Hachette and the German publisher Bonnier after they failed to agree to a business arrangement in which Amazon demanded broader discounts and extra marketing fees. "You know, the thing that is illegal when the Mafia does it."[42] As Brad Stone notes, Amazon is becoming "increasingly monolithic in markets like books and electronics," which is why he believes that antitrust authorities will inevitably come to scrutinize Amazon's market power.[43] Let's hope that there will be politicians bold enough to take on Bezos before Amazon becomes, quite literally, the Everything Store.

No, the Internet is *not* the answer, especially when it comes to the so-called sharing economy of peer-to-peer networks like Uber and Airbnb. The good news is that, as *Wired*'s Marcus Wohlsen put it, the "sun is setting on the wild west" of ride- and apartment-sharing networks.[44] Tax collectors and municipalities from Cleveland to Hamburg are recognizing that many peer-to-peer rentals and ride-sharing apps are breaking both local and national housing and transportation laws. What the *Financial Times* calls a "regulatory backlash"[45] has pushed Uber to limit surge pricing during emergencies[46] and forced Airbnb hosts to install smoke and carbon monoxide detectors in their homes.[47] "Just because a company has an app instead of a storefront doesn't mean consumer protection laws don't apply," notes the New York State attorney general Eric Schneiderman, who is trying to subpoena Airbnb's user data in New York City.[48] A group of housing activists in San Francisco is even planning a late 2014 ballot measure in the city that would "severely curb" Airbnb's operations.[49] "Airbnb is bringing up the rent despite what the company says," explains the New York City–based political party Working Families.[50]

The answer is to use the law and regulation to force the Internet out of its prolonged adolescence. Whether it's Philadelphia's 2013 decision to ban 3-D-printed weapons[51] or a 2014 European Court of Human Rights ruling on the responsibility of websites to police their users' comments[52] or California governor Jerry Brown's 2013 bill to outlaw online revenge porn[53] or the French so-called anti-Amazon law, which doesn't allow free shipping on discounted books,[54] or Thomas Piketty's call for a global tax on plutocrats like Mark Zuckerberg or Larry Page, active legislation is the most effective way to make the Internet a fairer and better place. Rather than asking what will life be like after the Internet, the real question is what life could be like if the Wild West openness of the Internet were tempered by the external authority of government.

But these external controls don't always need to originate from government. One of the most effective strategies for fighting online piracy has stemmed from voluntary, market-led solutions uniting private companies across the Internet economy—from content creators and ISPs to payment processors and even search providers. In 2011, for example, there was a US-based voluntary agreement, the so-called "six strikes" copyright enforcement plan, signed by AT&T, Cablevision, Comcast, Time Warner Cable, Verizon, and the major record labels, designed to reduce online piracy.[55] Beginning in June 2011, American

Express, Discover, MasterCard, PayPal, and Visa worked with the City of London Police on a set of best practices for withdrawing payment to websites that distribute stolen content.[56] And in July 2013, AOL, Condé Nast, Microsoft, Yahoo, and Google were among signatories of an Interactive Advertising Bureau plan designed to cut off the flow of advertising revenue to websites profiting from illegal content.[57] These kinds of voluntary efforts by the private sector should be seen as complementing rather than competing with government efforts to police the Internet. Indeed, as the then US Intellectual Property Enforcement coordinator, Victoria Espinel, noted about the 2013 Interactive Advertising Bureau plan, it would actually "further encourage the innovation made possible by an open Internet."[58]

Libertarian disruptors like John Perry Barlow and Alexis Ohanian would, no doubt, disagree with Espinel, arguing that any kind of external controls on the Internet would undermine innovation. But this is wrong, too. As AOL founder Steve Case has argued, the "coming Internet revolutions in areas such as education and health care" will require partnering with government.[59] And as Sussex University economist Mariana Mazzucato showed in her important 2013 book, *The Entrepreneurial State*, the most significant innovations—such as Tim Berners-Lee's invention of the World Wide Web at CERN in 1989—have come out of the public sector.[60] Even Google and Apple, Mazzucato notes, were originally funded by public money—Apple by a $500,000 government loan before it went public and Google by Sergey Brin's National Science Foundation grant to fund his graduate studies at Stanford.[61]

I'm not sure I'd go quite as far as the Canadian political theorist Michael Ignatieff, whose answer is "a new Bismarck to tame the machines." But Ignatieff's question is the most important one facing us all in the early twenty-first century. "A question haunting democratic politics everywhere," he says, "is whether elected governments can control the cyclone of technological change sweeping through their societies."[62]

The answer to Ignatieff's question is yes. Elected governments exist so that we can shape the society in which we live. There's no other alternative to controlling technological change. Not distributed capitalism or peer-to-peer government or MOOCs, data factories, or some other libertarian scheme to make a few Internet entrepreneurs obscenely rich and powerful. From downtown Rochester to London's Berwick Street to Silicon Valley itself, that cyclone is doing much more harm than good. The Internet's current Epic Fail isn't necessarily its final grade. But to improve, it needs to grow up quickly and take responsibility for its actions.

The Alien Spaceship

A couple of weeks after meeting Michael Birch, I had lunch with a friend at the Battery. There was no Soylent on the menu. Instead, we dined on grilled octopus and shared a vintage bottle of Russian River Chardonnay. The service, the wine, and the organic food produced by local, sustainable farms were all impeccable. We were treated like lords by the club's obsequious domestic staff—which wasn't surprising, since the Battery had been designed by Ken Fulk, the high-society event planner who organized Sean Parker's $10 million *Lord of the Rings* fantasy wedding and who is a big fan of television dramas like *Downton Abbey* that glorify two-tier societies.[63]

After lunch, I took a tour of the Battery, which, with its not-so-secret poker room and its wood-paneled library lined with unread books, resembled a nineteenth-century gentleman's club as imagined by a twenty-first-century fantasist. The Battery might have been a gigantic Instagram photo. *Hello this is us*, it was saying about a Silicon Valley that has seceded from time and space. Half a century ago, J. C. R. Licklider imagined a human-computer symbiosis that would "save humanity." Little did Licklider imagine, however, that his intergalactic computer network would end up financing the building of an alien spaceship in downtown San Francisco.

Chrystia Freeland, the author of *Plutocrats*[64] and an authority on the rise of the new global superrich and the fall of everyone else, has a compelling explanation of why fantasists like Fulk find nostalgic dramas like *Downton Abbey* so seductive. It's a contemporaneous show, she argues, because there is a "profound similarity between the vast economic, social, and political changes that drive the action in 'Downton Abbey' and our own time."[65] In our digital age of perpetual creative destruction, Freeland says, technology companies like Google, Uber, and Facebook are, on the one hand, enabling the vast personal fortunes of twenty-first-century Internet plutocrats like Mark Zuckerberg and Travis Kalanick; and, on the other, wrecking the lives of a woman like Pam Wetherington, the nonunionized worker at Amazon's Kentucky warehouse who was fired after suffering stress fractures in both feet after walking for miles on the warehouse's concrete floor.

But there is one important difference between *Downton Abbey* and Silicon Valley, Freeland reminds us. "With their lavish lifestyles, the aristocrats of 'Downton Abbey' may seem like a 20th-century version of our own plutocrats, but they are not," she says, because today's "aristocracy of talent" have "all the perks and few of the traditional values" of the old Downton Abbey aristocracy."[66] And so, in the Silicon Valley of 2014, there are all the social and economic hierarchies of 1914 without any of what Freeland calls "the social constraints" of the old aristocracy. We have Downton Abbey reinvented as the Battery. We have secession fantasies and $130 million yachts as long as football fields and billionaire uberlibertarians with staffs of black-clad blondes and white-coated butlers. We have massively meretricious wealth with minimal social responsibility. We have a new nobility without any noblesse oblige. What we have is certainly not the answer to the deepening economic and social inequalities and injustices of the early twenty-first century.

The answer, then, can't just be more regulation from government. Noblesse oblige, after all, can't be legislated. As critics like Tim Wu have argued, the answer lies in our new digital elite becoming accountable for the most traumatic socioeconomic disruption since the industrial revolution. Rather than thinking differently, the ethic of this new elite should be to think traditionally. Rather than seceding to Burning Man or Mars, this plutocracy must be beamed back down to earth. "Move fast and break things" was the old hacker ethic; "you break it, you own it" should be the new one. Rather than an Internet Bill of Rights, what we really need is an informal Bill of Responsibilities that establishes a new social contract for every member of networked society.

Silicon Valley has fetishized the ideals of collaboration and conversation. But where we need real collaboration is in our conversation about the impact of the Internet on society. This is a conversation that affects everyone from digital natives to the precariat to Silicon Valley billionaires. And it's a conversation in which we all need to take responsibility for our online actions—whether it's our narcissistic addiction to social media, our anonymous cruelty, or our lack of respect for the intellectual property of creative professionals. The answer lies in the kind of responsible self-regulation laid out in William Powers's *Hamlet's BlackBerry*, his excellent guide for building a good life in the digital age.[67]

"You have only one identity," Mark Zuckerberg so memorably trivialized the complexity of the human condition. In our conversation about the Internet, we need to recognize that our multiple identities are often at odds. For example, the Internet is generally excellent for consumers. But it's much more problematic for citizens. Internet evangelists, especially libertarian entrepreneurs like Jeff Bezos, see everything in terms of satisfying the customer. And while Amazon does indeed satisfy most of us as consumers, it is having a far less satisfactory outcome for citizens, who are more and more concerned with the reliability of information, the civility of discourse, and the respect for individual privacy.

It's a conversation that needs to take place in Silicon Valley, Silicon Alley, and the other centers of digital power in our networked world. The time is now ripe for this. Some of the more responsible entrepreneurs, academics, and investors are finally recognizing that the Internet—the technological revolution they believed would make the world a radically better place—hasn't been an unmitigated success. Sequoia Capital's Michael Moritz warns about the increasing inequality of our digital age. Union Square Ventures's Fred Wilson worries about the dangerous new monopolies of our digital economy. New York University's Clay Shirky is troubled by the tragic fate of journalists in a world without print newspapers. Charles Leadbeater says the Web has lost its way. Emily Bell frets about our new media one percent economy. Marc Andreessen is concerned with the impact of anonymous networks on civic life. MIT's Ethan Zuckerman worries that the Internet's "Original Sin," its reliance on free advertising's supporting content, has transformed the network into a fiasco. Distinguished bloggers, writers, and journalists like Dave Winer, Astra Taylor, John Naughton, Dan Gillmor, Om Malik, and Mathew Ingram all fear the power of large Internet companies like Google, Amazon, and Facebook. Jeff Jarvis is disgusted by the plague of trolls, abusers, harassers, lunatics, imposters, and assholes on the Internet.

"What society are we building here?" Jarvis asks.[68] And that question should be the beginning of every conversation about the Internet. Like it or not, the digital world is reshaping our society with a bewildering speed. The fate of employment, identity, privacy, prosperity, justice, and civility are all being transformed by networked society. The Internet may not (yet) be the answer, but it nonetheless remains the central question of the first quarter of the twenty-first century.

On my way out of the club, I passed by some words inscribed on a black marble slab. WE SHAPE OUR BUILDINGS; THEREAFTER THEY SHAPE US, they said. Outside, a cold fog had drifted in from the Bay. It felt good to be back in the anonymous city—that reassuring place of self-erasure and self-invention. I shivered and, dodging a couple of networked Uber limousines, hailed a licensed yellow cab.

"So what's that new club like?" the driver asked me as we sped off down Battery Street toward San Francisco's South of Market (SoMa) district, where the new offices of Internet companies like Twitter, Yelp, and Instagram are destroying local businesses.

"It's a failure," I replied. "An epic fucking failure."

AFTERWORD
ONE YEAR LATER

If, as the former British prime minister Harold Wilson once quipped, a week is a long time in politics, then a year is an eternity in Silicon Valley. Writing a year after I finished the hardcover version of *The Internet Is Not the Answer*, nothing—and yet everything—in the digital economy has changed. *Plus ça change, plus c'est la même chose*. Disruption remains the norm here. The technology industry is still in a perpetual, Moore's Law–driven upheaval. The Internet, with its billions of users, continues to turn the world upside down.

The last year has seen the appearance of tens of thousands of new startups and billions of dollars of fresh investment capital financing the digital revolution in markets as disparate as finance, education, health care, and transportation. Over the last twelve months, hitherto futuristic notions like the "sharing economy," the "Internet of Things," and "artificial intelligence" have become increasingly common parlance. In the last year, the valuations of cutting-edge private Internet startups have skyrocketed with Peter Thiel's creepy big-data corporation Palantir Technologies, worth $20 billion; Airbnb, worth $24 billion; and Travis Kalanick's notorious peer-to-peer transportation network Uber, worth a mind-boggling $50 billion. There has even been a spate of movies and television shows like Alex Garland's critically acclaimed *Ex Machina* and AMC's blockbuster television series *Humans*, about a future in which humans and networked robots have become indistinguishable.

The last year has also seen a sharp shift in the public mood about the digital revolution. The central warnings in my book—of the Internet's impact on unemployment and inequality, and an increasingly ubiquitous surveillance economy—have become a concern not only of technology writers but also of many entrepreneurs, investors, and politicians. There are more and more conferences, books, and television shows about the dark side of technological progress. The zeitgeist has clearly shifted. My skepticism about the benefits of network society, once considered by some critics to be reactionary, now represents conventional wisdom.

So, if I were writing *The Internet Is Not the Answer* today, in the summer of 2015, what would I add? What's really *changed* in the last year? How different does the digital revolution appear today than it did a year ago?

Making sense of the ever-changing digital landscape is rather like being imprisoned in the always-on culture of social media. The challenge is to escape the selfie-centric narcissism of the latest Twitter scandal or Facebook outrage. The challenge is to stand back and think in a broad historical context about the digital revolution.

And it's here that I'd like to add one new idea to my book. It's something that occurred to me in June 2015, while I was interviewing AOL founder and former CEO Steve Case at one of my Futurecast salons. Trying to establish some distance of his own from the day-to-day chaos of the digital revolution, Case presented the history of the Internet to me in terms of three historical stages. The first period, he explained, extended through the last quarter of the twentieth century, when infrastructure companies like AOL were building the foundations of the Internet. The second, he argued, was the so-called "Web 2.0" period between around 2000 and 2015, in which "free" media platform companies like Google and Facebook built their dominant Internet services and products. And the third stage, he concluded, beginning around now, is the period in which the Internet begins to revolutionize industries in the rest of the economy, such as education, health care, finance, and transportation.

While this economic take on Internet history certainly isn't wrong, it occurred to me that there's another, more political way of making sense of the digital revolution that can be understood in parallel with Steve Case's version. Like Case, I have a trinitarian reading of the Internet's history; unlike him, however, my version focuses on politics rather than economics.

The first period, as I've outlined in my first chapter, "The Network," lasted between the end of the Second World War and the early 1990s. This period was characterized by the public-spirited contributions of pioneering technologists like Vannevar Bush, Norbert Wiener, J. C. R. Licklider, Paul Baran, and the inventor of the World Wide Web, Tim Berners-Lee. In political terms, this first period was shaped by the investment from non-profit, public institutions like MIT's Lincoln Laboratory and the Advanced Research Projects Agency (ARPA). The British physicist Tim Berners-Lee—who, you'll remember, believed that charging for licensing fees for Web browser technology represented an "act of treason"—exemplifies this idealistic spirit.

The second period of the Internet's history, covered by my second chapter, "The Money," extended from the early 1990s to now. It is characterized by the Internet's radical deregulation and the transformation of Silicon Valley into an increasingly speculative market dominated by venture capitalists like Tom Perkins and Marc Andreessen and entrepreneurs like Travis Kalanick and Peter Thiel. This uncontrolled version of the Internet, a digital economy dominated by supposedly "free" technologies like Facebook and Google, is the reason why the Internet is currently *not* the answer. It is compounding the inequality between rich and poor, hollowing out the middle class, deepening our crisis of unemployment, and creating a surveillance economy in which we, the Internet user, have become its primary product.

Some people criticize me as a curmudgeon, a miserably pessimistic critic with nothing positive to say about technological progress. But they are wrong. In this afterword, I am, in fact, the bringer of good tidings. The good news is that we are now on the cusp of a much more positive stage in digital history. I confess that I missed this when I wrote *The Internet Is Not the Answer* in 2014. But today, I can see the digital forest for the trees, and, I'm glad to say, I can report positive news on the near horizon. A year is indeed a *very* long time in Silicon Valley.

In my concluding chapter, "The Answer," I argued that the solution to the excesses of the second period of Internet history was regulation—governmental, corporate, and self-regulation. But this conclusion was a little tentative and, I confess, more hopeful than confident. When I wrote it, I don't think I really believed that regulation could reign in radical disruptiveness of out-of-control libertarians like Travis Kalanick and Peter Thiel. I wasn't confident that politics could be the answer.

I was wrong. Over the last year, we have seen the emergence of the third stage in the history of the Internet. It represents the end of what President Barack Obama, in a Stanford University speech in February 2015, dubbed the "Wild Wild West" Internet period.[1] "The very technologies that can empower us to do great good can also be used to undermine us and do great harm," President Obama argued, as he called for what the *New York Times* described as a "new era of cooperation between the government and the private sector to defeat a range of fast-evolving online threats" in the big-data age of network surveillance.[2]

Over the last year, the emergence of the third stage in the history of the Internet, Obama's "new era of cooperation"—let's called it the Political Age—has been particularly pronounced in Europe. On August 31, 2014, the Danish politician Margrethe Vestager replaced Joaquín Almunia as the European Commissioner for Competition. The appointment represents a watershed moment in European relations with Silicon Valley. Dubbed "the Enforcer" by the *Economist*,[3] Vestager is, according to *Time*, Google's "worst nightmare."[4] Unlike Almunia, Vestager has been willing to challenge Google on its monopolistic behavior in Europe, filing antitrust charges against the Mountain View leviathan in April 2015.

Barack Obama's new era of cooperation between Silicon Valley and the outside world, of course, doesn't just happen. In 2015, it's politics, rather than economics, that's different. New sheriffs in town like Margrethe Vestager and Günther Oettinger, the EU commissioner in charge of the digital economy, appear committed to taking Silicon Valley's Wild Wild West. Senior EU officials in February 2015 even floated a plan to create a new EU-wide regulator for not only Google and Facebook, but also a swath of mainly U.S.-based Internet companies, including Amazon, Uber, and Twitter.

And Silicon Valley is also getting the message that the rules have changed both in Europe and in the United States. Today's new political stage calls for a different kind of technology company, one that recognizes that the Wild Wild West days of the Internet are now becoming history. Thus, even Uber, the wildest of all Silicon Valley's outlaw companies, appointed David Plouffe, Barack Obama's sweet-talking former campaign manager, as its SVP of Policy and Strategy in September 2014, while Marc Andreessen's venture capital firm, Andreessen Horowitz, has gone

one stage farther—appointing in April 2015 its first policy and regulatory affairs group, headed up by Facebook's former general council.[5]

So one year later, the news from Silicon Valley isn't bad. Of course, the Internet still isn't the answer. But over the last twelve months, things have improved, as more and more public figures have recognized the need to reshape the unregulated Internet of its "money" period. We can't—and shouldn't—want to return to the network's earliest history, with its intrinsic hostility to the market. But in this new political age of the Internet, a mixture of innovation and regulation promises that the Internet can indeed become a successful operating system for twenty-first-century connected life.

Andrew Keen
June 2015

ACKNOWLEDGMENTS

Sometimes one gets lucky. In March 2013, at Julia Hobsbawm's Names Not Numbers conference in the delightful little town of Adeburgh on the Suffolk coast, I had the great fortune to meet the Atlantic Books CEO Toby Munday. Over copious cups of tea at a little café on the seafront, Toby convinced me to write a book synthesizing all my ideas about the Internet. The book was originally entitled *Epic Fail.* But having sold the American rights to Morgan Entrekin, the publisher of Grove Atlantic in New York, Morgan wisely convinced us to change its name to *The Internet Is Not the Answer.*

Toby is a great salesman. "It'll be easy," he promised me in Aldeburgh. "Just summarize evrything you know about the Internet." But books, of course, are anything but easy and *The Internet Is Not the Answer* is as much Toby and Morgan's book (at least its good bits) as mine. Morgan was a particularly insightful editor, encouraging me to concentrate on the book's historical dimension and its structure. Thanks also to the teams at both Grove Atlantic in New York City and Atlantic Books in London. especially the excellent Peter Blackstock who has worked tirelessly with me throughout the editorial process. Many thanks also to my agent, George Lucas; to my researchers, Sophia Dominguez, Brittany

Sholes, Quan Nguyen, and Nico Appel; and to Dodi Axelson for kindly setting up my visit to the Ericsson offices in Stockholm.

I also got lucky in early 2010 when I recieved a call from my friend Keith Teare, Mike Arrington's cofounder at TechCrunch, who was setting up the TechCrunchTV network. Keith recommended me to Paul Carr and Jon Orlin at TechCrunchTV, and my show *Keen On . . .* was the first program on the network, running for four years and including over two hundred interviews with leading Internet thinkers and critics. In particular, I'd like to thank Kurt Andersen, John Borthwick, Stewart Brand, Po Bronson, Erik Brynjolfsson, Nicholas Carr, Clayton Christensen, Ron Conway, Tyler Cowen, Kenneth Cukier, Larry Downes, Tim Draper, Esther Dyson, George Dyson, Walter Isaacson, Tim Ferriss, Michael Fertik, Ze Frank, David Frigstad, James Gleick, Seth Godin, Peter Hirshberg, Reid Hoffman, Ryan Holiday, Brad Horowitz, Jeff Jarvis, Kevin Kelly, David Kirkpatrick, Ray Kurzweil, Jaron Lanier, Robert Levine, Steven Levy, Viktor Mayer-Schönberger, Andrew McAfee, Gavin Newsom, George Packer, Eli Pariser, Andrew Rasiej, Douglas Rushkoff, Chris Schroeder, Tiffany Shlain, Robert Scoble, Dov Seidman, Gary Shapiro, Clay Shirky, Micah Sifry, Martin Sorrell, Tom Standage, Bruce Sterling, Brad Stone, Clive Thompson, Sherry Turkle, Fred Turner, Yossi Vardi, Hans Vestberg, Vivek Wadhwa, and Steve Wozniak for appearing on *Keen On . . .* and sharing their valuable ideas with me.

NOTES

Preface

1 *The Cult of the Amateur: How Today's Internet Is Killing Our Culture* (New York: Currency/Doubleday, 2007), and *Digital Vertigo: How Today's Online Social Revolution Is Dividing, Diminishing, and Disorienting Us* (New York: St. Martin, 2012).

Introduction

1 Carolyne Zinko, "New Private S.F. Club the Battery," *SFGate*, October 4, 2013.

2 Renée Frojo, "High-Society Tech Club Reborn in San Francisco," *San Francisco Business Times*, April 5, 2013.

3 The Battery describes itself on its website: "Indeed, here is where they came to refill their cups. To tell stories. To swap ideas. To eschew status but enjoy the company of those they respected. Here is where they came to feel at home on an evening out." For more, see: thebatterysf.com/club.

4 Liz Gannes, "Bebo Founders Go Analog with Exclusive Battery Club in San Francisco," AllThingsD, May 21, 2013.

5 Zinko, "New Private S.F. Club the Battery."

6 Ibid.

7 "A lie can travel halfway around the world while the truth is putting on its shoes," Twain originally said. See Alex Ayres, *Wit and Wisdom*

of Mark Twain: A Book of Quotations (New York: Dover, 1999), p. 35.

8 Julie Zeveloff, "A Tech Entrepreneur Supposedly Spent $35 Million on San Francisco's Priciest House," *Business Insider*, April 16, 2013, businessinsider.com/trevor-traina-buys-san-francisco-mansion-2013-4?op=1.

9 Anisse Gross, "A New Private Club in San Francisco, and an Old Diversity Challenge," *New Yorker*, October 9, 2013.

10 Timothy Egan, "Dystopia by the Bay," *New York Times*, December 5, 2013.

11 David Runciman, "Politics or Technology—Which Will Save the World?," *Guardian*, May 23, 2014.

12 John Lanchester, "The Snowden Files: Why the British Public Should Be Worried About GCHQ," *Guardian*, October 3, 2013.

13 Thomas L. Friedman, "A Theory of Everything (Sort Of)," *New York Times*, August 13, 2011.

14 Saul Klein, "Memo to boards: the internet is staying," *Financial Times*, August 5, 2014.

15 Mark Lilla, "The Truth About Our Libertarian Age," *New Republic*, June 17, 2014.

16 Craig Smith, "By the Numbers: 30 Amazing Reddit Statistics," expandedramblings.com, February 26, 2014.

17 Alexis Ohanian, *Without Their Permission: How the 21st Century Will Be Made, Not Managed* (New York: Grand Central, 2013).

18 Alexis C. Madrigal, "It Wasn't Sunil Tripathi: The Anatomy of a Misinformation Disaster," *Atlantic*, April 2013.

19 Lilla, "The Truth About Our Libertarian Age."

20 Zeynep Tufekci, "Facebook and Engineering the Public," *Medium*, June 29, 2014.

21 Pew Research Center, "The Web at 25 in the U.S.: The Overall Verdict: The Internet Has Been a Plus for Society and an Especially Good Thing for Individual Users."

22 Esha Chhabra, "Ubiquitous Across Globe, Cellphones Have Become Tool for Doing Good," *New York Times*, November 8, 2013.

23 Julia Angwin, "Has Privacy Become a Luxury Good?," *New York Times*, March 3, 2014.

24 Marshall McLuhan, *Understanding Media: The Extensions of Man* (Cambridge, MA: MIT Press, 1994), p. xi.

25 Ibid.

Chapter One

1 "Ericsson Mobility Report," 2013.

2 Mat Honan, "Don't Diss Cheap Smartphones. They're About to Change Everything," *Wired*, May 16, 2014.

3 Tim Worstall, "More People Have Mobile Phones Than Toilets," *Forbes*, March 23, 2013.

4 "More Than 50 Billion Connected Devices," Ericsson white paper.

5 Michael Chui, Markus Loffler, and Roger Roberts, "The Internet of Things," *McKinsey Quarterly*, March 2010.

6 Matthieu Pelissie du Rausas, James Manyika, Eric Hazan, Jacques Burghin, Michael Chui, and Remi Said, "Internet Matters: The Net's Sweeping Impact on Growth, Jobs, and Prosperity," *McKinsey*, May 2011.

7 See: "Data Never Sleeps 2.0," infographic from the data company Domo, domo.com/learn/data-never-sleeps-2.

8 Clive Thompson, "Dark Hero of the Information Age: The Original Computer Geek," *New York Times*, March 20, 2005.

9 James Harkin, *Cyburbia: The Dangerous Idea That's Changing How We Live and Who We Are* (London: Little, Brown, 2009), p. 19.

10 John Naughton, *A Brief History of the Future: From Radio Days to Internet Years in a Lifetime* (Woodstock, NY: Overlook Press, 2000), p. 52.

11 Norbert Wiener, *Cybernetics: or Control and Communication in the Animal and the Machine* (Cambridge, MA: MIT Press,1948).

12 Harkin, *Cyburbia*, p. 22.

13 Vannevar Bush, "As We May Think," *Atlantic Monthly*, July 1945.

14 Naughton, *A Brief History of the Future*, p. 65.

15 "Science, The Endless Frontier," a report to the president by Vannevar Bush, director of the Office of Scientific Research and Development, July 1945.

16 Naughton, *A Brief History of the Future*, p. 70.

17 Katie Hafner and Matthew Lyon, *Where Wizards Stay Up Late: The Origins of the Internet* (New York: Simon & Schuster, 2006), p. 34.

18 Ibid.

19 Ibid., p. 38.

20 Paul Dickson, "Sputnik's Impact on America," PBS, November 6, 2007.

21 Hafner and Lyon, *Where Wizards Stay Up Late*, p. 20.

22 Ibid., p. 15.

23 Naughton, *A Brief History of the Future*, p. 95.

24 "I was driving one day to UCLA from RAND and couldn't find a single parking spot in all of UCLA nor the entire adjacent town of Westwood," Baran recalled. "At that instant I concluded that it was God's will that I should discontinue school. Why else would He have found it necessary to fill up all the parking lots at that exact instant?," Hafner and Lyon, *Where Wizards Stay Up Late*, p. 54.

25 Naughton, *A Brief History of the Future*, p. 92.

26 Hafner and Lyon, *Where Wizards Stay Up Late*, p. 55.

27 Ibid., p. 56.

28 Johnny Ryan, *A History of the Internet and the Digital Future* (London: Reaktion Books, 2010), p. 22.

29 Ibid., p. 16.

30 Hafner and Lyon, *Where Wizards Stay Up Late*, pp. 41–42.

31 Ibid., p. 263.

32 Ryan, *A History of the Internet and the Digital Future*, p. 39.

33 Ibid., p. 249.

34 Janet Abbate, *Inventing the Internet* (Cambridge, MA: MIT Press, 1999), p. 186.

35 Larry Downes and Chunka Mui, *Unleashing the Killer App: Digital Strategies for Market Dominance* (Boston: Harvard Business School Press, 1998).

36 Ibid.

37 Outlook Team, "The 41-Year History of Email," Mashable, September 20, 2012.

38 John Perry Barlow, "A Declaration of the Independence of Cyberspace," February 8, 1996.

39 David A. Kaplan, *The Silicon Boys and Their Valley of Dreams* (New York: Perennial, 2000), p. 229.

40 Naughton, *A Brief History of the Future*, p. 218.

41 Bush, "As We May Think."

42 Gary Wolf, "The Curse of Xanadu," *Wired*, June 1995.

43 Tim Berners-Lee, *Weaving the Web* (New York: HarperCollins, 1999), p. 5.

44 Ibid.

45 Ibid., p. 6.

46 Mariana Mazzucato, *The Entrepreneurial State: Debunking Public vs. Private Sector Myths* (London: Anthem Press, 2013), p. 105.

47 John Cassidy, *DOT.CON: The Real Story of Why the Internet Bubble Burst* (Penguin, 2002), p 19.

48 Naughton, *A Brief History of the Future*, ch. 15.

49 Ibid., p. 261.

Chapter Two

1 David Streitfeld, "Tom Perkins, Defender of the 1% Once Again," *New York Times*, February 14, 2014.

2 Peter Delevett, "Tom Perkins Apologizes for Holocaust Comments, but It's Hardly His First Controversy," *San Jose Mercury News*, February 14, 2014.

3 "Progressive Kristallnacht Coming?," Letters, *Wall Street Journal*, January 24, 2014.

4 Delevett, "Tom Perkins Apologizes for Holocaust Comments."

5 David Streitfeld and Malia Wollan, "Tech Rides Are Focus of Hostility in Bay Area," *New York Times*, January 31, 2014.

6 Tom Perkins, *Valley Boy: The Education of Tom Perkins* (New York: Gotham, 2007).

7 Ibid.

8 Jordan Weissmann, "Millionaire Apologizes for Comparing Progressives to Nazis, Says His Watch Is Worth a '6-Pack of Rolexes,'" *Atlantic*, January 27, 2014.

9 Brad Stone, *The Everything Store: Jeff Bezos and the Age of Amazon* (New York: Little, Brown, 2013), p. 12.

10 Berners-Lee was specifically responding to the University of Minnesota's spring 1993 decision to charge a licensing fee for its Gopher browser. See Tim Berners-Lee, *Weaving the Web* (San Francisco: HarperSanFrancisco, 1999), pp. 72–73.

11 John Cassidy, *Dot.Con: The Real Story of Why the Internet Bubble Burst* (London: Penguin, 2002).

12 Kaplan, *The Silicon Boys and Their Valley of Dreams*, pp. 157, 209. See also "John Doerr #23, The Midas List," *Forbes*, June 4, 2014.

13 Kevin Roose, "Go West, Young Bank Bro," *San Francisco*, February 21, 2014.

14 Cassidy, *Dot.Con*, p. 22.

15 Jim Clark, *Netscape Time: The Making of the Billion-Dollar Start-Up That Took on Microsoft* (New York: St. Martin's Griffin, 2000), p. 34.

16 Ibid., p. 68.

17 Cassidy, *Dot.Con*, p. 63.

18 Kaplan, *The Silicon Boys and Their Valley of Dreams*, p. 243.

19 Clark, *Netscape Time*, p. 261.

20 Ibid., p. 251.

21 Ibid., p. 249.

22 Ibid., p. 119.

23 Ibid., p. 67.

24 Thomson Venture Economics, special tabulations, June 2003.

25 Nicholas Negroponte, *Being Digital* (New York: Random House, 1996).

26 Kevin Kelly, *New Rules for the New Economy* (New York: Penguin, 1997).

27 Kevin Kelly, *What Technology Wants* (New York: Viking, 2010).

28 Kelly, *New Rules for the New Economy*, p. 156.

29 Robert H. Frank and Philip J. Cook, *The Winner-Take-All Society: How More and More Americans Compete for Ever Fewer and Bigger Prizes, Encouraging Economic Waste, Income Inequality, and an Impoverished Cultural Life* (New York: Free Press, 1995).

30 Ibid., p. 47.

31 Ibid., p. 48.

32 "The Greatest Defunct Web Sites and Dotcom Disasters," CNET, June 5, 2008.

33 Cassidy, *Dot.con*, pp. 242–45.

34 Stone, *The Everything Store*, p. 48.

35 Ibid.

36 Fred Wilson, "Platform Monopolities," AVC.com, July 22, 2014.

37 Ibid.

38 Ibid.

39 Matthew Yglesias, "The Prophet of No Profit," *Slate*, January 30, 2014.

40 Stone, *The Everything Store*, pp. 181–82.

41 Ibid., p. 173.

42 Jeff Bercovici, "Amazon Vs. Book Publishers, By The Numbers," *Forbes*, February 10, 2014.

43 George Packer, "Cheap Words," *New Yorker*, February 17, 2014.

44 Steve Wasserman, "The Amazon Effect," *Nation*, May 29, 2012.

45 Sarah Butler, "Independent Bookshops in Decline as Buying Habits Change," *Guardian*, February 21, 2014.

46 Stone, *The Everything Store*, p. 243.

47 Ibid, p. 340.

48 Stacy Mitchell, "The Truth about Amazon and Job Creation," Institute for Local Self-Reliance, July 29, 2013, ilsr.org/amazonfacts.

49 Simon Head, "Worse than Walmart: Amazon's Sick Brutality and Secret History of Ruthlessly Intimidating Workers," *Salon*, February 23, 2014.

50 Spencer Soper, "Amazon Warehouse Workers Fight for Unemployment Benefits," *Morning Call*, December 17, 2012.

51 Hal Bernton and Susan Kelleher, "Amazon Warehouse Jobs Push Workers to Physical Limit," *Seattle Times*, April 3, 2012.

52 Lara Stevens, "Amazon Vexed by Strikes in Germany," *New York Times*, June 19, 2013. See also Ollie John, "Amazon Fires 'Neo-Nazi' Security Firm at German Facilities," *Time*, February 19, 2013.

53 "Amazon workers face 'increased risk of mental illness,'" BBC Business News, November 20, 2013.

54 Bernton and Kelleher, "Amazon Warehouse Jobs Push Workers to Physical Limit."

55 Ibid.

56 "Amazon's Power Play," Editorial Board, *New York Times*, June 3, 2014.

57 Yglesias, "The Prophet of No Profit."

58 Ryan, *A History of the Internet and the Digital Future*, p. 125.

59 "Yahoo! Still First Portal Call," BBC News, June 5, 1998.

60 Steven Levy, *In the Plex: How Google Thinks, Works, and Shapes Our Lives* (New York: Simon & Schuster, 2011), pp. 69–120.

61 Ryan, *A History of the Internet and the Digital Future*, p. 115.

62 Levy, *In the Plex*, p. 22.

63 Ibid.

64 Ibid.

65 Ibid., p. 32.

66 Ibid., p. 33.

67 Ibid., p. 73.

68 Ibid., p. 99.

69 Ibid., p. 93.

70 Ibid.

71 "Google's Income Statement Information," investor.google.com/financial/tables.html. See also Seth Rosenblatt, "Google Demolishes Financial Expectations to Close 2013," CNET, January 30, 2014.

72 Danny Sullivan, "Google Still World's Most Popular Search Engine by Far, but Share of Unique Search Dips Slightly," SearchEngineLand, February 11, 2013.

73 Moises Naim, *The End of Power: From Boards to Battlegrounds and Churches to States, Why Being in Charge Isn't What It Used to Be* (New York: Basic Books, 2013).

74 Viktor Mayer-Schönberger and Kenneth Cukier, *Big Data: A Revolution That Will Transform How We Live, Work, and Think* (Boston: Houghton Mifflin, 2013), p. 113.

75 "What Is Web 2.0: Design Patterns and Business Models for the Next Generation of Software," O'Reilly.com, September 30, 2005.

76 Astra Taylor, *The People's Platform: Taking Back Power and Culture in the Digital Age* (New York: Metropolitan Books, 2014), p. 202.

77 Josh Constine, "The Data Factory—How Your Free Labor Lets Tech Giants Grow the Wealth Gap," *TechCrunch*, September 9, 2013, techcrunch.com/2013/09/09/the-data-factory.

78 Anoushka Sakoul, "Concentrated Cash Pile Puts Recovery in Hands of the Few," *Financial Times*, January 22, 2014.

79 John Plender, "Apple, Google and Facebook Are Latter-Day Scrooges," *Financial Times*, December 29, 2013.

80 Ibid.

81 Ben Mezrich, *The Accidental Billionaires* (New York: Heinemann, 2009), pp. 62, 73, 74, 175.

82 Stephen Silberman, "The Geek Syndrome," *Wired*, September 2001.

83 Rebecca Savastio, "Facebook Founder Zuckerberg's Asperger's Problem," *Las Vegas Guardian*, September 5, 2013.

84 Nicholas Carlson, "Coping with Asperger's: A Survival Manual for Mark Zuckerberg," *Business Insider*, July 25, 2008.

85 Austin Carr, "Facebook Everywhere," *Fast Company*, July/August 2014.

86 Felix Gillette, "The Rise and Inglorious Fall of MySpace," *Bloomberg Businessweek*, June 22, 2011.

87 David Kirkpatrick, *The Facebook Effect: The Inside Story of the Company That Is Connecting the World* (New York: Simon & Schuster), p. 16.

88 Carr, "Facebook Everywhere."

89 Kirkpatrick, *The Facebook Effect*, p. 305.

90 Carr, "Facebook Everywhere."

91 Kirkpatrick, *The Facebook Effect*, p. 316.

92 Ibid., p. 332.

93 Ibid., p. 313.

94 "Journal That Published Facebook Mood Study Expresses 'Concern' at Its Ethics," Associated Press, July 3, 2014.

95 Kirkpatrick, *The Facebook Effect*, p. 314.

96 Charlie Warzel, "Your Next Phone Will Be the Ultimate Surveillance Machine," *Buzzfeed*, November 27, 2013.

97 Kirkpatrick, *The Facebook Effect*, p. 199.

98 Ibid., p. 210.

99 Matthew Sparkes, "Young Users See Facebook as 'Dead and Buried,'" *Daily Telegraph*, December 27, 2013.

100 Maria Konnikova, "How Facebook Makes Us Unhappy," *New Yorker*, September 10, 2013.

101 Charlie Warzel, "Americans Still Don't Trust Facebook with Their Privacy," *Buzzfeed*, April 3, 2014.

102 Alexandra Sifferlin, "Why Facebook Makes You Feel Bad About Yourself," *Time*, January 24, 2003.

103 Berners-Lee, *Weaving the Web*, p. 36.

104 Michael Sandel, *What Money Can't Buy: The Moral Limits of Markets* (New York: Farrar, Straus & Giroux, 2012), p. 5.

105 Evan Spiegel, LA Hacks Keynote Address, April 11, 2014.

106 Joseph A. Schumpeter, *Capitalism, Socialism and Democracy* (New York: Routledge, 2005), p. 83.

107 Marc Andreessen, "Why Bitcoin Matters," *New York Times*, January 21, 2014.

108 Ibid.

109 Colin Lecher, "How Did a $10 Potato Salad Kickstarter Raise More than $30,000?," *Verge*, July 7, 2014.

110 Sarah Eckel, "You Want Me to Give You Money for What?," *BBC Capital*, May 1, 2014.

111 Ryan Lawler, "Airbnb Tops 10 Million Guest Stays Since Launch, Now Has 550,000 Properties Listed Worldwide," *TechCrunch*, December 19, 2013.

112 Sydney Ember, "Airbnb's Huge Valuation," *New York Times*, April 21, 2014. See also Carolyn Said, "Airbnb's Swank Digs Reflect Growth, but Controversy Grows," *SFGate*, January 27, 2014.

113 Thomas L. Friedman, "And Now for a Bit of Good News . . ." *New York Times*, July 19, 2014.

114 Will Oremus, "Silicon Valley Uber Alles," *Slate*, June 6, 2014.

115 See Dan Amira, "Uber Will Ferry Hampton-Goers Via Helicopter This July 3rd," *New York*, July 2013, nymag.com/daily/intelligencer/2013/07/uber-helicopter-uberchopper-hamptons-july-3rd.html.

116 Jessica Guynn, "San Francisco Split by Silicon Valley's Wealth," *Los Angeles Times*, August 14, 2013.

117 Paul Sloan, "Marc Andreessen: Predictions for 2012 (and Beyond)," CNET, December 19, 2011, news.cnet.com/8301-1023_3-57345138-93/marc-andreessen-predictions-for-2012-and-beyond.

118 Mark Scott, "Traffic Snarls in Europe as Taxi Drivers Protest Against Uber," *New York Times*, June 11, 2014.

119 Kevin Roose, "Uber Might Be More Valuable than Facebook Someday. Here's Why," *New York*, December 6, 2013, nymag.com/daily/intelligencer/2013/12/uber-might-be-more-valuable-than-facebook.html.

120 Erin Griffith, "Meet the Uber Rich," *Fortune*, June 5, 2014.

Chapter Three

1 In his afterword to the 2000 edition of *Neuromancer*, the American science fiction writer Jack Womack speculated that the book might have inspired the creation of the World Wide Web. "What if the act of writing it down, in fact, *brought it about*," Womack wrote.

2 Michael Keene, "Rochester Crime Rates," Examiner.com, February 4, 2010. For data on Rochester's very high 2012 murder rate, see Karyn Bower, John Klofas, and Janelle Duda, "Homicide in Rochester, NY 2012: Comparison of Rates for a Selection of United States and International Cities," Center of Public Initiatives, January 25, 2013.

3 Rory Carroll, "Silicon Valley's Culture of Failure . . . and the 'Walking Dead' It Leaves Behind," *Guardian*, June 28, 2014.

4 "How I Failed," Cultivate Conference, New York City, October 14, 2013, cultivatecon.com/cultivate2013/public/schedule/detail/31551.

5 "'Fail Fast' Advises LinkedIn Founder and Tech Investor Reid Hoffman," BBC, January 11, 2011.

6 "Failure: The F-Word Silicon Valley Loves and Hates," NPR.org, June 19, 2012, npr.org/2012/06/19/155005546/failure-the-f-word-silicon-valley-loves-and-hates.

7 Eric Markowitz, "Why Silicon Valley Loves Failure," *Inc.*, August 16, 2012, inc.com/eric-markowitz/brilliant-failures/why-silicon-valley-loves-failures.html/1.

8 *MIT Technology Review*, September/October 2013, technologyreview.com/magazine/2013/09. The young entrepreneur featured on the cover was Ben Milne, the founder and CEO of a digital payments startup called Dwolla, who, the magazine claimed, was seeking to "demolish" the finance industry. Milne seems to think of himself as a big-time demolisher. On his own Instagram page, for example, he posted an image saying: "MOVE FAST AND BREAK THINGS." instagram.com/p/epyqnEHQwg.

9 David Wills, *Hollywood in Kodachrome* (New York: HarperCollins, 2013), p. xiii.

10 Ibid. Kodachrome film was also used to make eighty Oscar winners of the Best Picture award. See Rupert Neate, "Kodak Falls in

the Creative Destruction of the Digital Age," *Guardian*, January 19, 2013, theguardian.com/business/2012/jan/19/kodak-bankruptcy-protection.

11 Ellen Gamerman, "I Snap Therefore I Am," *Wall Street Journal*, December 13, 2013.

12 Ibid.

13 John Naughton, "Could Kodak's Demise Have Been Averted?," *Guardian*, January 21, 2012.

14 Jason Farago, "Our Kodak Moments—and Creativity—Are Gone," *Guardian*, August 23, 2013, theguardian.com/commentisfree/2013/aug/23/photography-photography.

15 Nick Brown, "US Judge Approves Kodak Plan to Exit Bankruptcy," Reuters, August 20, 2013, reuters.com/article/2013/08/20/us-kodak-idUSBRE97J0W820130820.

16 Julie Creswell, "Kodak's Fuzzy Future," *New York Times*, May 3, 2013, dealbook.nytimes.com/2013/05/03/after-bankruptcy-a-leaner-kodak-faces-an-uphill-battle.

17 Derek Thompson, "What Jobs Will the Robots Take?," *Atlantic*, January 23, 2014.

18 Daniel Akst, "Automation Anxiety," *Wilson Quarterly*, Summer 2013.

19 "Coming to an Office Near You . . ." *Economist*, January 18, 2014.

20 Martin Wolf, "If Robots Divide Us, They Will Conquer," *Financial Times*, February 4, 2014.

21 Tim Harford, "The Robots Are Coming and Will Terminate Your Jobs," *Financial Times*, December 28–29, 2013.

22 Ibid.

23 Nicholas Carr, *The Big Switch: Rewiring the World, from Edison to Google* (New York: Norton, 2008), p. 113.

24 Nicholas Carr, *The Glass Cage: Automation and Us* (New York: Norton, 2014), p. 198.

25 Carole Cadwallader, "Are the Robots About to Rise? Google's New Director of Engineering Thinks So . . ." *Guardian*, February 22, 2014.

26 Samuel Gibbs, "What Is Boston Dynamics and Why Does Google Want Robots?," *Guardian*, December 17, 2013.

27 Lorraine Luk, "Foxconn Working with Google on Robotics," *Wall Street Journal*, February 11, 2014.

28 Dan Rowinski, "Google's Game of Moneyball in the Age of Artificial Intelligence," ReadWrite.com, January 29, 2014.

29 Chunka Mui, "Google Car + Uber = Killer App," *Forbes*, August 23, 2013.

30 395,000 at UPS (pressroom.ups.com/Fact+Sheets/UPS+Fact+Sheet) and 300,000 at FedEx (about.van.fedex.com/company-information).

31 Claire Cain Miller, "FedEx's Price Rise Is a Blessing in Disguise for Amazon," *New York Times*, May 9, 2014.

32 David Streitfeld, "Amazon Floats the Notion of Delivery Drones," *New York Times*, December 1, 2013.

33 Charles Arthur, "Amazon Seeks US Permission to Test Prime Air Delivery Drones," *Guardian*, July 11, 2014.

34 Katie Lobosco, "Army of Robots to Invade Amazon Warehouse," *CNNMoney*, May 22, 2014.

35 George Packer, "Cheap Words," *New Yorker*, February 17, 2014.

36 "John Naughton, Why Facebook and Google Are Buying into Drones," *Observer*, April 19, 2014.

37 Reed Albergotti, "Zuckerberg, Musk Invest in Artificial-Intelligence Company," *Wall Street Journal*, March 21, 2014.

38 Ibid.

39 Emily Young, "Davos 2014: Google's Schmidt Warning on Jobs," BBC, January 23, 2014.

40 Carl Benedikt Frey and Michael A. Osborne, "The Future of Employment: How Susceptible Are Jobs to Computerization?," Oxford Martin Programme on the Impacts of Future Technology, September 17, 2013, oxfordmartin.ox.ac.uk/downloads/academic/The_Future_of_Employment.pdf.

41 Derek Thompson, "What Jobs Will the Robots Take?," *Atlantic*, January 23, 2014.

42 Ibid.

43 Erik Larson, "Kodak Reorganization Approval Affirms Move from Cameras," Bloomberg, August 21, 2013, bloomberg.com/news/2013-08-20/kodak-bankruptcy-reorganization-plan-approved-by-new-york.html.

44 "Kodak, Smaller and Redirected, Leaves Bankruptcy," Associated Press, September 3, 2013.

45 Julie Creswell, "Kodak's Fuzzy Future," *New York Times*, May 3, 2013, dealbook.nytimes.com/2013/05/03/after-bankruptcy-a-leaner-kodak-faces-an-uphill-battle.

46 For a helpful timeline of Kodak's 2013 emergence from bankruptcy, see "Key Events in the History of Eastman Kodak Company," *Wall Street Journal*, September 3, 2013, nytimes.com/2013/09/04/business/kodak-smaller-and-redirected-leaves-bankruptcy.html?ref=eastmankodakcompany&_r=0&pagewanted=print; online.wsj.com/article/AP6b640447eb8a41418c01e4110720d4e4.html.

47 Larson, "Kodak Reorganization Approval Affirms Move from Cameras."

48 For an introduction to the Eastman House collection see *Photography from 1839 to Today: George Eastman House, Rochester, NY* (London: Taschen, 1999).

49 Greg Narain, "The New Kodak Moment: Why Storytelling Is Harder Than Ever," Briansolis.com, November 21, 2013.

50 Andrew Keen, *The Cult of the Amateur: How Today's Internet Is Killing Our Culture*, p. 115.

51 Ibid.

52 Neate, "Kodak Falls in the Creative Destruction of the Digital Age."

53 Ibid. The comment was made by Robert Burley, a professor of photography at Ryerson University in Toronto, whose work on the collapse of film photography, *The Disappearance of Darkness*, was shown at the National Gallery of Canada in late 2013: gallery.ca/en/see/exhibitions/upcoming/details/robert-burley-disappearance-of-darkness-5324.

54 John Naughton, "Could Kodak's Demise Have Been Averted?," *Observer*, January 21, 2012, theguardian.com/technology/2012/jan/22/john-naughton-kodak-lessons.

55 Clayton Christensen, *The Innovator's Dilemma: The Revolutionary Book That Will Change the Way You Do Business* (New York: Harper Business, 2011). For an introduction to Christensen's ideas, see my TechCrunchTV interview with him. "Keen On . . . Clay Christensen: How to Escape the Innovator's Dilemma," April 2, 2012, techcrunch.com/2012/04/02/keen-on-clay-christensen-how-to-escape-the-innovators-dilemma-tctv. For a more critical view on the cult of Christensen, see Jill Lepore, "The Disruption Machine," *New Yorker*, June 23, 2014.

56 "The Last Kodak Moment?," *Economist*, January 14, 2012. economist.com/node/21542796/print.

57 Stone, *The Everything Store*, p. 348.

58 Joshua Cooper Ramo, *The Age of the Unthinkable: Why the New World Disorder Constantly Surprises Us and What We Can Do About It* (New York: Bay Back Books, 2010).

59 Paul F. Nunes and Larry Downes, "Big Bang Disruption: The Innovator's Disaster," *Outlook*, June 2013, accenture.com/us-en/outlook/Pages/outlook-journal-2013-big-bang-disruption-innovators-disaster.aspx.

60 Larry Downes and Paul F. Nunes, "Big-Bang Disruption," *Harvard Business Review*, March 2013, hbr.org/2013/03/big-bang-disruption.

61 Ibid.

62 Larry Downes and Paul Nunes, *Big Bang Disruption: Strategy in the Age of Devastating Innovation* (New York: Portfolio/Penguin, 2014), p. 193.

63 Jason Farago, "Our Kodak Moments—and Creativity—Are Gone," *Guardian*, August 23, 2013, theguardian.com/commentisfree/2013/aug/23/photography-photography.

64 George Packer, "Celebrating Inequality," *New York Times*, May 19, 2013.

65 Ibid.

66 "The Onrushing Wave," *Economist*, January 18, 2014, p. 25.

67 Josh Constine, "The Data Factory—How Your Free Labor Lets Tech Giants Grow the Wealth Gap," *TechCrunch*, September 9, 2013.

68 David Brooks, "Capitalism for the Masses," *New York Times*, February 20, 2014.

69 Ibid.

70 George Packer, "No Death, No Taxes: The Libertarian Futurism of a Silicon Valley Billionaire," *New Yorker*, November 28, 2011.

71 Ibid.

72 Ibid.

73 Robert M. Solow, "We'd Better Watch Out," *New York Times* Book Review, July 12, 1987.

74 Timothy Noah, *The Great Divergence: America's Growing Inequality Crisis and What We Can Do About It* (New York: Bloomsbury, 2012), p. 7.

75 Eduardo Porter, "Tech Leaps, Job Losses and Rising Inequality," *New York Times*, April 15, 2014.

76 Loukas Karabarbounis and Brent Neiman, "The Global Decline of Labor Share," *Quarterly Journal of Economics*, 2014.

77 Thomas B. Edsall, "The Downward Ramp," *New York Times*, June 10, 2014.

78 Tyler Cowen, *Average Is Over: Powering America Beyond the Age of the Great Stagnation* (New York: Dutton, 2013), p. 53.

79 Ibid., p. 229.

80 Ibid., pp. 198–200.

81 Joel Kotkin, "California's New Feudalism Benefits a Few at the Expense of the Multitude," *Daily Beast*, October 5, 2013.

82 Paul Krugman, "Sympathy for the Luddites," *New York Times*, June 13, 2013, nytimes.com/2013/06/14/opinion/krugman-sympathy-for-the-luddites.html?_r=0&pagewanted=print.

Chapter Four

1 Kara Swisher, "The Money Shot," *Vanity Fair*, June 2013.

2 Steve Bertoni, "The Stanford Billionaire Machine Strikes Again," *Forbes*, August 1, 2013.

3 Ibid.

4 Swisher, "The Money Shot."

5 Systrom denies that there was a bidding war between Facebook and Twitter. But, according to Nick Bilton, the author of the bestselling *Hatching Twitter* (New York: Portfolio, 2013), there was one. See

Nick Bilton, "Instagram Testimony Doesn't Add Up," *New York Times*, December 16, 2012, bits.blogs.nytimes.com/2012/12/16/disruptions-instagram-testimony-doesnt-add-up-2/?_r=1.

6 Emil Protalinski, "Thanksgiving Breaks Instagram Records: Over 10M Photos Shared at a Rate of Up to 226 per Second," Next Web, November 23, 2012, thenextweb.com/facebook/2012/11/23/instagram-sees-new-record-during-thanksgiving-over-10m-photos-shared-at-a-rate-of-226-per-second.

7 Emil Protalinski, "Instagram Says Thanksgiving 2013 Was Its Busiest Day So Far, but Fails to Share Exact Figures," Next Web, November 29, 2013.

8 Ingrid Lunden, "73% of U.S. Adults Use Social Networks, Pinterest Passes Twitter in Popularity, Facebook Stays on Top," *TechCrunch*, December 31, 2013.

9 Sarah Perez, "An App 'Middle Class' Continues to Grow: Independently Owned Apps with a Million-Plus Users Up 121% Over Past 18 Months," *TechCrunch*, November 8, 2013.

10 Ingrid Lunden, "Instagram Is the Fastest-Growing Social Site Globally, Mobile Devices Rule Over PCs for Access," *TechCrunch*, January 21, 2014, techcrunch.com/2014/01/21/instagram-is-the-fastest-growing-social-site-globally-mobile-devices-rule-over-pcs-for-social-access.

11 See, for example, Ellis Hamburger, "Instagram Announces Instagram Direct for Private Photo, Video and Text Messaging," *Verge*, December 12, 2013.

12 Alex Williams, "The Agony of Instagram," *New York Times*, December 13, 2013.

13 Sarah Nicole Prickett, "Where the Grass Looks Greener," *New York Times*, November 17, 2013.

14 Ibid.

15 Williams, "The Agony of Instagram."

16 Tim Wu, "Sign of the Times: The Intimacy of Anonymity," *New York Times*, June 3, 2014.

17 Teddy Wayne, "Of Myself I Sing," *New York Times*, August 24, 2014.

18 *Time*, December 25, 2006.

19 Packer, "Celebrating Inequality."

20 See, for example, Jean Twenge and W. Keith Campbell, *The Narcissism Epidemic: Living in the Age of Entitlement* (New York: Free Press, 2009), and Elias Aboujaoude, *Virtually You* (New York: Norton, 2011).

21 David Brooks, "High-Five Nation," *New York Times*, September 15, 2009.

22 Parmy Olson, "Teenagers Say Goodbye to Facebook and Hello to Messenger Apps," *Observer*, November 9, 2013.

23 Keen, *Digital Vertigo*, p. 12.

24 Malkani, *Financial Times*, December 28, 2013.

25 Charles Blow, "The Self(ie) Generation," *New York Times*, March 7, 2014.

26 James Franco, "The Meanings of the Selfie," *New York Times*, December 26, 2013, nytimes.com/2013/12/29/arts/the-meaning-of-the-selfie.html.

27 Sophie Heawood, "The Selfies at Funerals Tumblr Tells Us a Lot About Death," Vice.com, November 1, 2013.

28 Stacy Lambe, "14 Grindr Profile Pics Taken at the Holocaust Memorial," *Buzzfeed*, January 31, 2013.

29 Craig Detweiler, "'Auschwitz Selfies' and Crying into the Digital Wilderness," CNN, July 22, 2014.

30 Stuart Heritage, "Selfies of 2013—the Best, Worst and Most Revealing," *Guardian*, December 22, 2013.

31 Rachel Maresca, "James Franco Allegedly Attempts to Meet Up with 17-Year-Old Girl via Instagram: Report," New York *Daily News*, April 3, 2014.

32 Ibid.

33 "Selfie Is Oxford Dictionaries' Word of the Year," *Guardian*, November 18, 2013, theguardian.com/books/2013/nov/19/selfie-word-of-the-year-oed-olinguito-twerk/print.

34 This number is from the research advisory firm mobileYouth. See Olson, "Teenagers Say Goodbye to Facebook and Hello to Messenger Apps." Interestingly, the mobileYouth research shows that the proportion of selfies on Snapchat is even higher than 50%.

35 Steven Johnson is perhaps the most relentlessly optimistic of Web believers. See, for example, his latest book: *Future Perfect: The Case for Progress in a Networked Age* (New York: Riverhead, 2012).

36 Tom Standage, *Writing on the Wall: Social Media—The First 2,000 Years* (New York: Bloomsbury, 2013).

37 Ibid., epilogue, pp. 240–51.

38 Williams, "The Agony of Instagram."

39 Rhiannon Lucy Coslett and Holly Baxter, "Smug Shots and Selfies: The Rise of Internet Self-Obsession," *Guardian*, December 6, 2013.

40 Nicholas Carr, "Is Google Making Us Stupid?," *Atlantic*, July/ August 2008. Also see Nicholas Carr, *The Shallows: What the Internet Is Doing to Our Brains* (New York; Norton, 2011).

41 Eli Pariser, *The Filter Bubble: What the Internet Is Hiding From You* (Penguin, 2011). See also my June 2011 TechCrunchTV interview with Eli Pariser: Andrew Keen, "Keen On . . . Eli Pariser: Have Progressives Lost Faith in the Internet?," *TechCrunch*, June 15, 2011, techcrunch.com/2011/06/15/keen-on-eli-pariser-have-progressives-lost-faith-in-the-internet-tctv.

42 Claire Carter, "Global Village of Technology a Myth as Study Shows Most Online Communication Limited to 100-Mile Radius," BBC, December 18, 2013; Claire Cain Miller, "How Social Media Silences Debate," *New York Times*, August 26, 2014.

43 Josh Constine, "The Data Factory—How Your Free Labor Lets Tech Giants Grow the Wealth Gap."

44 Derek Thompson, "Google's CEO: 'The Laws Are Written by Lobbyists,'" *Atlantic*, October 1, 2010.

45 James Surowiecki, "Gross Domestic Freebie," *New Yorker*, November 25, 2013.

46 Monica Anderson, "At Newspapers, Photographers Feel the Brunt of Job Cuts," Pew Research Center, November 11, 2013.

47 Robert Reich, "Robert Reich: WhatsApp Is Everything Wrong with the U.S. Economy," *Slate*, February 22, 2014.

48 Alyson Shontell, "Meet the 20 Employees Behind Snapchat," *Business Insider*, November 15, 2013, businessinsider.com/snapchat-early-and-first-employees-2013-11?op=1.

49 Douglas Macmillan, Juro Osawa, and Telis Demos, "Alibaba in Talks to Invest in Snapchat," *Wall Street Journal*, July 30, 2014.

50 Mike Isaac, "We Still Don't Know Snapchat's Magic User Number," All Things D, November 24, 2013.

51 Josh Constine, "The Data Factory—How Your Free Labor Lets Tech Giants Grow the Wealth Gap," *TechCrunch*.

52 Alice E. Marwick, *Status Update: Celebrity, Publicity and Branding in the Social Media Age* (New Haven, CT: Yale University Press, 2013). See chapter 3: "The Fabulous Lives of Micro Celebrities."

53 Surowiecki, "Gross Domestic Freebie."

54 Amanda Holpuch, "Instagram Reassures Users over Terms of Service After Massive Outcry," *Guardian*, December 18, 2013.

55 The American Society of Media Photographers (ASMP), "The Instagram Papers," Executive Summary, July 25, 2013, p. 3.

56 Ethan Zuckerman, The Internet's Original Sin," *Atlantic*, August 14, 2014.

57 Annie Leonard, "Facebook Made My Teenager into an Ad. What Parent Would Ever 'Like' That?," *Guardian*, February 15, 2014.

58 Caroline Daniel and Maija Palmer, "Google's Goal: to Organise Your Daily Life," *Financial Times*, May 22, 2007.

59 Derek Thompson, "Google's CEO: The Laws Are Written by Lobbyists," *Atlantic*, October 1, 2010.

60 Amir Efrati, "Google Beat Facebook for DeepMind, Creates Ethics," *The Information*, January 26, 2014.

61 Jaron Lanier, *Who Owns the Future?* (New York: Simon & Schuster, 2013), p. 366.

Chapter Five

1 Kunal Dutta, "The Revolution That Killed Soho's Record Shops," *Independent*, May 12, 2010.

2 Annie O'Shea, "Oasis (What's the Story) Morning Glory?," Radio Nova, January 14, 2014, nova.ie/albums/oasis-whats-the-story-morning-glory-3.

3 Philip Beeching, "Why Companies Fail—the Rise and Fall of HMV," Philipbeeching.com, August 6, 2012.

4 Alexander Wolfe, "Digital Pennies from Analog Dollars Are Web Content Conundrum," *InformationWeek*, March 12, 2008.

5 David Carr, "Free Music, at Least While It Lasts," *New York Times*, June 8, 2014.

6 Grant Gross, "Pirate Sites Draw Huge Traffic," *Computerworld*, January 1, 2013.

7 "NetNames Piracy Analysis: Sizing the Piracy Universe 3," September 2013.

8 IFPI Digital Music Report, 2011, "Music at the Touch of a Button," p. 14.

9 OFCOM, online copyright infringement tracker benchmark study, Q3 2012, November 20, 2012.

10 David Goldman, "Music's Lost Decade: Sales Cut in Half in 2000s," *CNN Money*, February 3, 2010.

11 Derek Thompson, "Why Would Anybody Ever Buy Another Song?," *Atlantic*, March 17, 2014.

12 Thair Shaikh, "HMV Closes Historic Oxford Street Store," *Independent*, January 14, 2014.

13 Dave Lee, "'Netflix for Piracy' Popcorn Time Saved by Fans," BBC News, March 17, 2014.

14 Andrew Stewart, "Number of Frequent Young Moviegoers Plummets in 2013," *Variety*, March 25, 2014.

15 IFPI Digital Music Report, 2011, p. 5.

16 TERA Consultants, "Building a Digital Economy: The Importance of Saving Jobs in the EU's Creative Industries," International Chamber of Commerce/BASCAP, March 2010.

17 "45% Fewer Professional Working Musicians Since 2002," *Trichordist*, May 21, 2013.

18 For a summary of the corrosive impact of piracy on the creative industries, see my white paper "Profiting from Free: The Scourge of Online Piracy and How Industry Can Help" (ICOMP, October 2013). Some of the research from my white paper has also been deployed

in this book.

19 Ananth Baliga, "Pirate Websites Roped in $227 Million in Ad Revenues in 2013," UPI, February 18, 2014.

20 Duncan Grieve, "Kim Dotcom: 'I'm Not a Pirate, I'm an Innovator,'" *Guardian*, January 14, 2014.

21 Robert Levine, *Free Ride: How Digital Parasites Are Destroying the Culture Business and How the Culture Business Can Fight Back* (New York: Doubleday, 2011), p. 4.

22 Ibid., p. 13.

23 "Know Your Rights on Social Media—Legal Considerations and More," American Society of Media Photographers, 2013.

24 "Understanding the Role of Search in Online Piracy," Millward Brown Digital, September 2013.

25 "comScore Releases March 2014 U.S. Search Engine Rankings," comScore.com, April 15, 2014.

26 "comScore Releases '2013 UK Digital Future in Focus Report,'" comScore.com, February 14, 2013.

27 Josh Holiday, "Google Pledge to Downgrade Piracy Sites Under Review," *Guardian*, November 5, 2012.

28 See Glenn Peoples, "RIAA Report Criticizes Google's Efforts to Limit Infringing Search Results," *Billboard*, February 21, 2013. Also Glenn Peoples, "Business Matters: MP3 Stores Harder to Find as Google Search Removal Requests Accumulate," *Billboard*, February 4, 2013.

29 Andrew Albanese, "Artists and Photographers Sue Over Google Book Search," *Publishers Weekly*, April 7, 2010.

30 Erik Kirschbaum, "Merkel Criticizes Google for Copyright Infringement," Reuters, October 10, 2009.

31 Stuart Dredge and Dominic Rushe, "YouTube to Block Indie Labels Who Don't Sign Up to New Music Service," *Guardian*, June 17, 2014.

32 Leslie Kaufman, "Chasing Their Star, on YouTube," *New York Times*, February 1, 2014.

33 Jason Calacanis, "I Ain't Gonna Work on YouTube's Farm No More," Launch, June 2, 2013.

34 Carr, "Free Music, at Least While It Lasts."

35 Michael Wolff, "New Cash, New Questions for Business Insider," *USA Today*, March 16, 2014.

36 Levine, *Free Ride*, p. 4.

37 Ibid., p. 113.

38 Henry Mance, "Trust-Fund Newspaper? Not Us," *Financial Times*, March 7, 2014. See also Ravi Somaiya, "*Guardian* to Make Management Changes," *New York Times*, March 6, 2014.

39 Lucia Moses, "The *Guardian*'s Robot Newspaper Comes to the U.S.," *Digiday*, April 13, 2014.

40 Tom Kutsch, "The Blurred Lines of Native Advertising," Al Jazeera America, March 8, 2014.

41 Alan D. Mutter, "The Newspaper Crisis, by the Numbers," Newsosaur.blogspot.com, July 16, 2014.

42 Monica Anderson, "At Newspapers, Photographers Feel the Brunt of Job Cuts," Pew Research Center, November 11, 2013.

43 Lawrie Zion, "New Beats: Where Do Redundant Journalists Go?," TheConversation.com, December 1, 2013.

44 Rachel Bartlett, "A Quarter of Spanish Journalists Made Redundant Since the Recession, Suggests Report," Journalism.co.uk, December 15, 2010.

45 Andres Cala, "Spain's Economic Crisis Has an Unexpected Victim: Journalism," *Christian Science Monitor*, February 28, 2013.

46 Clay Shirky, "Last Call: The End of the Printed Newspaper," Medium.com, August 21, 2014.

47 Rory Carroll, "Silicon Valley's Culture of Failure . . . and 'the Walking Dead' It Leaves Behind," *Guardian*, June 28, 2014.

48 Alyson Shontell, "$4 Billion Is the New $1 Billion in Startups," *Business Insider*, November 13, 2013.

49 Joshua Brustein, "Spotify Hits 10 Million Paid Users. Now Can It Make Money?," *Bloomberg Businessweek*, May 21, 2014.

50 David Byrne, "The Internet Will Suck All Creative Content Out of the World," *Guardian*, October 11, 2013.

51 Charles Arthur, "Thom Yorke Blasts Spotify on Twitter as He Pulls His Music," *Guardian*, July 15, 2013.

52 Paul Resnikoff, "16 Artists That Are Now Speaking Out Against Streaming," *Digital Music News*, February 2, 2013.

53 Ellen Shipley, "My Song Was Played 3.1 Million Times on Pandora. My Check Was $39," *Digital Music News*, July 29, 2013.

54 David Carr, "A New Model for Music: Big Bands, Big Brands," *New York Times*, March 16, 2014.

55 Ibid.

56 Ibid.

57 TERA Consultants, "Building a Digital Economy: The Importance of Saving Jobs in the EU's Creative Industries."

Chapter Six

1 European Observatory on Infringements of Intellectual Property Rights, "Intellectual Property Rights Intensive Industries: Contribution to Economic Performance and Employment in the European Union," September 2013, p. 6.

2 Motion Picture Association of America, "2011 Economic Contribution of the Motion Picture and Television Industry to the United States."

3 Michael Cass, "Commerce Secretary Gives Music Row Some Good News," *Tennessean*, August 7, 2013.

4 Keen, *The Cult of the Amateur*, p. 113.

5 Packer, "Celebrating Inequality."

6 Heather Havrilesky, "794 Ways in Which Buzzfeed Reminds Us of Impending Death," *New York Times*, July 3, 2014.

7 Anita Elberse, *Blockbusters: Hit-Making, Risk-Taking and the Big Business of Entertainment* (New York: Henry Holt, 2013), p. 11.

8 Robert H. Frank, "Winners Take All, but Can't We Still Dream?," *New York Times*, February 22, 2014.

9 Elberse, *Blockbusters*, p. 160.

10 "The Death of the Long Tail," MusicIndustryBlog, March 4, 2014.

11 Helienne Lindvall, "The 1 Percent: Income Inequality Has Never Been Worse Among Touring Musicians," *Guardian*, July 5, 2013.

12 John Gapper, "The Superstar Still Reigns Supreme over Publishing," *Financial Times*, July 17, 2013.

13 Alison Flood, "Most Writers Earn Less Than £600 a Year, Survey Reveals," *Guardian*, January 17, 2014.

14 Colin Robinson, "The Loneliness of the Long-Distance Reader," *New York Times*, January 4, 2014.

15 Amanda Ripley, *The Smartest Kids in the World* (New York: Simon & Schuster, 2013), pp. 169–70.

16 Tamar Lewin, "Professors at San Jose State Criticize Online Courses," *New York Times*, May 2, 2013.

17 Ki Mae Heussner, "'Star' Coursera Prof Stops Teaching Online Course in Objection to MOOCs," GigaOm, September 3, 2013.

18 William Deresiewicz, *Excellent Sheep: The Miseducation of the American Elite* (New York: Simon & Schuster, 2014), p. 186.

19 Jessica McKenzie, "More Evidence That MOOCs Are Not Great Equalizers," Techpresident.com, March 17, 2014.

20 Emily Bell, "Journalists Are on the Move in America—and Creating a New Vitality," *Guardian*, November 17, 2013.

21 Riva Gold, "Newsroom Diversity: A Casualty of Journalism's Financial Crisis," *Atlantic*, July 2013.

22 Emily Bell, "Journalism Startups Aren't a Revolution if They're Filled with All These White Men," *Guardian*, March 12, 2014.

23 Suzanne Moore, "In the Digital Economy, We'll Soon All Be Working for Free—and I Refuse," *Guardian*, June 5, 2013.

24 Tim Kreider, "Slaves of the Internet, Unite!," *New York Times*, October 26, 2013.

25 Alina Simone, "The End of Quiet Music," *New York Times*, September 25, 2013.

26 Joe Pompeo, "The *Huffington Post*, Nine Years On," CapitalNewYork.com, May 8, 2014.

27 Ibid.

28 Mathew Ingram, "The Unfortunate Fact Is That Online Journalism Can't Survive Without a Wealthy Benefactor or Cat GIFs," GigaOm, September 22, 2013.

29 Julie Bosman, "To Stay Afloat, Bookstores Turn to Web Donors," *New York Times*, August 11, 2013.

30 Teddy Wayne, "Clicking Their Way to Outrage," *New York Times*, July 3, 2014.

31 Ben Dirs, "Why Stan Collymore's Treatment on Twitter Is Not Fair Game," BBC Sport, January 23, 2014.

32 Raphael Minder, "Fans in Spain Reveal Their Prejudices, and Social Media Fuels the Hostilities," *New York Times*, May 22, 2014.

33 Jeff Jarvis, "What Society Are We Building Here?," BuzzMachine, August 14, 2014.

34 Farhad Manjoo, "Web Trolls Winning as Incivility Increases," *New York Times*, August 14, 2014.

35 Ibid.

36 Amanda Hess, "Why Women Aren't Welcome on the Internet," Pacific Standard, January 6, 2014.

37 Simon Hattenstone, "Caroline Criado-Perez: 'Twitter Has Enabled People to Behave in a Way They Wouldn't Face to Face," *Guardian*, August 4, 2013. For Twitter's lack of response, see Jon Russell, "Twitter UK Chief Responds to Abuse Concerns After Campaigner Is Deluged with Rape Threats," The Next Web, July 27, 2013.

38 "Blog Death Threats Spark Debate," BBC News, March 27, 2007.

39 Deborah Fallows, "How Women and Men Use the Internet," Pew Internet and American Life Project, December 28, 2005.

40 Stuart Jeffries, "How the Web Lost Its Way—and Its Founding Principles," *Guardian*, August 24, 2014.

41 Alex Hern, "'We Need the Mary Beard Prize for Women Online,' Author Claims," *Guardian*, August 7, 2014.

42 Seth Stephens-Davidowitz, "The Data of Hate," *New York Times*, July 12, 2014.

43 Emily Bazelton, "The Online Avengers," *New York Times Magazine*, January 15, 2014.

44 Jon Henley, "Ask.fm: Is There a Way to Make It Safe?" *Guardian*, August 6, 2013.

45 Lizette Alvarez, "Felony Counts for 2 in Suicide of Bullied 12-Year-Old," *New York Times*, October 15, 2013.

46 Ben Wedeman, "Facebook May Face Prosecution over Bullied Teenager's Suicide in Italy," CNN, July 31, 2013.

47 Schumpeter, "Anonymous Social Networking: Secrets and Lies," *Economist*, March 22, 2014.

48 David Gardner, "Tribes and Sects Rule as the Old Order Crumbles," *Financial Times*, July 31, 2014.

49 Sam Jones, "Jihad by Social Media," *Financial Times*, March 28, 2014.

50 Rod Nordland, "Iraq's Sunni Militants Take to Social Media to Advance Their Cause and Intimidate," *New York Times*, June 28, 2014.

51 Shiv Malik and Michael Safi, "Revealed: The Radical Clerics Using Social Media to Back British Jihadists in Syria," *Guardian*, April 15, 2014.

52 Harriet Sherwood, "Israel and Hamas Clash on Social Media," *Guardian*, July 16, 2014.

53 Lisa Chow, "Top Reviewers on Amazon Get Tons of Free Stuff," NPR, *Planet Money*, October 29, 2013.

54 David Streitfeld, "Give Yourself 5 Stars? Online, It Might Cost You," *New York Times*, September 22, 2013.

55 Charles Arthur, "How Low-Paid Workers at 'Click Farms' Create Appearance of Online Popularity," *Guardian*, August 2, 2014.

56 Tim Wu, "Little Lies the Internet Told Me," *New Yorker*, April 17, 2014.

57 Pippa Stephens, "Trust Your Doctor, Not Wikipedia, Say Scientists," BBC Health News, May 27, 2014.

58 Tom Simonite, "The Decline of Wikipedia," *MIT Technology Review*, October 22, 2013.

59 Ibid.

60 Anne Perkins, "Whose Truth Is Wikipedia Guarding?," *Guardian*, August 7, 2014.

61 James R. Hagerty and Kate Linebaugh, "Next 3-D Frontier: Printed Plane Parts," *Wall Street Journal*, July 14, 2012.

62 Stuart Dredge, "30 Things Being 3D Printed Right Now (and None of Them Are Guns)," *Guardian*, January 29, 2014.

63 Chris Anderson, *Makers: The New Industrial Revolution* (New York: Crown, 2012), p. 12.

64 Eliza Brooke, "Why 3D Printing Will Work in Fashion," *TechCrunch*, July 20, 2013.

65 Alice Fisher, "3D-Printed Fashion: Off the Printer, Rather Than Off the Peg," *Guardian*, October 12, 2013.

66 Rebecca Hiscott, "Will 3D Printing Upend Fashion Like Napster Crippled the Music Industry?," Mashable, March 3, 2014.

67 Katrina Dodd, "Monetize Me: Selfies, Social and Selling," *Contagious*, May 19, 2014.

68 Alex Hudson, "Is Digital Piracy Possible on Any Object?," BBC News, December 8, 2013.

69 Paul Krugman, "Sympathy for the Luddites," *New York Times*, June 18, 2013.

70 Chris Myant, "Reuben Falber: Key Figure in British Communism," *Independent*, May 31, 2006.

Chapter Seven

1 Noam Cohen, "Borges and the Foreseeable Future," *New York Times*, January 6, 2008.

2 Victor Sebestyen, *Revolution 1989: The Fall of the Soviet Empire* (New York: Pantheon 2009), p. 121.

3 Ibid.

4 Anna Funder, *Stasiland* (London: Granta, 2003), p. 57.

5 Viktor Mayer-Schönberger and Kenneth Cukier, *Big Data: A Revolution That Will Transform How We Live, Work and Think* (Boston: Houghton-Mifflin, 2013), p. 150.

6 Andrew Keen, "Opinion: Beware Creepy Facebook," CNN, February 3, 2012.

7 Ibid.

8 Karin Matussek, "Google Fined 145,000 Euros Over Wi-Fi Data Collection in Germany," Bloomberg News, April 22, 2013.

9 Robert Booth, "Facebook Reveals News Feed Experiment to Control Emotions," *Guardian*, June 29, 2014.

10 Natasha Lomas, "Facebook's Creepy Data-Grabbing Ways Make It the Borg of the Digital World," *TechCrunch*, June 24, 2013.

11 Patrick Kingsley, "Julian Assange Tells Students That the Web Is the Greatest Spying Machine Ever," *Guardian*, March 15, 2011.

12 Charles Arthur, "European Watchdogs Order Google to Rewrite Privacy Policy or Face Legal Action," *Guardian*, July 5, 2013.

13 Claire Cain Miller, "Google Accused of Wiretapping in Gmail Scans," *New York Times*, October 1, 2013.

14 Las Vaas, "Google Sued for Data-Mining Student Email," *Naked Security*, March 18, 2014.

15 Stefan Wolle, *Die heile Welt der Diktatur*, p. 186.

16 "The NSA's Secret Spy Hub in Berlin," *Spiegel Online*, October 27, 2013.

17 Ian Traynor and Paul Lewis, "Merkel Compared NSA to Stasi in Heated Encounter with Obama," *Guardian*, December 17, 2013.

18 Duncan Campbell, Cahal Milmo, Kim Gengupta, Nigel Morris, and Tony Patterson, "Revealed: Britain's 'Secret Listening Post in the Heart of Berlin,'" *Independent*, November 5, 2013.

19 David Sellinger, "Big Data: Getting Ready for the 2013 Big Bang," *Forbes*, January 15, 2013. See also Ase Dragland, "Big Data, for Better or Worse: 90% of World's Data Generated over the Last Two Years," SINTEF.com.

20 Patrick Tucker, "Has Big Data Made Anonymity Impossible?," *MIT Technology Review*, May 7, 2013.

21 Tim Bradshaw, "Wearable Devices Pump Up the Technology," *Financial Times*, January 7, 2014.

22 "Where to Wear Your Technology? Torso to Toe," *Wall Street Journal*, January 7, 2014.

23 Michael Chertoff, "Google Glass, the Beginning of Wearable Surveillance," CNN, May 1, 2013.

24 Claire Cain Miller, "Privacy Officials Worldwide Press Google About Glass," *New York Times*, June 19, 2013.

25 Tucker, "Has Big Data Made Anonymity Impossible?"

26 Neil McAllister, "You THINK You're Watching Your LG Smart TV—but IT'S WATCHING YOU, Baby," *Register*, November 20, 2013.

27 Chris Bryant and Henry Foy, "VW Chief Warns over Big Brother Vehicle Data," *Financial Times*, March 10, 2014.

28 Ibid.

29 Holman W. Jenkins Jr., "When Your Car Is Spying on You," *Wall Street Journal*, August 31, 2013.

30 Brandon Bailey, "Google's Working on a Phone That Maps Your Physical Surroundings," *San Jose Mercury News*, February 21, 2014.

31 Berners-Lee, *Weaving the Web*, p. 123.

32 Dan Gillmor, "The Real CES Takeaway: Soon We'll Be Even More Connected and Have Even Less Privacy," *Guardian*, January 10, 2014.

33 Bryant and Foy, "VW Chief Warns over Big Brother Vehicle Data."

34 Sophie Gadd, "Five Things I've Learned from Being at the Heart of a Twitter Storm," *Guardian*, December 19, 2013.

35 Ibid.

36 Daniel Bates, "I Am Ashamed," *MailOnline*, December 22, 2013.

37 Gadd, "Five Things I've Learned."

38 Simon Sebag Montefiore, *Potemkin: Catherine the Great's Imperial Partner* (New York: Vintage, 2005), p. 299.

39 John Dinwiddy, *Bentham* (Oxford: Oxford University Press, 1989).

40 Ibid., p. 109.

41 Parmy Olson, "The Quantified Other: Nest and Fitbit Chase a Lucrative Side Business," *Forbes*, April 17, 2014.

42 Meglena Kuneva, Keynote Speech, "Roundtable on Online Data Collection, Targeting and Profiling," Brussels, March 31, 2009.

43 Dan Gillmor, "Is the Internet Now Just One Big Human Experiment?," *Guardian*, July 29, 2014.

44 Zeynep Tufekci, "Facebook and Engineering the Public."

45 Christopher Caldwell, "OkCupid's Venal Experiment Was a Poisoned Arrow," *Financial Times*, August 1, 2014.

46 Vanessa Thorpe, "Google Defends Listing Extremist Websites in Its Search Results," *Guardian*, May 25, 2014.

47 Ana Marie Cox, "Who Should We Fear More with Our Data: The Government or Companies?," *Guardian*, January 20, 2014.

48 Charlie Savage, Edward Wyatt, Peter Baker, and Michael D. Shear, "Surveillance Leaks Likely to Restart Debate on Privacy," *New York Times*, June 7, 2013.

49 John Naughton, "Edward Snowden's Not the Story. The Fate of the Internet Is," *Observer*, July 27, 2013.

50 Ibid.

51 James Risen and Nick Wingfield, "Web's Reach Binds N.S.A. and Silicon Valley Leaders," *New York Times*, June 19, 2013.

52 Michael Hirsh, "Silicon Valley Doesn't Just Help the Surveillance State—It Built It," *Atlantic*, June 10, 2013.

53 Claire Cain Miller, "Tech Companies Concede to Surveillance Program," *New York Times*, June 7, 2014.

54 David Firestone, "Twitter's Surveillance Resistance," *New York Times*, June 10, 2013.

55 Sue Halpern, "Partial Disclosure," *New York Review of Books*, July 10, 2014.

56 Andy Greenberg and Ryan Mac, "How a 'Deviant' Philosopher Built Palantir, a CIA-Funded Data-Mining Juggernaut," *Forbes*, August 14, 2013.

57 Ibid.

58 Ashlee Vance and Brad Stone, "Palantir, the War on Terror's Secret Weapon," *Bloomberg Businessweek*, November 22, 2011.

59 Robert Cookson, "Internet Launches Fightback Against State Snoopers," *Financial Times*, August 23, 2013.

60 This letter was sent by AOL, Facebook, LinkedIn, Google, Apple, Microsoft, Twitter, and Yahoo. See reformgovernmentsurveillance.com.

61 "Silicon Valley's Hypocrisy on Spying," *Bloomberg Businessweek*, December 11, 2013.

62 Bruce Schneier, "The Public-Private Surveillance Partnership," *Bloomberg Businessweek*, July 31, 2013.

63 Daniel Etherington, "Google Patents Tiny Cameras Embedded in Contact Lenses," *TechCrunch*, April 13, 2014.

64 James Robinson, "*Time* Magazine Shows Just How Creepy Smart Homes Really Are," *Pando Daily*, July 7, 2014.

65 Quentin Hardy, "How Urban Anonymity Disappears When All Data Is Tracked," *New York Times*, April 22, 2014.

66 Ibid.

Chapter Eight

1 This remains the FailCon credo. See thefailcon.com/about.html.

2 Jessi Hempel, "Hey, Taxi Company, You Talkin' to Me?," *CNN Money*, September 23, 2013, money.cnn.com/2013/09/19/magazines/fortune/uber-kalanick.pr.fortune.

3 On Kalanick's Ayn Rand fetish, see Paul Carr, "Travis Shrugged: The Creepy, Dangerous Ideology Behind Silicon Valley's Cult of Disruption," *Pando Daily*, October 24, 2012, pandodaily.com/2012/10/24/travis-shrugged.

4 Julie Zauzmer and Lori Aratani, "Man Visiting D.C. Says Uber Driver Took Him on Wild Ride," *Washington Post*, July 9, 2014.

5 Olivia Nuzzi, "Uber's Biggest Problem Isn't Surge Pricing. What If It's Sexual Harassment by Drivers?," *Daily Beast*, March 28, 2014.

6 See, for example, Ryan Lawler, "Uber Prepares for Another Fight with DC Regulators," *TechCrunch*, May 17, 2013, techcrunch .com/2013/05/17/uber-prepares-for-another-fight-with-dc-regulators. See also Jeff John Roberts, "Cabbies Sue to Drive Car Service Uber out of San Francisco," GigaOm, November 14, 2012, gigaom.com/2012/11/14/cabbies-sue-to-drive-car-service-uber-out-of-san-francisco.

7 Salvador Rodriguez, "Uber Claims Its Cars Attacked by Cab Drivers in France," *Los Angeles Times*, January 13, 2014.

8. Mark Scott and Melissa Eddy, "German Court Bans Uber Service Nationwide," *New York Times*, September 2, 2014.

9 David Streitfeld, "Rough Patch for Uber's Challenge to Taxis," *New York Times*, January 26, 2014.

10 Paul Sloan, "Marc Andreessen: Predictions for 2012 (and Beyond)," CNET, December 19, 2011, news.cnet.com/8301-1023_3-57345138-93/marc-andreessen-predictions-for-2012-and-beyond.

11 Jordan Novet, "Confirmed: Uber Driver Killed San Francisco Girl in Accident," *VentureBeat*, January 2, 2014.

12 Michael Hiltzik, "Uber Upholds Capitalism, (Possibly) Learns Downside of Price Gouging," *Los Angeles Times*, December 16, 2013.

13 "Uber's Snow Storm Surge Pricing Gouged New Yorkers Big Time," *Gothamist*, December 16, 2013.

14 Aly Weisman, "Jerry Seinfeld's Wife Spent $415 During Uber's Surge Pricing to Make Sure Her Kid Got to a Sleepover," *Business Insider*, December 16, 2013.

15 Airbnb's investigation by US tax authorities is well documented. See, for example, April Dembosky, "US Taxman Peers into Holiday Rental Sites," *Financial Times*, May 29, 2011; Brian R. Fitzgerald and Erica Orden, "Airbnb Gets Subpoena for User Data in New York," *Wall Street Journal*, October 7, 2013; and Elizabeth A. Harris, "The Airbnb Economy in New York: Lucrative but Often Unlawful," *New York Times*, November 4, 2013.

16 Alexia Tsotsis, "TaskRabbit Gets $13M from Founders Fund and Others to 'Revolutionize the World's Labor Force,'" *TechCrunch*, July 23, 2012.

17 Brad Stone, "My Life as a TaskRabbit," *Bloomberg Businessweek*, September 13, 2012.

18 Sarah Jaffe, "Silicon Valley's Gig Economy Is Not the Future of Work—It's Driving Down Wages," *Guardian*, July 23, 2014.

19 Guy Standing, *The Precariat: The New Dangerous Clas*s (Bloomsbury Academic, 2001).

20 Natasha Singer, "In the Sharing Economy, Workers Find Both Freedom and Uncertainty," *New York Times*, August 16, 2014.

21 George Packer, "Change the World," *New Yorker*, May 27, 2013, newyorker.com/reporting/2013/05/27/130527fa_fact_packer. For my TechCrunchTV interview with Packer about his *New Yorker* piece, see "Keen On . . . How We Need to Scale Down Our Self-Regard and Grow Up," *TechCrunch*, June 19, 2013, techcrunch.com/2013/06/19/keen-on-silicon-valley-how-we-need-to-scale-down-our-self-regard-and-grow-up.

22 For a video of Kalanick's FailCon speech, see youtube.com/watch?v=2QrX5jsiico.

23 See invitation to FailChat: culturesfirststeps.eventbrite.com.

24 Stephen E. Siwek, "The True Cost of Sound Recording Piracy," Institute of Policy Research, August 21, 2007. See executive summary: ipi.org/ipi_issues/detail/the-true-cost-of-sound-recording-piracy-to-the-us-economy.

25 IFPI Digital Music Report, 2011, "Music at the Touch of a Button," ifpi.org/content/library/dmr2011.pdf, p. 15.

26 Ibid.

27 See, for example, Ellen Huet, "Rideshare Drivers' Unexpected Perk: Networking," *San Francisco Chronicle*, December 29, 2013.

28 Gideon Lewis-Kraus, *No Exit: Struggling to Survive a Modern Gold Rush* (*Kindle Single*, 2014).

29 Jessica Guynn, "San Francisco Split by Silicon Valley's Wealth," *Los Angeles Times*, August 14, 2013.

30 Rebecca Solnit, "Google Invades," *London Review of Books*, February 7, 2013.

31 Michael Winter and Alistair Barr, "Protesters Vandalize Google Bus, Block Apple Shuttle," *USA Today*, December 20, 2013.

32 Alexei Oreskovic and Sarah McBride, "Latest Perk on Google Buses: Security Guards," Reuters, January 16, 2014.

33 Tom Perkins, "Progressive Kristallnacht Coming?," Letters to the Editor, *Wall Street Journal*, January 24, 2014.

34 Nick Wingfield, "Seattle Gets Its Own Tech Bus Protest," *New York Times*, February 10, 2014.

35 Packer, "Change the World."

36 Ibid.

37 Guynn, "San Francisco Split by Silicon Valley's Wealth."

38 Stephanie Gleason and Rachel Feintzeig, "Startups Are Quick to Fire," *New York Times*, December 12, 2013.

39 See, for example, Eric Ries, *The Lean Startup: How Today's Entrepreneurs Use Continuous Innovation to Create Radically Successful Businesses* (New York: Crown, 2011).

40 Quentin Hardy, "Technology Workers Are Young (Really Young)," *New York Times*, July 5, 2013.

41 Vivek Wadhwa, "A Code Name for Sexism and Racism," *Wall Street Journal*, October 7, 2013.

42 Jon Terbush, "The Tech Industry's Sexism Problem Is Only Getting Worse," *The Week*, September 12, 2013.

43 Jessica Guynn, "Sexism a Problem in Silicon Valley, Critics Say," *Los Angeles Times*, October 24, 2013.

44 Terbush, "The Tech Industry's Sexism Problem Is Only Getting Worse."

45 Elissa Shevinsky, "That's It—I'm Finished Defending Sexism in Tech," *Business Insider*, September 9, 2013.

46 Max Taves, "Bias Claims Surge Against Tech Industry," *Recorder*, August 16, 2013.

47 Colleen Taylor, "Key Details of the Kleiner Perkins Gender Discrimination Lawsuit," *TechCrunch*, May 22, 2012.

48 Alan Berube, "All Cities Are Not Created Unequal," Brookings Institution, February 20, 2014.

49 Timothy Egan, "Dystopia by the Bay," *New York Times*, December 5, 2013.

50 Marissa Lagos, "San Francisco Evictions Surge, Reports Find," *San Francisco Chronicle*, November 5, 2013.

51 Carolyn Said, "Airbnb Profits Prompted S.F. Eviction, Ex-Tenant Says," *San Francisco Chronicle*, January 22, 2014.

52 Ibid.

53 Casy Miner, "In a Divided San Francisco, Private Tech Buses Drive Tension," NPR.org, December 17, 2013.

54 Andrew Gumbel, "San Francisco's Guerrilla Protest at Google Buses Wells into Revolt," *Observer*, January 25, 2014.

55 Carmel DeAmicis, "BREAKING: Protesters Attack Google Bus in West Oakland," *Pando Daily*, December 20, 2013.

56 Robin Wilkey, "Peter Shih '10 Things I Hate About You' Post Draws San Francisco's Ire, Confirms Startup Stereotypes," *Huffington Post*, August 16, 2013.

57 Jose Fitzgerald, "Real Tech Worker Says SF Homeless 'Grotesque,' 'Degenerate,' 'Trash,'" *San Francisco Bay Guardian*, December 11, 2013.

58 Yasha Levine, "Occupy Wall Street Leader Now Works for Google, Wants to Crowdfund a Private Militia," *Pando Daily*, February 7, 2014.

59 J. R. Hennessy, "The Tech Utopia Nobody Wants: Why the World Nerds Are Creating Will Be Awful," *Guardian*, July 21, 2014.

60 Krissy Clark, "What Did the Tech CEO Say to the Worker He Wanted to Automate?," Marketplace.org, August 28, 2013.

61 Solnit, "Google Invades."

62 Justine Sharrock, "How San Francisco Tech Companies Justify Their Tax Breaks," *Buzzfeed*, October 8, 2013.

63 Sam Biddle, "This Asshole Misses the Shutdown," *Valleywag*, October 17, 2013.

64 Max Read, "Oakland Residents Are Crowdfunding a Private Police Force," *Valleywag*, October 4, 2013.

65 Lisa Fernandez, "Facebook Will Be First Private Company in U.S. to Pay for Full-Time Beat Cop," NBCBayArea.com, March 5, 2014.

66 Geoffrey A. Fowler and Brenda Cronin, "Freelancers Get Jobs Via Web Services," *Wall Street Journal*, May 29, 2013.

67 Greg Kumparak, "Larry Page Wants Earth to Have a Mad Scientist Island," *TechCrunch*, May 2015.

68 Sean Gallagher, "Larry Page Wants You to Stop Worrying and Let Him Fix the World," Ars Technica, May 20, 2013.

69 "What Is Burning Man?," burningman.com/whatisburningman.

70 Nick Bilton, "A Line Is Drawn in the Desert," *New York Times*, August 20, 2014.

71 Kevin Roose, "The Government Shutdown Has Revealed Silicon Valley's Dysfunctional Fetish," *New York*, October 16, 2013.

72 Chris Anderson, "Elon Musk's Mission to Mars," *Wired*, October 21, 2010.

73 Peter Delevett, "Tech Investor Tim Draper Launches 'Six Californias' Ballot Measure to Divide the Golden State," *San Jose Mercury News*, December 23, 2013.

74 Aaron Kinney, "Martins Beach: Lawmaker Proposes Eminent Domain for Access on Khosla's Property," *San Jose Mercury News*, February 6, 2014.

75 Bill Wasik, "Silicon Valley Needs to Lose the Arrogance or Risk Destruction," *Wired*, February 2, 2014.

76 Chris Baker, "Live Free or Down: Floating Utopias on the Cheap," *Wired*, January 19, 2009.

77 Egan, "Dystopia by the Bay."

78 Alex Hern, "Google Execs Saved Millions on Private Jet Flights Using Cheaper NASA Fuel," *Guardian*, December 12, 2013.

79 Paul Goldberger, "Exclusive Preview: Google's New Build-from-Scratch Googleplex," *Vanity Fair*, February 22, 2013.

80 Allen Martin, "Google Launches Private SF Bay Ferry Service to Shuttle Workers," CBS Local News, January 7, 2014.

81 Philop Matier and Andrew Ross, "Google Barge Mystery Unfurled, *SFGate*, November 8, 2013.

82 Tony Romm, "Senate Investigators: Apple Sheltered $44 Billion from Taxes," *Politico*, May 20, 2103.

83 Bob Duggan, "Are Tech Giants' Offices the Cathedrals of the Future?," BigThink.com, December 12, 2013.

84 Thomas Schulz, "From Apple to Amazon: The New Monuments to Digital Domination," Spiegel Online, November 29, 2013.

85 Brandon Bailey, "Mark Buys Four Houses Near His Palo Alto Home," *San Jose Mercury News*, October 11, 2013.

86 Allison Arieff, "What Tech Hasn't Learned from Urban Planning," *New York Times*, December 13, 2013.

87 Charlotte Allen, "Silicon Chasm: The Class Divide on America's Cutting Edge," *Weekly Standard*, December 2, 2013.

88 Tom Foremski, "Fortune Asks 'Why Does America Hate Silicon Valley?'," *Silicon Valley Watcher*, October 4, 2013.

Conclusion

1 Thomas Friedman, "The Square People, Part One," *New York Times*, May 13, 2014. See also "The Square People, Part Two," *New York Times*, May 17, 2014.

2 Edward Luce, "America Must Dump Its Disrupters in 2014," *Financial Times*, December 22, 2014.

3 Nick Cohen, "Beware the Lure of Mark Zuckerberg's Cool Capitalism," *Observer*, March 30, 2013.

4 Fred Turner, *From Counterculture to Cyberculture* (University of Chicago Press, 2008).

5 For more on Apple, Steve Jobs, and Foxconn, see my TechCrunchTV interview with Mike Daisey, who starred in the Broadway hit *The Agony and Ecstasy of Steve Jobs*: "Apple and Foxconn, TechCrunchTV, February 1, 2011.

6 Lyn Stuart Parramore, "What Does Apple Really Owe Taxpayers? A Lot, Actually," Reuters, June 18, 2013.

7 Jo Confino, "How Technology Has Stopped Evolution and Is Destroying the World," *Guardian*, July 11, 2013.

8 Alexis C. Madrigal, "Camp Grounded, 'Digital Detox,' and the Age of Techno-Anxiety," *Atlantic*, July 2013.

9 Oliver Burkman, "Conscious Computing: How to Take Control of Our Life Online," *Guardian*, May 10, 2013.

10 Jemima Kiss, "An Online Magna Carta: Berners-Lee Calls for Bill of Rights for Web," *Guardian*, March 11, 2014.

11 "Bitcloud Developers Plan to Decentralize Internet," BBC Technology News, January 23, 2014.

12 Suzanne Labarre, "Why We're Shutting Off Our Comments," *Popular Science*, September 24, 2013; Elizabeth Landers, "*Huffington Post* to Ban Anonymous Comments," CNN, August 22, 2013.

13 "Data Protection: Angela Merkel Proposes Europe Network," BBC News, February 15, 2014.

14 Philip Oltermann, "Germany 'May Revert to Typewriters' to Counter Hi-Tech Espionage," *Guardian*, July 15, 2014.

15 Lanier, *Who Owns the Future?*, p. 263.

16 John Gapper, "Bitcoin Needs to Grow out of Its Obsessive Adolescence," *Financial Times*, March 12, 2014. See also new.livestream.com/theNYPL/businessasusual.

17 David Byrne, "The NSA Is Burning Down the Web, but What if We Rebuilt a Spy-Proof Internet?," *Guardian*, March 24, 2014.

18 On the impracticality of this law, see, for example, this rather self-serving piece by Google's legal czar David Drummond: "We Need to Talk About the Right to Be Forgotten," *Guardian*, July 10, 2014.

19 Roger Cohen, "The Past in Our Future," *New York Times*, November 27, 2013.

20 Jonathan Freedland, "From Memory to Sexuality, the Digital Age Is Changing Us Completely," *Guardian*, June 21, 2013.

21 Mark Lilla, "The Truth About Our Libertarian Age," *New Republic*, June 17, 2014.

22 Ibid.

23 Douglas Rushkoff, *Present Shock: When Everything Happens Now* (New York: Current, 2014), p. 9.

24 Mic Wright, "Is 'Shadow' the Creepiest Startup Ever? No, CIA Investment Palantir Owns That Crown," *Telegraph*, September 21, 2013.

25 Cass R. Sunstein, *Why Nudge: The Politics of Libertarian Paternalism* (New Haven, CT: Yale University Press, 2014), p. 116.

26 Cohen, "Beware the Lure of Mark Zuckerberg's Cool Capitalism."

27 europarl.europa.eu/ep_products/poster_invitation.pdf.

28 John Naughton, "Amazon's History Should Teach Us to Beware 'Friendly' Internet Giants," *Guardian*, February 22, 2014.

29 Richard Sennett, "Real Progressives Believe in Breaking Up Google," *Financial Times*, June 28, 2013.

30 Ibid.

31 Rebecca Solnit, "Who Will Stop Google?," *Salon*, June 25, 2013.

32 Philip Oltermann, "Google Is Building Up a Digital Superstate, Says German Media Boss," *Guardian*, April 16, 2014.

33 Mathew Ingram, "Giants Behaving Badly. Google, Facebook and Amazon Show Us the Downside of Monopolies and Black-Box Algorithms," GigaOm, May 23, 2014.

34 Polly Toynbee, "Snowden's Revelations Must Not Blind Us to Government as a Force for Good," *Guardian*, June 10, 2013.

35 Simon Bowers and Rajeev Syal, "MP on Google Tax Avoidance Scheme: 'I Think That You Do Evil,'" *Guardian*, May 16, 2013.

36 Marc Rotenberg, "Put Teeth in Google Privacy Fines," CNN, April 29, 2013.

37 Alex Hern, "Italy Gives Google 18 Months to Comply with European Privacy Regulations," *Guardian*, July 22, 2014.

38 "When Will the Justice Department Take On Amazon?," *Nation*, July 16, 2014.

39 Ingrid Lunden, "More Woe for Amazon in Germany as Antitrust Watchdog Investigates Its 3rd Party Pricing Practices," *TechCrunch*, October 21, 2013.

40 "Amazon Sued by US Regulators over Child In-App Purchases," BBC Business News, July 10, 2014.

41 Brad Stone, "Amazon May Get Its First Labor Union in the U.S.," *Bloomberg Businessweek*, December 17, 2013.

42 David Streitfeld and Melissa Eddy, "As Publishers Fight Amazon, Books Vanish," *New York Times*, May 23, 2014.

43 Stone, *The Everything Store*, p. 340.

44 Marcus Wohlsen, "Why the Sun Is Setting on the Wild West of Ride-Sharing," *Wired*, August 2, 2013.

45 April Dembosky and Tim Bradshaw, "Start-ups: Shareholder Societies," *Financial Times*, August 7, 2013.

46 Ben Popper, "Uber Agrees to New National Policy That Will Limit Surge Pricing During Emergencies," *Verge*, July 8, 2014.

47 Chris Welch, "Airbnb Hosts Must Install Smoke and Carbon Monoxide Detectors by End of 2014," *Verge*, February 21, 2014.

48 Eric T. Schneiderman, "Taming the Digital Wild West," *New York Times*, April 22, 2014.

49 Carolyn Said, "S.F. Ballot Would Severely Limit Short-Term Rentals," *SFGate*, April 29, 2014.

50 Cale Guthrie Weissman, "Working Families Party Joins the Anti-Airbnb Brigade," *Pando Daily*, May 2, 2014.

51 Kevin Collier, "Philadelphia Jumps the Gun, Bans 3-D-Printed Guns," *Daily Dot*, November 22, 2013.

52 John Sunyer, "No Comment?," *Financial Times*, May 24, 2014.

53 Associated Press, "'Revenge Porn' Outlawed in California," *Guardian*, October 1, 2013.

54 Pamela Druckerman, "The French Do Buy Books. Real Books," *New York Times*, July 9, 2014.

55 Andrew Wallenstein, "Cable Operator Pitching TV Industry on Plan to Convert Illegal Downloads to Legal Transaction Opportunities," *Variety*, August 5, 2013, variety.com/2013/digital/news/comcast-developing-anti-piracy-alternative-to-six-strikes-exclusive-1200572790.

56 "Recording Industry Welcomes Support by Payment Providers to Tackle Illegal Online Sale of Unlicensed Music," International Federation of the Phonographic Industry, March 2, 2011, ifpi.org/content/section_news/20110302.html.

57 Bill Rosenblatt, "Ad Networks Adopt Notice-and-Takedown for Ads on Pirate Sites," Copyright and Technology Blog, July 21, 2013, copyrightandtechnology.com/category/economics.

58 Victoria Espinel, "Coming Together to Combat Online Piracy and Counterfeiting," Whitehouse.gov, July 15, 2013.

59 Kyle Alspach, "Steve Case: Silicon Valley Has Wrong Mindset for Next Internet Revolution," *Techflash*, October 10, 2013.

60 Mariana Mazzucato, *The Entrepreneurial State: Debunking Public vs.*

Private Sector Myths (London: Anthem, 2013), p. 105.

61 Joseph Schumpeter, "The Entrepreneurial State," *Economist*, August 31, 2013.

62 Michael Ignatieff, "We Need a New Bismarck to Tame the Machines," *Financial Times*, February 11, 2014.

63 Catherine Bigelow, "An Honor for Danielle Steel and a Downton for All," *SFGate*, January 9, 2014.

64 Chrystia Freeland, *Plutocrats: The Rise of the New Global Super Rich and the Fall of Everyone Else* (New York: Penguin, 2012).

65 Chrystia Freeland, "Sympathy for the Toffs," *New York Times*, January 24, 2014.

66 Ibid.

67 William Powers, *Hamlet's BlackBerry: A Practical Philosophy for Building a Good Life in the Digital Age* (HarperCollins, 2010).

68 Jeff Jarvis, "What Society Are We Building Here?," Buzzmachine, August 14, 2014.

Afterword

1 Nicole Perlroth and David E. Sanger, "Obama Calls for New Cooperation to Wrangle the 'Wild West' Internet," *New York Times*, February 13, 2015.

2 Ibid.

3 "The Enforcer," *Economist*, May 2, 2015.

4 Lisa Abend, "Why This Woman Is Google's Worst Nightmare," *Time*, May 20, 2015.

5 Miguel Helft, "Ted Ullyot Joins Andreessen Horowitz to Build First Policy Group at a VC Firm," *Forbes*, April 16, 2015.

INDEX

Aboujaoude, Elias, 106
Acxiom, 181
Advanced Research Projects Agency (ARPA), 20–21, 25
advertisements for ourselves, 104–105, 107–108
advertising, 6, 37–43, 63, 110–119, 126–127, 128, 134–135
Airbnb, 72, 187, 198, 221–222, 229
Akst, Daniel, 81
Allen, Charlotte, 207
Amazon.com. *See also* Bezos, Jeff: as business, 43, 47–48, 51–52, 220–221; FedEx and, 83–84; investment in, 46; publishing industry and, 48–49, 50–51; robots and, 84–85; top reviewers on, 154; workforce of, 49–50, 179
Anderson, Chris, 123, 127, 143, 157
Andreessen, Marc, 39–41, 42, 71, 73–74, 112, 152, 186, 227
Andreessen Horowitz, 71, 72–73, 101, 142, 152, 233–234
anger, online, 148–149
Angwin, Julia, 9
anonymity, online, 152
Apple, 206, 211–212
Arieff, Allison, 207
ARPANET, 25–27
artificial intelligence, 82–83, 85–86, 118
Ash, Timothy Garton, 180
Ask.fm, 151
Assange, Julian, 165
attention economy, 17, 115
audience, people formerly known as, 148–155
AudioCafe, 127–128, 190
automation anxiety, 81–82, 85–90
Autor, David, 97

Baran, Paul, 23–25, 26, 37–38
Barlow, John Perry, 29, 126, 131, 211, 215
Battery social club, 1–4, 209–210, 224–225, 228
Beaudry, Paul, 97
Bebo, 59, 60
Bell, Emily, 145, 146, 227
Bentham, Jeremy, 176–178, 183, 217
Bentham, Samuel, 176, 177
Bercovici, Jeff, 48
Berners-Lee, Tim, 31–32, 37–38, 68, 90, 173, 212
Bezos, Jeff, 37, 43, 46, 48, 49, 51–52, 69, 84, 147
Big Brother, 173–174, 180

Birch, Michael, 1–3, 9, 59, 60, 209–210
Birch, Xochi, 1–3, 9, 59, 60
Bitcoin, 71
Blow, Charles, 107
Boorstin, Daniel, 21
Borders, Louis, 45
Borges, Jorge Luis, 162
Boston Dynamics, 81
Bowden, Mark, 182
Brand, Stewart, 211
Brin, Sergey, 52–55, 57, 69, 205
Brooks, David, 94, 106
Brynjolfsson, Erik, 98, 111, 216
Burley, Robert, 91
Burning Man, 202
Bush, Vannevar, 15, 16–19, 30, 37–38, 96
Busque, Leah, 187–188
Buzzfeed, 142–143
Byrne, David, 137, 213

Calacanis, Jason, 134
Caldwell, Christopher, 179
Campbell, Keith, 104, 106
capitalism, distributed, 68–74, 188
Carlson, Nicholas, 64
Carlyle, Thomas, 177
Carr, Austin, 66
Carr, David, 128, 134, 137–138
Carr, Nicholas, 82, 109, 168, 213
cars, connected and driverless, 172–173
Case, Steve, 223, 230–231
Caspar, Johannes, 165
Cassidy, John, 45
catastrophe of abundance, 128–138
Cerf, Vint, 28
Cerwall, Patrik, 11, 12, 70, 174
Chertoff, Michael, 171
Chesky, Brian, 72
Christensen, Clayton, 91, 92
Chuang, Joshua, 79
Churchill, Winston, 2
Clark, Jim, 38, 40–42
Clark, Wesley, 19, 26
Cohen, Nick, 210–211, 217
Cohen, Roger, 214
Cold War, 21–23, 33
collective narrative, authority of, 215–217
Collymore, Stan, 149
communications network, vulnerable, 23–25
Consumer Electronics Show (CES), 168–172, 174
Cook, Philip, 44–45, 96, 98
Cowen, Tyler, 97–98, 110
Cox, Ana Marie, 180
creative destruction, 70, 74, 77–78, 90
Criado-Perez, Caroline, 150
crystal man metaphor, 166
Cukier, Kenneth, 58, 164
cult: of celebrity, 105; of failure, 76, 105, 184–190; of social, 62–68, 164
Cult of the Amateur, The (Keen), 140–141

data factories, 60–62, 113, 114–119
Davies, Donald, 25
DeepMind, 82–83, 118
DeLong, J. Bradford, 97
democratization of media, 140–142, 148
Deresiewicz, William, 145
digital photographs, 79, 87–88, 91. *See also* photography
digital revolution, 92–93, 147, 191–193, 214–215, 230
digital technologies, 24–25, 28–29, 30, 32, 160–161
disrupting disruptors, 212–217
disruptive qualities of Internet, 5–6, 10, 92–93
distributed capitalism, 68–74, 188
distributed networks, 24, 28
diversity, as casualty, 144, 145–146
Dodd, Katrina, 159
Doerr, John, 38–39, 41, 46, 55, 72, 73
Dopfner, Mathias, 220
Dorsey, Jack, 101, 102
Dotcom, Kim, 131
dot-com boom, 42, 45

Dougherty, Dale, 58, 156, 157–158
Downes, Larry, 28, 92–93
Draper, Tim, 203
drone revolution, 83–84
Duneier, Mitchell, 145

Eastman House, 89–90
Eastman Kodak, 78–80, 87–88, 91–92, 111
eBay, 52
e-commerce, 13, 47. *See also* Amazon.com
economy. *See also* winner-take-all economy: attention, 17, 115; "blockbuster," 143; class warfare, 198–202; cracking code on profits, 51–58; creative destruction, 70, 74, 77–78, 90; data factories, 60–62, 113, 114–119; digital revolution and, 92–93; elimination of jobs, 81–82, 83–85; feudal aspect of, 98, 106, 198, 204–208; industrial, 111; inequality in, 94, 96–99, 110–111, 195–196; maker, 155–161; monetization of Internet, 37–43, 51–58; networked, 70–74, 125–126; one percent, 34–36; reshaping of, 33
Efrati, Amir, 118
Egan, Timothy, 4, 204
Eggers, Dave, 175
Eisenhower, Dwight, 20, 21–22
Elberse, Anita, 143
e-learning industry, 144–145
email, 28–29
employees and market caps, 61–62
enabling products, 59, 71
Ericsson, 11–12
Espinel, Victoria, 223
European Particles Physics Laboratory (CERN), 31
European Union, 220–221, 233
Evans, Robin, 177

Facebook: acquisitions of, 113–114; artificial intelligence and, 85; cult of social and, 63–68; images of children and, 117–118; Instagram and, 102–103, 112; IPO of, 60; office for, 164, 207; spying of, 165
FailCon, 184–185, 189–191
failure, 76–80, 105, 191–193
Falber, Reuben, 151
Falbers Fabrics, 121, 124
Fanning, Shawn, 129
Farago, Jason, 79, 93
fashion business, 155, 158–159
feudal aspect of new economy, 98, 106, 198, 204–208
Filo, David, 52
Fi magazine, 125, 126
Fisher, Alice, 158
Fitbit, 170–171
FOO Camp, 7, 139–141
Foster, Norman, 206
Foucault, Michel, 177
Foxconn, 83, 211
Franco, James, 107
Frank, Robert, 44–45, 96, 98
"free" apps and content, 116–117, 128–138
Freedland, Jonathan, 214
Freeland, Chrystia, 225
Frey, Carl Benedikt, 86
Friedman, Patri, 204
Friedman, Thomas, 5, 210
Fukuyama, Francis, 33
Fulk, Ken, 224
Funder, Anna, 164

Gadd, Sophie, 174–175, 176
Gamerman, Ellen, 79
Gapper, John, 213
Gardner, David, 152
Gebbia, Joe, 185
Gehry, Frank, 164, 207
Geller, Jonny, 144
Ghonim, Wael, 152
Gibson, William, 7, 75–76
Gillmor, Dan, 174, 178, 227
Goldhaber, Michael, 17
Goldin, Claudia, 93, 219
Goodman, Peter, 147

Google: acquisitions of, 81, 82–83; advertising and, 6, 63, 118; AI and, 85–86; driverless cars, 172–173; as feudal, 204–206; history of, 52–58; as monopoly, 219–220; partnering with, 133–134; personal data and, 165, 220; piracy and, 132–133; Web 2.0 and, 59
Google Bus, 195, 198
Google Glass, 171
Gore, Al, Jr., 162–163
Graham, Paul, 76–77
Green, David, 97
Gross, Anisse, 4
Guardian (newspaper), 135, 136

Hachette Book Group, 50, 221
Hafner, Katie, 22, 24, 28
Halpern, Sue, 181
Hardy, Quentin, 183
Harford, Tim, 81–82
Harkin, James, 16
Hart, H. L. A., 177
hatred, online expressions of, 149–152
Havrilesky, Heather, 143
Head, Simon, 49
Hennessy, J. R., 199
Herzfeld, Charles, 25–26
Hess, Amanda, 150, 196
Heym, Stefan, 164
Hirsh, Michael, 181
Hiscott, Rebecca, 159
Hobsbawn, Eric, 161
Hoffman, Reid, 64, 76, 146
Honecker, Erich, 163–164
Huffington, Arianna, 147, 148
Huffington Post, 146–147
Hughes, Chris, 147

Ignatieff, Michael, 223–224
Indiegogo, 72, 169
inequality, 94, 96–99, 110–111, 195–196
information overload, 53
Ingram, Mathew, 147, 220, 227
Instagram, 100–105, 106–107, 111–112, 115–117
Internet: borderless idealism of, 211; history of, 27–30, 37–38, 162, 230–234; need for conversation about, 226–228
Internet of Things, 13, 156, 172–174
Ito, Joi, 5

Jaffe, Sarah, 188
Jarvis, Jeff, 150, 227
Jenkins, Holman, 173
jobs, elimination of, 81–82, 83–85
Jobs, Steve, 211
Johnson, Dennis Loy, 221
Johnson, Steven, 108

Kahn, Robert, 27, 28
Kalanick, Travis, 73, 83, 98, 185, 188, 189–190
Kamiya, Gary, 35
Kaplan, David, 29, 30, 42
Karabarbounis, Loukas, 97
Karp, David, 114
Katz, Lawrence, 93, 219
Kay, Larry, 125–126
Kelly, Kevin, 43–44, 46, 47, 57, 62–63, 98, 157
Khosla, Vinod, 185, 203–204
Kim, Andrew, 144–145
Kirkpatrick, David, 65–66
Kiva Systems, 84
Kodachrome, 78, 79, 104
Kodak, 78–80, 87–88, 91–92, 111
Kotkin, Joel, 98, 106, 196, 204
KPCB: Amazon and, 46, 50; anonymous networks and apps and, 152; discrimination suit against, 197; Google and, 55; Gore and, 163; investments by, 38, 41, 42–43; origins of, 34; Perkins on, 35–36
Kreider, Tim, 146
Kreiger, Mike, 112
Kross, Ethan, 68
Krugman, Paul, 44–45, 98–99, 160–161
Krzanich, Brian, 170
Kuneva, Meglena, 178, 183

Kurzweil, Ray, 82
Kutcher, Ashton, 85

Lanchester, John, 5, 178
Lanier, Jaron, 119, 124, 213
Leadbeater, Charles, 151, 227
Leonard, Annie, 118
Levine, Robert, 132, 160
Levy, Steven, 54, 55, 56
libertarian age, 5–6, 58–59, 95–96, 180, 199–200, 211, 215
Licklider, J. C. R., 15, 16, 19–20, 25
Lilla, Mark, 5, 6, 214–215
Lindvall, Helienne, 144
Lindvist, Jonas, 12, 13, 70–71
Lomas, Natasha, 165
Luce, Edward, 210
Lyft, 72–73
Lyon, Matthew, 22, 24, 28

maker economy, 155–161
Maker Media, 156
Malkani, Gautam, 107, 108
Manjoo, Farhad, 150
Martin, Ryan, 148–149
Marwick, Alice, 115
Massachusetts Institute of Technology (MIT), 14–15, 16, 19
massive online open courses (MOOCs), 145
Mayer-Schönberger, Viktor, 58, 164
Mazzucato, Mariana, 32, 223
McAfee, Andrew, 98, 111, 216
McClure, Dave, 77
McCue, T. J., 83
McKenzie, Jessica, 145
McLuhan, Marshall, 3, 9–10, 16, 25, 66, 218
Meeker, Mary, 46
Megaupload, 131
Merkel, Angela, 166, 212
Merton, Robert, 68, 155
Metcalfe, Bob, and Metcalfe's law, 42
Mezrich, Ben, 63
middleman services, 59, 71
Mielke, Erich, 163, 164, 166, 167
Miller, Claire Cain, 83–84, 181
Mishel, Larry, 97
misogyny in culture, 150–151, 197
mobile networks, 11–13
monetization of Internet, 37–43, 51–58
monopolies, 47–48, 219–221
Moore, Gordon, and "Moore's law," 30
Moore, Suzanne, 146
Moritz, Michael, 55, 60–61, 62, 80, 94, 104, 111, 227
Mosaic Web browser, 39–40
movie industry, 130, 131–133
Mui, Chunka, 28, 83
music industry, 91, 120–121, 122–124, 127–132, 133, 136–138, 143–144, 189, 191
Musk, Elon, 85, 95, 203
MySpace, 64–65

Naim, Moises, 57
Napster, 128–129
narcissism, online, 104, 106
Narrative, 170–171
narrative fallacy, 37, 43, 51, 66, 67
National Center for Supercomputing Applications (NCSA), 39–40
National Security Agency (NSA), 166, 167, 180–181, 182
Naughton, John, 15, 23, 32, 181, 218, 227
Negroponte, Nicholas, 43, 57
Neiman, Brent, 97
Nelson, Ted, 30
Nest Labs, 83, 178
Netscape Communications, 41–42, 52
Netscape Moment, 41, 42, 43, 45
networked market/economy, 70–74, 125–126
networked society, 5–10, 11–14, 178–179, 212, 217–218
news industry, 135–136, 145–146, 147
Noah, Timothy, 97
NSFNET, 27, 38
Nunes, Paul F., 92–93

Obama, Barack, 232–233
Ohanian, Alexis, 6, 218
OkCupid, 178–179
Omidyar, Pierre, 148
one percent economy, 34–36
one percent rule, 142–148
online piracy, 129–133, 222–223
O'Reilly, Tim, 7, 58–59, 76, 139, 149
original sin of WWW, 117, 128
Orwell, George, 173
Osborne, Michael, 86
Owen, Jennifer, 50

Packer, George, 84–85, 93, 94, 96, 105, 142, 188, 196, 219
Page, Larry, 52–55, 57, 69, 202, 205
paid work, discrimination against, 146–147
Palantir Technologies, 181–182, 216, 229
Palihapitiya, Chamath, 200
Pandora, 136, 137, 138
Panopticon, 176–178
Pariser, Eli, 109
Parker, Sean, 4, 5, 95, 129, 136, 216, 224
Perkins, Anne, 155
Perkins, Tom, 34–36, 38, 44
personal revolution, 61, 100–105, 106–119
Pettis, Bre, 160
Phillips, Whitney, 150
Phoenix, Scott, 85
photography, 89–90, 107–110, 112–113, 132. *See also* digital photographs; Eastman Kodak; Instagram
Piketty, Thomas, 44–45, 222
piracy epidemic, 129–133, 222–223
Pishevar, Shervin, 201
Plender, John, 62
Pompeo, Joe, 147
Popcorn Time, 130
Powers, William, 226
Prickett, Sarah Nicole, 104
Pritzker, Penny, 141
privacy issues, 9, 165–167, 172–174, 180–182, 212–213, 220
publishing industry, 48–49, 50–51, 144

Ramos, Joshua Cooper, 92
Rand, Ayn, 189
RAND Corporation, 22, 23–24
regulation, need for, 217–224, 232–234
Reich, Robert, 44–45, 113
Ries, Eric, 185, 196
Ripley, Amanda, 144–145
Risen, James, 181
Robinson, Colin, 144
Rochester, New York, 75–81, 86–87, 88–89. *See also* Eastman Kodak
Roose, Kevin, 39, 203
Rosen, Jay, 148, 149
Ross, Alec, 217–218
Rowinski, Dan, 83
Runciman, David, 5
Rushkoff, Douglas, 215

Sacco, Justine, 175
Sand, Benjamin, 97
Sandberg, Sheryl, 67, 146
Sandel, Michael, 69, 145
San Francisco, 4, 34–35, 126, 127, 194–196, 197–202. *See also* Battery social club; Silicon Valley
Saverin, Eduardo, 63–64
Schmidt, Eric, 55, 85, 118, 146, 163, 180, 205
Schneier, Bruce, 182
Schumpeter, Joseph, 69–70
Scour, 189
Sebestyen, Victor, 164
secession from real world, 202–208
selfie culture, 107–110, 112–113
Sennett, Richard, 219
Sequoia Capital, 55, 152
Shipley, Ellen, 137
Shirky, Clay, 136, 227
Sierra, Kathy, 150
Silicon Valley. *See also* failure: FOO Camp, 139–141; government and, 180–181, 200–201; inequality and, 94, 195–197;

NSA critique by, 182; secession fantasy of, 202–208; values of, 225–226
Simon, Paul, 78, 79, 91, 92, 141
Simone, Alina, 146
Simonite, Tom, 154
Singer, Natasha, 188
smart televisions, 172
Snapchat, 106, 114
Snowden, Edward, 166–167, 180
social media, 106–107, 109–110, 152–153. *See also* Facebook; Instagram
Soho area in London, 120–124
Solnit, Rebecca, 195, 198, 200, 219
Solow, Robert, 96–97
Spiegel, Evan, 69, 114
Spotify, 136–137, 138
Sputnik Crisis, 21–22
Srinivasan, Balaji, 204
Standage, Tom, 108
Standing, Guy, 188
Stasi of East Germany, 163–164, 166–167
Stephens-Davidowitz, Seth, 151
Sterling, Bruce, 159–160
Stone, Brad, 36, 47, 49, 50, 188, 221
Strickland, Don, 91
suicide and online abuse, 151–152
Sullivan, Andrew, 135
Sum, Andrew, 97
Sunstein, Cass, 217
Surowiecki, James, 112, 115
surveillance: in East Germany, 163–168; by government, 166–167, 180–183; in networked society, 178–179; Panopticon, 176–178; technologies for, 168–174
Systrom, Kevin, 4, 5, 100–103, 104, 112, 115

Taleb, Nassim Nicholas, 36
TaskRabbit, 187–188, 201
Taylor, Bob, 25–26, 27, 38
TCP/IP, 27, 28
Thiel, Peter, 94–96, 98, 136, 181–182, 200, 204, 216
Thompson, Derek, 81, 86
3-D printers, 156–157, 158–160
Traina, Trevor, 4
truth, as casualty, 153–154
Tucker, Patrick, 170, 172
Tufekci, Zeynep, 8, 178
Tumblr, 114
Tunney, Justine, 199
Turkle, Sherry, 110
Turner, Fred, 211
Twenge, Jean, 106
Twitter, 174–176, 207

Uber, 73, 83, 186–187, 230, 233
unintended consequences, 8, 68, 155

venture capital, 42–43, 45–46, 71–73, 197. *See also specific companies*
Vicarious, 85
voyeurism, 105, 108–109

Wadhwa, Vivek, 197
war: nuclear, 22–23; social media and, 153
Wasik, Bill, 204
Wasserman, Steve, 220
wearable technologies, 170–171
Web 1.0, 51–52, 58–59
Web 2.0, 58, 59–60, 91, 156, 157
Weber, Max, 63, 68
Webvan, 45–46
Wetherington, Pam, 50
WhatsApp, 106, 113
Wiener, Norbert, 14–15, 16, 18
Wikipedia, 115, 154–155
Williams, Alex, 104, 108
Williams, Ev, 7
Wills, David, 78
Wilson, Fred, 46–47, 48, 160, 227
Wingfield, Nick, 181
winner-take-all economy: Andreessen and, 39; distributed capitalism and, 68–74, 188; evidence of, 193–198; IT and, 96–99; of Internet, 43–51; search engine for, 53; social network for, 64
Winterkorn, Martin, 174

Wiseman, Eva, 103
Wohlsen, Marcus, 221
Wolf, Martin, 81
Wolff, Michael, 134
Wolle, Stefan, 166
women, 150–151, 196–197
Wong, Yishan, 64
World Wide Web (WWW), 30–33, 68, 117, 128
Wu, Tim, 104, 154, 213, 226

Yahoo, 52, 60, 114
Yang, Jerry, 52
Yglesias, Matthew, 51–52
Yorke, Thom, 137
YouTube, 60, 133–134

Zucker, Jeff, 128
Zuckerberg, Mark, 63–64, 66–67, 69, 95, 100, 102, 164, 207, 226
Zuckerman, Ethan, 117, 227